W9-BDJ-069

JEFFREY K. MANN

WHEN BUDDHISTS ATTACK

THE CURIOUS RELATIONSHIP BETWEEN ZEN AND THE MARTIAL ARTS

TUTTLE Publishing

Tokyo | Rutland, Vermont | Singapore

The Tuttle Story: "Books to Span the East and West"

Most people are surprised to learn that the world's largest publisher of books on Asia had its humble beginnings in the tiny American state of Vermont. The company's founder, Charles E. Tuttle, belonged to a New England family steeped in publishing. And his first love was naturally books—especially old and rare editions.

Immediately after WW II, serving in Tokyo under General Douglas MacArthur, Tuttle was tasked with reviving the Japanese publishing industry. He later founded the Charles E. Tuttle Publishing Company, which thrives today as one of the world's leading independent publishers.

Though a westerner, Tuttle was hugely instrumental in bringing a knowledge of Japan and Asia to a world hungry for information about the East. By the time of his death in 1993, Tuttle had published over 6,000 books on Asian culture, history and art—a legacy honored by the Japanese emperor with the "Order of the Sacred Treasure," the highest tribute Japan can bestow upon a non-Japanese.

With a backlist of 1,500 titles, Tuttle Publishing is more active today than at any time in its past—inspired by Charles Tuttle's core mission to publish fine books to span the East and West and provide a greater understanding of each.

Published by Tuttle Publishing,
an imprint of Periplus Editions (HK) Ltd.

www.tuttlepublishing.com

Library of Congress Cataloging-in-Publication Data
Mann, Jeffrey K., 1970-
When Buddhists attack : the curious relationship between Zen and the martial arts / by Jeffrey K.Mann.
p. cm.
ISBN 978-4-8053-1230-8 (hardcover)
1. Martial arts--Religious aspects--Zen Buddhism. I. Title.
GV1102.7.R44M36 2012
796.815--dc23
2012006359

ISBN 978-4-8053-1230-8

14 13 12 10 9 8 7 6 5 4 3 2 1 1206RP
Printed in China

Distributed by

Asia Pacific
Berkeley Books Pte. Ltd.
61 Tai Seng Avenue #02-12, Singapore 5341
Tel: (65) 6280-1330; Fax: (65) 6280-6290
inquiries@periplus.com.sg; www.periplus.cc

Japan
Tuttle Publishing
Yaekari Building 3rd Fl, 5-4-12 Osaki
Shinagawa-ku, Tokyo 141 0032, Japan
Tel: 81 (3) 5437-0171; Fax: 81 (3) 5437-07
sales@tuttle.co.jp; www.tuttle.co.jp

North America, Latin America & Europe
Tuttle Publishing
364 Innovation Drive North Clarendon,
VT 05759-9436 U.S.A
Tel: 1 (802) 773-8930; Fax: 1 (802) 773-69
info@tuttlepublishing.com;
www.tuttlepublishing.com

Contents

Foreword

Even the layman knows that Zen has always played an important role in Japanese combat. What we have not clearly understood, however, is what lies at the core of this relationship, and how, why and to what extent Zen's role in the fighting arts has been exaggerated and distorted. If you've ever wanted to understand the true role Zen Buddhism plays in the martial arts, then look no further. This book not only explains this relationship; it gives the student and martial artist much, much more.

Dr. Jeffrey Mann's reputation for understanding Eastern religion and philosophy, along with their historic and contemporary cultural landscape and social mindset, predates this work and makes him an ideal candidate to address the Zen/Budo relationship. His articles in leading journals and martial arts magazines throughout the world impressed me before I ever read his manuscript.

An old Japanese term, "Bun bu ryo do" (文武両道), aptly describes the twin paths of the pen and sword and denotes the importance placed upon balancing physical training with academic study. Mann Sensei epitomizes the scholar-warrior—one who clearly appreciates the value of meditation and knows what it's like to forge a fighting spirit in the blazing furnace of personal austerity. His book brings together solid academic resources and well-rounded personal experiences... and some simply brilliant anecdotes. What I most enjoy about this treasure trove of information is the simplicity with which it reveals the actual relationship between Zen and the Japanese fighting arts.

Although I have been passionate about the fighting arts since childhood, it really wasn't until I was living in Japan and picked up the wonderful little book *Zen in the Art of Archery*, by Eugen Herrigel, that I first took notice of the interesting connection between Zen and physical violence. One passage in particular, in the foreword written by the eminent Zen prelate D. T. Suzuki, challenged my Western archetypical mindset:

"One of the most significant features we notice in the practice of Archery, and in fact all the arts as they are practiced in Japan, and probably also in all other far Eastern countries, is that they are not intended for utilitarian purposes only or for purely aesthetic enjoyments, but are meant to train the mind; indeed to bring it into contact with the ultimate reality."

While my passion for the fighting arts remains as strong as ever, the intensity of my physical training lessens as I get older. Yet, as I continue to study, I find myself being drawn more deeply into the philosophical, holistic and spiritual depths of these arts. Looking to Zen as a guide I discovered something valuable: The fighting arts are a pathway, and if you travel on it long enough it becomes evident that the destination is not the intended goal; rather, the goal consists of the journey itself. That simple truth is the heart of this book.

When Buddhists Attack provided me with an extraordinary understanding of the role Zen has played, and continues to play, in the fighting arts. I only wish Dr. Mann had written it forty years earlier! It provides a unique foundation upon which further study and exploration of Zen can and will take you on a wonderful journey... without distance.

I am confident that *When Buddhists Attack* is destined to become a modern classic. I applaud Dr. Mann's work and believe it should be mandatory reading for anyone serious about the fighting arts, Japanese culture and Zen Buddhism.

Patrick McCarthy
Karatedo 9th Dan Hanshi
Director IRKRS
Brisbane Australia

January 28, 2012

Introduction

What does a religion known for teaching non-violence have to do with disciplines that are designed to cripple, maim and kill? A great deal, it turns out. Consider samurai meditating in Buddhist temples before heading off to decapitate each other, Zen priests teaching Imperial Japanese soldiers to die bravely in battle, or a karate teacher lecturing on both compassion and how to break a clavicle during the same afternoon. As it turns out, Zen and *budō* (the martial arts of Japan) have a long history—and ongoing relationship—with one another.

We in the West are prone to see conflict in this association; we perceive something incongruous. While we may focus on the incompatibility of thesis and antithesis, our neighbors in the East appear more adept at finding the synthesis. Consider *yin* and *yang* (or *go* and *ju*), and you will find that contrast can become harmony rather than dissonance. A man may be a tremendous practitioner of a violent art and a paragon of compassion who shuns hostility; there is no necessary contradiction.

This contrast is only one part of the fascinating relationship between Zen and *budō*. Aside from how they co-exist are questions pertaining to how they were brought together and why, and why they are still practiced together. This book is an introduction to Zen as it relates to Japanese *budō*, both historically and today. It considers what value the samurai found in Zen centuries ago, and what value we may still find today. To provide the foundation needed for addressing these issues, this book begins with an introduction to Buddhism and Zen. While the focus of these first chapters is on the fundamentals of this religious tradition, I have attempted to keep them connected and relevant to the experiences of those studying *budō*. With the groundwork laid, we may then explore the interrelatedness of these disciplines with more precision and care.

Personal Confession

My initial exposure to both Japanese martial arts and Buddhism took place nearly simultaneously, although it was well over a decade before any real connection between the two became clear to me. While I was aware of an historical relationship, it appeared to me as a cultural artifact rather than something relevant for my own training. Today I hold a different view, as my understanding and practice of Zen Buddhism informs my martial training, and my practice in the dojo deepens my understanding of Zen.

I have been infatuated with Asian martial arts since I was kid. Like many other red-blooded American boys of my generation, I grew up watching "Black Belt Theatre" on Saturday afternoons, much to my mother's chagrin. Yet I would have to wait until I was eighteen before I had the chance to study formally. I was a freshman in my first semester at Kenyon College when I joined our school's karate club. At that time, I trained in shito-ryu on Mondays, Wednesdays and Fridays and jujutsu on Tuesdays, Thursdays and Saturdays. Looking back, my teachers and I had relatively little understanding of the disciplines we were studying, but we loved it and threw ourselves into it. On my first belt test I dislocated both my shoulders, but I was hooked. I still am.

It was during that same year that I discovered my other great passion—the academic study of religion. I enrolled in a world religions class at Kenyon, taught by one of the college's most learned professors, Dr. Royal Rhodes. While much of what I learned in that class is long lost, buried somewhere deep in my cortex, Buddhism's four noble truths made a profound and lasting impact on me. And while I had no intention of becoming a Buddhist, over the years that followed I found myself returning to that lens in order to make sense of the world around me. Graduate study in religion eventually led me to Vanderbilt University in Nashville. While my primary area of focus was historical Christian theology, I had more exposure to Buddhism, specifically Zen. During my time at Vanderbilt, I also became involved in Okinawan goju-ryu karate—the art I currently study and teach. I was delving deeper into both Buddhism and karate, yet there was still no meaningful association between the two in my mind.

It was a number of years more before I realized the fundamental connection between Zen and *budō*. While at a professional conference in Minneapolis, I dropped into a used book store. I was looking for something on Church history, but came across a copy of D. T. Suzuki's *Zen and Japanese Culture*. Glancing at the table of contents, the chapters on Zen and swordsmanship caught my eye, and I decided to purchase it. Like many other westerners, it opened my eyes to an understanding of both Buddhism and martial arts that led to greater understanding of this remarkable relationship, both in terms of its historical role and its relevance for practice today. Suddenly, Buddhism was more than a cultural artifact in its relationship to martial arts, more than legends about Bodhidharma, more than the occasional teacher who practiced meditation. I caught a glimpse of the mind and mindfulness that Japanese *budōka* have sought to develop and realized its value for my own practice. Moreover, I realized that what was being cultivated was not some supernatural power or controversial energy force, but philosophical principles that generally mesh with my own western, Christian worldview.

In the years that followed, I gobbled up everything I could find on the subject. Books by D. T. Suzuki, Eugen Herrigel, Taisen Deshimaru, Shunryu Suzuki , among others, began to fill my bookcase. There were also the historical works of figures like Miyamoto Musashi, Yagyū Munenori and Takuan Sōhō that begged to be read. I began to scour libraries, the internet, academic journals and various print publications. I found intriguing articles and uninformed rubbish. Likewise, I sought out conversation partners and found something similar. I was also fortunate enough to find opportunities to "sit" and learn at Mt. Equity Zendo in Pennsylvania and Kozenji Zendo in Okinawa. While no one would ever confuse me with a great martial artist or enlightened Buddhist, I have made progress.

The reason for this book, then, is to offer a basic introduction to the theory, history and practice of Zen as it relates to the martial arts of Japan. I write as one who is familiar with the essential beliefs and discipline of Zen, a longtime student of Japanese martial arts, and a college professor who teaches religious principles to students. While I am not a leading authority in any one of these disciplines, I hope my familiarity with all three allows me the vantage point to offer a clear and cohesive introduction to this material, serving as one who directs the reader on to greater teachers once a foundation has been laid. It would be disappointing if a reader never went on to find authorities on Zen or *budō* more experienced and knowledgeable than I am.

A final word of caution: when it comes to the relationship between Zen and Japanese martial arts, there has been a great deal of romanticism, misinformation, caricature and stereotype that have made their way into popular and academic circles. The role that Zen has played among the Japanese has certainly been exaggerated. Moreover, there have been numerous philosophical and religious influences on *budō*, not just Zen. And *budō* has been understood and practiced differently at different times. As Professor Kōhei Irie has said, it is "a complex mesh of overlapping influences."* Readers should be clear that the majority of samurai, imperial Japanese soldiers and contemporary practitioners of *budō* have not been adherents of Zen. However, I believe the backlash that may be witnessed in recent years, denying any special significance for Zen, is also problematic. The pendulum rarely stops dead center. I believe Zen has been quite important, an essential element in the development and practice of *budō*.

By virtue of writing a book about Zen, I may be complicit in overstating its importance in Japanese culture. I have tried to temper this, pointing out embellishments in the narrative where I find them. Also, this book concludes with an epilogue wherein I consider this issue of what is Zen, and what is not, in *budō*. I invite the reader to consider with me the role of Zen in the history, contemporary practice and future of Japanese martial arts.

---

* Irie Kōhei, "*Budō* as a Concept: An Analysis of Budō's Characteristics," *Budo Perspectives*, Ed. Alexander Bennett (Auckland, New Zealand: Kendo World Publications, 2005), 167.

A brief explanation may be helpful regarding my use of foreign words, names and transliteration. Unless otherwise indicated, I have chosen to use Sanskrit rather than Pali when discussing Indian Buddhism. Whereas the former is more familiar to most readers, I thought it best to use more recognizable terminology. In transliterating Chinese, I have opted for Pinyin over Wade-Giles, as it is currently the choice of scholars on mainland China, which is where our narrative takes us. In the case of Japanese, I have included relevant macrons above Latin letters. They are easy to understand and use, and it is my hope that they will facilitate more accurate pronunciation of Japanese terms. Japanese words that have become commonplace in the English language (e.g., Zen, karate, judo), and appear as such in the Oxford English Dictionary, do not appear in italics. Lastly, in regard to Japanese names, I have chosen to maintain the traditional Japanese style of placing the family name first only with pre-modern figures. Individuals who lived after the Meiji Restoration (1868) are cited according to the western style of placing the family name last.

Chapter One

The Life and Teachings of the Buddha

"The purpose of studying Buddhism is not to study Buddhism, but to study ourselves." –Shunryu Suzuki

The Life of the Buddha

For many people raised within a western culture, the word "Buddha" brings to mind images of a chubby and jovial bald Chinese man. For others, a gold-covered statue of a serene east-Asian sage is the mental picture that first presents itself. Many, in fact, are unaware that the man we call the Buddha was an historical individual. Siddhartha Gautama, born in modern-day Nepal roughly 2500 years ago, was a man whose religious insights and teachings led others to give him the title of Buddha, or "awakened one." Like Jesus of Nazareth after him, he never commanded an army or government, wrote a book, or sought worldly fame. Likewise, his title became the basis for the name of one of the world's great religions. And so there is no better place to begin an examination of Buddhism than with the man we call the Buddha.

The biography of Siddhartha Gautama found in Buddhism's many sutras combines history, legend and speculation into a narrative that is familiar to countless people around the world. What is fact and what is fiction is often difficult to differentiate. It is not my intention here to attempt such a herculean undertaking, but to relate the story as it is commonly told. However, in certain places I will deconstruct aspects of the narrative to help readers attain a deeper understanding of the story.

While there remains some discussion of when he lived, the most common dates offered for the life of the Buddha are 563–483 BCE. We are told that, coinciding with his conception, his mother, Queen Maya, had a dream in which a white elephant appeared to her and penetrated her side. With this auspicious beginning, she enjoyed a pregnancy free of physical duress, able to see the perfect baby in her womb. When the time came near for her to deliver, she journeyed from the capital city of Kapilavastu to be with her family. During her travels, while passing the beautiful Lumbinī grove, she went into labor. When she walked into the nearby woods, the branch of a Sāl tree presented itself to her, and she was able to support herself there while giving birth, not sitting or lying down as is common. She was also blessed by being spared the normal pains of childbirth, her son entering the world, according to the Acchariya-abbhūta, "undefiled by fluids, mucous, or blood, or by any other kind of impurity."* Immediately he was able to stand. This sutra goes on to tell us that, while facing north, he took seven strides and announced to those present, "I am the highest, the most excellent, the first in the world. This is my final birth; now I will be reborn no more." By doing this, he was indicating that he would achieve the highest goal and ambition of a living being: to reach enlightenment and transcend life, death and rebirth.

Shortly thereafter, depending on the version of the story, one or more oracles examined his body and made predictions of the potential greatness of the boy. He would grow up to be either a great cakravartin king (i.e., a world-ruler) or a great religious teacher who would become enlightened and lead others to enlightenment. The path would be determined by whether or not he was made aware of the suffering of the world.

Siddhartha's father was King Śuddhodana. Not surprisingly, he had every intention of ensuring that his son would continue in the "family business," exceeding his father in worldly power. Acting on the prophecies of the soothsayers, he went to great lengths to shelter

* Quoted in John S. Strong, *The Experience of Buddhism: Sources and Interpretations* (Thomson Wadsworth, 2008), 8.

his son from the reality of suffering in the world. He was destined to rear his child without the help of his wife, who died seven days after Siddhartha's birth.

Young Siddhartha's youth and early adulthood were spent in three magnificent palaces. He moved from one to the other according to the seasons so that he would always enjoy the most favorable climate. Within each he was provided with every luxury, surrounded by beautiful women and attendants who were healthy and strong. He was raised at ease and educated as befits a young prince with a military career ahead of him, becoming quite expert in archery. (According to one story, he shot five arrows into the sky simultaneously, bringing down five flying ravens.*) As he traveled from palace to palace, his father made certain that the roads were cleared of anything unpleasant or offensive to the eye. While Prince Siddhartha was spared the dreadful realities of the world, he recognized that something was amiss. The real world, however, was about to make itself known to him in what are called the Four Passing Sights.

Again, the legends vary when telling of Siddhartha's life-changing exposure to suffering. Typically we find the young prince on a trip outside the palace grounds during which his father's efforts to shield him were insufficient, either by chance or the intervention of the gods. In either case, the experience could not have been more profound for the young man, now in his twenties.

Siddhartha first encountered an old man. While this may seem a rather mundane experience, we must remember that his father had only allowed him to be exposed to people who were healthy, strong and attractive. To encounter a man ravaged by many years on this earth, toothless, hunched and inflicted with senility, was a shocking experience. We should also bear in mind that old age throughout most of the world and throughout most of human history is significantly more debilitating and distressing than we privileged children

---

* John Stevens, *Zen Bow, Zen Arrow: The Life and Teachings of Awa Kenzo* (Boston: Shambhala, 2007), 31.

of the first world, living in these times, can often recognize. The sheltered prince was obliged to ask his charioteer what he was witnessing. The sight of the aged man, coupled with the explanation that this is the fate of all men, affected him profoundly.

The experience with the old man is followed by an encounter with a sick man. Again, Siddhartha had never encountered anyone suffering from illness, racked with pain, being destroyed from within by some disease. In this case as well, an explanation of the sight was required of his charioteer and, again, the new knowledge that all of humanity faces sickness and its effects weighed heavily on his mind.

The third of the Four Passing Sights was his first sight of a corpse. Having never been exposed to death, he once again turned to his servant in order to comprehend what he witnessed. This first encounter with death, an introduction to the very concept of mortality, forced Siddhartha into a deep existential crisis. He was struggling with his own inevitable demise, the suffering of the world, and the very meaning of existence. When combined with a worldview which believes in an endless series of rebirths, the weight of these sudden realizations was overwhelming.

The final sight was that of a sādhu, or wandering holy man. It was at this moment that Siddhartha realized that there are those who renounce this world and all that it has to offer in pursuit of something greater. There are individuals who forsake the life of a householder in order to pursue the religious life with the utmost effort and devotion, seeking to overcome the suffering and death that the prince had just faced in such starkness.

While we understand that the Four Passing Sights had a tremendous effect on Siddhartha, it is easy to conclude that the story is a bit silly. After all, even those who live sheltered and privileged lives cannot truly be oblivious to all pain until they are in their twenties! In addition, Prince Siddhartha is the son of a king, from a caste of warriors. His father was preparing him to conquer the world. While in his palatial luxury, he still learned the military arts and carried a sword at his side. Surely he could not be ignorant of the realities and possibilities of pain in the world.

On the contrary, I think it is at this point that Siddhartha's story is quite similar to many of our own. While all of us understand the concepts of illness, old age and death, many of us have difficulty personally appropriating these realities in our lives. In western societies, those who are seriously ill are confined to hospitals. Unless we work in the medical profession, we do not regularly see disease wreaking havoc on a person's body. Similarly, the elderly who are not strong and independent are often shipped off to nursing homes. For most of us, it is only occasionally that we visit such places, and catch a glimpse of our possible future: completely dependent on others and in various states of mental decay. What is more, we tend to shun such places, whispering to one another how unpleasant we find the odd necessary visit. As for death, rarely if ever do we witness the life of a fellow human being departing a once-vigorous body. Most times our exposure to death is at a funeral, where its reality is visible but presented with as much beauty and dignity as we can muster. Looking on as a body submits to the flames of a funeral pyre would affect many of us as powerfully as it did Siddhartha.

Even for students of combat, who train for fighting and discuss breaking bones and slashing knives, the violence that is simulated is usually far removed from reality, tucked safely in the protective environment of the training facility. As a white belt, I remember talking casually about how one could break an arm or wrist, this way or that. I suspect that if I had actually seen someone's arm snapped at the elbow, I would have passed out. Both Siddhartha and I may have studied martial science as young men, but even the disciplines of violence can be engaged in without a true understanding of the suffering they create.

There is a difference between knowing about illness, old age and death and staring them in the face. Siddhartha's story is not all that different from many of ours. In our world we hide, disguise and remove such things, and so the moments when we encounter such realities directly often affect us overpoweringly. At such times, one often considers the religious life more seriously than during our moments of contented denial.

We might imagine another objection to this story as well. How is it, one might ask, that the newborn baby Siddhartha could be so aware, so blessed, and demonstrate incomparable abilities, but then, more than twenty years later, demonstrate such naïveté and ignorance of the world? This certainly does seem to be a blatant inconsistency in his biography. However, when reading the various myths and legends about his life, you may find that the point is not to reconcile one with the other, or distill fact from fiction, but rather to understand the meaning that was being communicated by their various authors. In contrasting the wise infant with the later encounter of the imperceptive young man, we can see the tension regarding the personhood of Siddhartha Gautama with which Buddhism has struggled for more than two millennia. On the one hand, the Buddha is the great blessed one, the fully enlightened being to whom there is no equal in this eon of time. On the other, he is a human being like you and me, who walked a path from delusion and ignorance to wisdom and enlightenment, just as any human being may do. Embracing both of these beliefs simultaneously can be a juggling act, a bit awkward, just as we find them in his biography.*

Returning to our story, Siddhartha struggled deeply with the existential crisis which the Four Passing Sights awakened in him. Realizing that his palatial estate functioned more as a cage than an opportunity, he decided to leave. With his mind intent on pursuing the religious life, he planned to flee the prison his father had created for him. One night, while all were asleep, Siddhartha went in to see his father and spoke to the sleeping man. "Father, I am not leaving out of lack of respect, not out of lack of reverence, but for no other reason than that I wish to liberate the world, which is afflicted by old age and death, from the fear of the suffering that comes with old age

* Cf. Jonathan A. Silk, "The Fruits of Paradox: On the Religious Architecture of the Buddha's Life Story," *Journal of the American Academy of Religion*, 71:4, 863-881.

and death."* Despite his father's recent efforts to physically confine him to the palace grounds, Siddhartha was able to escape this night, while everyone slept, thanks to a spell cast upon them by the gods. With his servant Chandaka at his side, Siddhartha left behind his father, wife and newborn son in order to pursue enlightenment. After crossing the river Anomā on horseback, Siddhartha left his steed, removed his jewelry, then drew his sword from its sheath and cut off his long hair to a length of two inches—the length it remained for the rest of his life. He also shed his garments of Benares silk, trading them with an old hunter (who may actually have been the god Indra in disguise) for the hempen clothes befitting a religious wanderer. Ordering Chandaka to return to the palace, Siddhartha began his Great Going Forth at the age of twenty-nine.

Siddhartha sought out various teachers of yoga. Contrary to the stereotype in the West, the Hindu concept of "yoga" is a path which one travels on the way to spiritual maturity and, perhaps, enlightenment. One takes up the yoke of such a discipline in order to pursue liberation from this world. There are many such paths and disciplines, and the physical exercises of hatha yoga are only one component of one such religious system. Siddhartha is said to have studied with one teacher after another, excelling in the practices of various mystical trances. His spiritual guides recognized the genius of their student and offered him a position as a teacher, but he turned them down and continued his quest.

After his rapid progress within these various yogic disciplines, Siddhartha found himself dissatisfied with what they offered. Seeking to move beyond what his teachers were able to provide, he took up the self-denying life of an ascetic. Joining five others, Siddhartha pursued the life of denial with unequaled passion and commitment. Spending long hot days sitting under the sun, surrounded by four fires; subsisting on one grain of rice daily; standing on one leg throughout the day; and pursuing other such physical disciplines, he

---

* As in John S. Strong, *The Experience of Buddhism: Sources and Interpretations*, 15.

was determined to shed his attachment to his body and the world in order to realize that which exists beyond the illusions and distractions of this world. It is said that his asceticism was so extreme that he could grasp his stomach and take hold of his spine.*

After attaining to the most extreme discipline of asceticism, Siddhartha collapsed one day at the riverside. While there, he overheard a conversation between two musicians regarding their stringed instrument. The advice Siddhartha overheard, which had an intense effect on the religious seeker, were the words, "If the string is too loose, it will not play. If it is too tight, it will snap." With those simple words Siddhartha made a tremendous breakthrough. The true path is not found in extremes but in "the middle way." Neither a life of luxury nor a life of asceticism is the way to enlightenment. This path of moderation, the middle way, not only prompted Siddhartha to reject asceticism but would become a paradigm for later Buddhists to understand many aspects of the dharma, or teachings of the Buddha.†

It was shortly after this that Siddhartha proceeded to sit down under a pipul tree, determined not to move from the spot until he had realized the truth about the nature of the cosmos, himself and how to overcome suffering. He declared, "Either I will solve the problem, or I will fall dead on this meditation seat." For seven days he sat in profound meditation, penetrating deeper into the laws of karma, perceiving his past lives, overcoming the illusions that keep us shackled to this world of decay and suffering.

His extraordinary progress worried the evil deity Mara, who was determined to prevent Siddhartha's realization of full enlightenment. He sent his three beautiful daughters to distract the young man with those feminine wiles which have been known to divert more than a

---

* I had regarded this as but another legend about his life until I heard about prisoners in Japanese camps during World War II who also claimed to be able to do such a thing.

† Buddhists speak of the life of the monk or nun as a lifestyle between that of solitary mendicant and the householder, living within a community of full-time religious seekers. The Mahayana tradition extended the language of the "middle way" to other doctrinal issues. For example, in regard to questions about final nirvana, they explained that Buddhism teaches a middle position between eternalism and annihilationism.

few men throughout history. Due to the strength of his great virtue and will power, Siddhartha was not swayed. Mara continued with frightful attacks, but still to no avail. When challenged as to whether or not he was deserving of becoming a fully enlightened being, Siddhartha reached down and touched the ground, calling on the earth itself to validate his worthiness. This particular scene has been depicted quite often in Buddhist artwork over the centuries, and will be immediately recognizable to those familiar with Buddhist iconography.

Finally, at dawn of the seventh day, Siddhartha's years of effort and striving came to an end with a full and complete awakening to the truth. From this moment on, he would be known as Buddha, the awakened one. At the age of thirty-five he had realized the truth, without the benefit of another's direction, achieving an absolute and full enlightenment—an accomplishment so rare that the next time this is expected to happen will be in more than five billion years with the advent of the future Buddha Maitreya.

After remaining under the pipul tree for six more weeks—a tree better known today as the bodhi tree—the Buddha set off on a hundred mile trek to the Isipatana deer park, beginning his work of sharing what he discovered with others, a task that consumed the remainder of his life. Once again finding the five ascetics with whom he had spent much time, he preached his first sermon. It was in this first discourse that he taught the Four Noble Truths, in many ways the heart of Buddhist thought. Even today, these four short and pithy claims often function as a student's introduction to Buddhist thought.

The Four Noble Truths

While the Four Noble Truths may be expressed in different ways, one of the clearest and simplest formulations is:

1. To live is to suffer.
2. The cause of suffering is desire.
3. To eradicate suffering, one must eradicate desire.
4. Follow the eightfold path.

In order to shed some light on these four fundamental principles of Buddhism, and avoid some misunderstandings, let us look at each Noble Truth in turn.

To live is to suffer. The first thing to discern is that being alive and suffering necessarily go hand in hand. The Buddha is not saying that life is full of suffering, but that life itself is suffering. Our birth into this world takes place amidst suffering; our death is an event associated with suffering. For each of us life is filled throughout with pain and sickness, sorrow and loss, and is concluded with the ravages of old age, if we are fortunate enough to live so long. Suffering cannot be avoided, even though we do our best to flee its approach, relying on wealth, modern medicine, or various means of trying to escape reality.

The Buddha was not suggesting that life does not also provide us with joy and happiness. It certainly does; the Buddha was not being pessimistic. Rather, he taught us that suffering and life necessarily go together. Moments of even the greatest bliss and delight are still compromised by discontent. We continue to exist in a world where distress is inevitable and inescapable. We should not, however, associate this suffering solely with physical, emotional and mental pain. The Pali word *dukkha* conveys a much broader meaning, more concerned with inner suffering and dissatisfaction at the deepest level. The word literally refers to a wheel that is off its axle or a bone that is out of joint. Our lives exist in a state of dissatisfaction from which we can never find peace; pursuing the happiness we crave cannot free us.

To many, this first of the Noble Truth seems too harsh. After all, most of the people we interact with do not seem to have lives that are characterized by suffering. When I look out at a class of American college students, I often wonder if the Buddha's words resonate with them. They are, after all, pretty much at the peak of human potential for joy and happiness. They are young, bright achievers who live in the protective bubble of an American college campus in the twenty-first century. Most grew up in the wealthiest country in the world without ever seriously worrying about issues like hunger, violence, injustice, or adequate shelter. On the contrary, many of their childhoods were replete with trips to Disney World, Caribbean islands, or weekends jet-skiing at a vacation resort. And yet, when I discuss how, despite having all the benefits in the world, they know that their own struggles, unhappiness, depression and anger mire them in a world of psychological discontent, they sit forward in their chairs with rapt attention. They contemplate the suffering we rarely acknowledge, considering their own pain, or that of their friends. For some, they consider the unexpected suicide of a classmate who appeared to have everything going his way. Despite our best efforts at camouflage and denial, we recognize the truth in the Buddha's claim, to live is to suffer.

The cause of suffering is desire. From where does this suffering arise and what is its cause? The Buddha had an answer. Our state of disjointedness, living in dukkha, is due to our desires. For the sake of clarity, the word used in Pali—*tanha*—is perhaps better translated as "craving," even if the word "desire" is more commonly used when discussing the Buddha's thought. So, it is our craving that causes us pain and misery. At a basic level, this is apparent to most people who stop to reflect on their thoughts and behaviors. When I wish and hope for something I do not have, I create my own unhappiness. I want a nicer car. I want a bigger pay check. And this craving makes me unhappy. My wife can be enjoying a wonderful day, but if the Home Depot advertisement comes in the mail, and she sees the big beautiful kitchens full of sparkling appliances on the glossy pages, her mood immediately changes; she finds herself wanting something she does not have. She creates her own pain through craving.

The Buddha was certainly not the only person to observe this simple correlation. However, the Buddha was saying a great deal more than that we should stop craving things we do not have. There are many variations on the saying that "happiness is found not in getting the things you want, but in wanting the things you have," and the Buddha might have given the idea partial credit. But it fails to achieve an important insight that the Buddha did not want us to overlook: craving what you already have creates *dukkha* as well.

One of the central ideas of Buddhism is that everything is subject to change, nothing is permanent. Therefore, there are no guarantees that what we have today will not be taken from us tomorrow. Perhaps more than our desires for things we do not have, it is our desire to keep what we presently have that truly brings us misery. I want my hairline to stop receding. I want my joints to work like they did last year. I want my favorite shirt to look new again.

This grasping attachment to what we have today encompasses more than such superficial things; it extends to people. I tease the seniors in my classes, saying that while they eagerly count down the days until their graduation, when the day comes, and they see their best friends climb into over-packed cars and drive away, they are going to cry like babies. The friendships we have today are not guaranteed to last forever, and when we try to hold on to them too long, we create misery for ourselves and others. More significantly, the pain we experience when a loved one dies reflects this as well. I don't want my parents to die. I don't want my wife to die. And yet I recognize that I live in a world of impermanence, wherein it is inevitable and necessary that our loved ones will leave us, if we don't leave them first. Our craving for their presence in our lives for all time creates a great deal of suffering.

In the words of samurai-turned-Zen-monk Suzuki Shōsan (1579–1655), "Every moment is impermanent and the passing of the months and years is not unlike the flowing of a mountain stream. And are not bodies as bubbles on that water?... Though there are rosy cheeks in the morning, by nightfall there may be whitened bones."*

What is offered in the brief paragraphs above is only a quick introduction and glimpse into the nature of craving and its effects. Those who wish to explore the nature of our self-defeating desires will have to look beyond this short introduction.† Nevertheless, with this modest beginning, we now turn to the third noble truth.

---

* As in Winston L. King, *Death Was His Kōan: The Samurai-Zen of Suzuki Shōsan,* (Asian Humanities Press, 1986), 277.

† I highly recommend Walpola Rahula, *What the Buddha Taught* (New York: Grove Press, 1974).

To eradicate suffering, one must eradicate desire. The good news that the Buddha taught is that the pain and suffering that attend our living in *dukkha* can be overcome. (Please note, suffering is not always eliminated, but overcome.) What we must do is stop our constant craving. When my wife can appreciate looking at a beautiful kitchen without coveting it for herself, she can eliminate suffering. When I can come to grips with the fact that my body heals from injuries more slowly, without craving for my youth, I am more at peace. When we can compete with our peers without the overwhelming need for victory, we purge the agony of defeat and the fleeting excitement from victories that we cannot maintain forever.

This is not to say that life will be pain-free for the one who overcomes desire. Such a person can still hit his thumb with a hammer or contract a painful disease. We are finite creatures living in a mutable world; we are not immune from physical pain. However, much of our suffering is only triggered by physical pain. If I sprain my ankle while exercising, there is certainly physical pain, but there is even greater pain from what I perceive to be lost. Now, I will not be able to compete in next week's tournament. I will have to go everywhere more slowly on crutches. I won't be able to work out and I'm going to get fat. In other words, all those things I thought were mine are being taken from me, and that is what causes the greater pain. Closer to home, while I struggle with arthritis, I often drive myself to misery craving for the body of my younger days. Or, I can learn to concede that this happens as one ages and learn how to live with it.

Imagine stepping into a martial arts class and letting go of the craving for respect which compels so many of us. Instead of practicing basics and hoping that others around you appreciate your great skill, you could train for the sake of training. Rather than losing control—both physical and mental—while sparring, you could be content with your best performance, not feeling the need to show others that you can beat your partner. The drive to be your best certainly remains, but the unhealthy and destructive lust for respect could be checked at the door.

While it is one thing to stop craving nice things, or the absence of hardship, it is quite another to let go of certain other desires. In our twenties we may struggle with the loss of grandparents, in our fifties perhaps our parents, and later on even our spouses. Moreover, we also come to realize that anyone and everyone we know can be taken from us in a moment. The pain is real, and the Buddha had no illusions that such losses do not cause grief. At the same time, the pain we experience is manageable when we live our lives recognizing that we are unable to hold on to everything we enjoy. Our hold on the things we cherish is like our grasping the blade of a knife; the tighter we grasp, the more pain and damage when it is pulled from our hand.

Perhaps the most difficult desire to overcome is the craving for our own life. That too can be taken away at any moment. And while it is normal and desirable to struggle in order to stay alive in this world, especially for the sake of what we can offer to others, it is our failure to understand that the impermanence of the universe applies to us as well that creates great suffering. In the Zen tradition, as well as the warrior traditions of Japan, overcoming the desire for one's own life is the necessary goal to which all must strive. We shall return to this again when we consider the traditions and values of the samurai, as well as the mindset of Japanese soldiers in World War II.

Shunryu Suzuki (1904–1971), a Zen master well known in the West, explained, "So if you see things without realizing the background of Buddha nature, everything appears to be in the form of suffering. But if you understand the background of existence, you realize that suffering itself is how we live, and how we extend our life. So in Zen sometimes we emphasize the imbalance or disorder of life."* Suffering is not eradicated, but understood.

Follow the eightfold path. At this point, if one decides that the Buddha was really on to something here, and tries for oneself to eradicate craving in order to find peace and eliminate suffering, another problem may arise: this isn't easy! For a Buddhist to stop craving is

* Shunryu Suzuki, *Zen Mind, Beginner's Mind* (New York: Weatherhill, 1973), 32.

about as easy as it is for a Christian to stop sinning. The fourth of the Noble Truths, then, amounts to a program or method to assist the disciple in a life dedicated to overcoming craving. It consists of eight principles that one is to follow in one's daily being. They are:

1. Right view
2. Right thought, or intention
3. Right speech
4. Right action
5. Right livelihood
6. Right effort
7. Right mindfulness, or meditation
8. Right concentration

A great deal could be written about each one of these values, but this short work doesn't allow us to delve as deeply into them as we might like. Put simply, therefore, we should realize that the one who strives to eradicate suffering in her life may be enabled to overcome her craving by being careful to perceive the world correctly and not dwell on ideas informed by misdirected thinking. She should not allow herself to speak falsely, which is so often practiced in the pursuit of undeserved gain. She should act daily in accord with peace, rather than engaging in destructive behavior, which is driven by covetousness. She should pursue a career and calling that furthers such goals and does not demand violence of her. She should not tire from this struggle, but strive to progress in her efforts every day. She should actively pursue the life of the mind, careful to cultivate her self-awareness and attentiveness in all that she does. In doing so, she may be said to be traveling the noble eightfold path.

The Buddha spent fifty years traveling throughout India, instructing in the eightfold path and the other noble truths. During this time he attracted disciples who became the first Buddhist monks. After some prodding the Buddha allowed women to join the *sangha* (the Buddhist community) as ordained nuns. A distillation of his original teachings from the hundreds of volumes of sutras accredited to him is, again, beyond the scope of this book, but I will attempt to articulate here a few of the central themes of his thought.

Impermanence

Impermanence, often mentioned in discussions of Buddhism, essentially points to the belief that everything that exists is constantly in a state of change. There is nothing that is static and unchanging, fixed or permanent. While contemporary students of physics will immediately detect commonality with modern science, the Buddha's point was not so much scientific as existential. That is to say, the Buddha was not interested in questions about the structure of the universe as much as about the lived experiences of individuals. By insisting that everything is impermanent, we are being taught that the perception of the world as full of static and unchanging things is an illusion. The buildings we work in, the cars we drive, the trees we climb, these will all one day be gone.

More importantly, we begin to understand that those items we possess at the moment are not ours forever. There is no guarantee that I will have my job next week. All of my possessions could be consumed in a fire this very day. And even more important, the teaching of impermanence reminds me that my loved ones will not always be here. The connection between the right understanding of impermanence and the Four Noble Truths is then quite obvious. According to Shunryu Suzuki, "The teaching of the cause of suffering and the teaching [that] everything changes are thus two sides of one coin."*

The notion of impermanence in the Buddha's thought goes much deeper, however, than things and relationships. To say that everything is subject to change, and that nothing is permanent, is then to deny the orthodox notion of God in western thought. If impermanence is to be accepted, then there can be no eternal being we can call God. Even current notions in Process Theology—that God is

* Ibid., 103.

ever-changing and developing—are incompatible, as God remains an eternal being. Does this mean that the Buddha was an atheist? By many definitions, yes. Most likely, the Buddha accepted the notion that there are gods and goddesses that exist within this universe, but these are beings who will not live forever and are subject to the same universal laws as the rest of us.

Even closer to home, the belief in a constantly changing reality means that we individuals have no essential self. This represents a break from the Hinduism in which the Buddha was raised. There is no static soul or spirit (*atman* in Hinduism) which was present at my birth and remains with me throughout my whole life. There is no ghost in the machine. I do not have a translucent soul that looks like me, animates my body, and will rise from my corpse after my death. No, that which I call myself is nothing more than five *skandhas*, or aggregates: matter, sensation, perception, mental formation and consciousness. What makes me the person I am is not a concrete self or eternal spirit, but these five cognitive functions working in conjunction with each other. There is no underlying soul. (This monistic notion of the self often troubles those with dualistic notions of a person consisting of both body and soul. However, it is not very far from biblical Judaism and, in my opinion, completely compatible with Christianity.)

It was the hope of the Buddha that his hearers would understand this observation not just intellectually, but experientially. Zen master Shunryu Suzuki wrote, "When we realize the everlasting truth of 'everything changes' and find our composure in it, we find ourselves in *Nirvana*."* As we shall see later on, within discussions of *mushin* and the samurai attitude toward death, it was believed that recognizing the impermanence and illusory nature of self is essential to reach one's potential as a human being and as a warrior. The existential embrace of this principle enables one to overcome the fear of death and act resolutely in all situations.

---

* Shunryu Suzuki, 102f..

Samsara, Karma and Nirvana

One may ask, at this point, how a belief system can reject the notion of a self or soul, and at the same time accept reincarnation. It is true that Buddhism has taught the principle of rebirth (a term Buddhists prefer to reincarnation). But if there is no self, who or what is being reborn? To say that we have no essential underlying self, however, is not to say that there is no continuity in life or existence. For Buddhists, there is continuity that does not simply stop after this life. Consider this image: A candle is lit. While the burning flame has no static existence, but is obviously an entity in a constant state of flux, it is still real. If, as the candle burns down, right before the wax is exhausted, another candle is lit from the flame as the first disappears, we could point to a continuity of energy and existence. It is still the same flame, but a flame with a constantly changing nature. It is the same with rebirth.

The Buddhist sutras convey copious stories about the Buddha's previous lifetimes—who he was and what he did. There is also a great deal written about the transmigration of an individual's soul from this life to a future existence as an animal or human being, or a temporary stay in a heaven or hell. In fact, this cycle of birth, death and rebirth, known by the name *samsara,* is quintessential *dukkha.* That is, being reborn into another form is not a pleasant way of continuing one's existence after this life. We are all caught in *samsara,* destined to be reborn repeatedly in this cycle of pain and suffering.

What determines our rebirth, and the conditions of our present lives, is *karma*. Karma is the moral law of cause and effect. While we all know how cause and effect works in the physical realm, those who accept the idea of karma believe that there is a natural law at work in regard to the moral realm as well. Morally virtuous behavior is rewarded, in this life or in another to come. Morally repugnant behavior is punished. There is no God or powerful being who determines this; karma is simply a law of the universe. And so, while we often speak of "good karma" or "bad karma," this makes no more sense than talking about "good gravity" or "bad gravity." There are good and bad fruits of karma, but karma itself is something neutral. Hence, we can see that the individual who lives her life in service of others will reap what she sows, obtaining a good rebirth, while the one who does evil will be reborn with a serious debt to pay.

If this is the cycle of *samsara* in which we are all caught, is there anything to do other than work with karma in order to earn a good rebirth? The Buddha believed so. The one who awakens to the truth –one who is enlightened to perceive reality correctly and overcomes the illusions and craving that create our own suffering—attains liberation. Therein one may find *nirvana*. The one who attains this enlightenment is liberated from *samsara* and *dukkha*; there is no more rebirth, but only nirvana. We can then speak of the one who has found enlightenment as attaining *nirvana,* but it is only at the point of death that the individual reaches *parinirvana,* or final *nirvana*. Until then, such a person does remain in the world.

Unfortunately, to the reader who is hoping to learn what *nirvana* is, I have little to offer. In fact, *nirvana* is something outside of normal human comprehension, and so any definition is inherently flawed. However, we can say what *nirvana* and *parinirvana* are not. *Parinirvana* is not a place, a heaven to which you go. It is not some other location. *Parinirvana* is not the complete extinction of being, although it has been compared to extinguishing of the candle mentioned above. When the Buddha was asked if an enlightened being continues to exist in *parinirvana,* the Buddha remained quiet and did not answer. A positive answer would have been wrong, as it would suggest that there is some self or soul that could remain. A negative answer would have been erroneous as well, as it would convey the idea of extinctionism, which he also rejected. In the end, we are left with a notion beyond human language and concepts wherein one is liberated from *dukkha* and *samsara* and the false notion of a self in unending bliss.

One final comment about *samsara,* enlightenment and *nirvana*: We in the West often tend to project our own religious categories onto eastern religions. This is natural, and I do not pretend to be immune to this myself. However, we should be clear that the western notion, especially strong in Christianity and Islam, of actively pursuing the ultimate goal of salvation is not so common in the East. Whether speaking of Hinduism or Buddhism, most adherents of these traditions are not very interested in pursuing enlightenment in this lifetime. Most people's concerns are focused on improving the circumstances of this life and ensuring a good rebirth or reincarnation. This will become clearer when we discuss the apparent inconsistency of the samurai studying Buddhism but continuing a lifestyle apparently at odds with Buddhist ethics.

Ahimsa

Another principle that the Buddha carried over from the Hindu tradition was that of *ahimsa*. Often defined as non-violence or non-harm, *ahimsa* extends much further than traditions of pacifism in the West. The ideal of *ahimsa* requires living in a way that causes no living being any harm. While followers of the Jain religion took this to the extreme of sweeping the ground before them as they walked, in order to avoid accidentally stepping on an insect, Buddhists believe that it is only the volitional killing or injuring of another that is subject to moral critique. In practice, this means not only that one should avoid bloodshed (e.g., serving as a soldier), but also that one reject the livelihood of a weapon-maker. In modern terms, being employed by a company that produces fighter jets is a violation of this principle. Even sports and recreation that cause others harm are to be avoided, so that Buddhist rugby or ice-hockey players might find themselves facing a certain battle of conscience, to say nothing of martial arts enthusiasts ... an issue we will obviously need to return to later on.

In terms of diet, one should strive to be a vegetarian. And, of course, pursuing a career as a fisherman or butcher is a good way to ensure that karma will direct you to an unpleasant rebirth. However, because of the need to balance *ahimsa* with graciousness, Buddhist monks were taught that if anyone ever offered them meat to eat, they should receive and eat it. The only exception was in the case that the monk discovered that the animal had been killed specifically for him. In that case he should refuse. Interestingly, in 1872, the Meiji government of Japan declared that Buddhist monks were officially given permission to eat meat. And so, while it is more common to find such omnivorous behavior among Buddhists there today, it rests on the individual to decide how closely to follow the *ahimsa* ideal.

The Death of the Buddha

While many religious leaders have faced early deaths at the hands of their enemies, the Buddha lived to the age of eighty, making good use of his longevity by preaching throughout India and converting many to his new faith. As the legend goes, a blacksmith named Chunda offered the Buddha some food to eat, not realizing that it had spoiled. After consuming the food, the Buddha became quite ill. As he lay dying, his disciples gathered around him, filled with great sadness. Their teacher told them not to cry, reminding them that every living being is subject to death. Before parting, he explained that he had taught them everything that they needed to know. There was no secret knowledge reserved for a select group of initiates. Buddhism was not to be a secret gnostic religion. He also made clear to them that they should be their own lights and their own refuges. In his final words the Buddha demonstrated one of the most central and essential differences between his belief system and many others, especially those of the West: One should not take refuge in another, whether a priest, God, or the Buddha himself. Enlightenment is not found by relying on another, but through finding the strength, truth and resources within oneself.

With this, the Buddha passed on to *parinirvana*. His students, believing that they had been given a tremendous gift and opportunity in hearing the message of their teacher, wanted to share what they had learned with the world. And, as we shall see in the next chapter, they did just that.

Chapter Two

Zen in Buddhist Context

"If you live the sacred and despise the ordinary, you are still bobbing in the ocean of delusion." –Linji Yixuan

From Buddha to Buddhisms

After the death of a religion's founder, those left behind must struggle to keep the spirit and unity of the movement intact. This is always difficult. Almost invariably, there are splintering and competing claims for authority and legitimacy. Christianity's early centuries were filled with competing groups, all claiming to represent the true spirit of Jesus; Gnostics, Marcionites and Docetists competed with the catholic and apostolic church. Only a few short decades after Muhammad's death, the Muslim community permanently divided into the Sunni and Shi'a. In the case of Buddhism, maintaining unity was even more difficult. The *sangha*, or community of Buddhist disciples, had to wait nearly four centuries until the writing of the first sutras (recorded sayings of the Buddha). While they were passed down orally during this time, scholars today cast serious doubt on the historicity of most of these teachings of the Buddha.

In addition to the delay in creating a canon of Buddhist scriptures, the followers of the tradition took the good news of their teacher far and wide, encountering various other philosophies and social forces as they did so. Buddhism spread throughout India and into Sri Lanka. It made its way into the Southeast Asian countries of Burma, Laos, Thailand, Cambodia and Vietnam. It crossed the Himalayas and reached into China, Tibet, Mongolia, Korea and Japan. Buddhist emissaries also made their way westward into what is today Afghanistan, Iraq and possibly Greece. Wherever it went, the Buddha's message necessarily adapted itself to accommodate the local cultures it encountered.

Divisions within Buddhism developed within a century over different interpretations of the dharma, or Buddha's teaching. Over the millennia that followed, the appearance and disappearance of hundreds of sects took place. Today, numerous Buddhist traditions remain, enough to keep any academic researcher busy for a lifetime trying to track them. There are, however, three major branches that scholars identify, which makes it considerably easier for the novice to make sense of the variety of Buddhist religious experiences worldwide. These are typically referred to as the Theravada, Mahayana and Vajrayana. For those seeking a more complete account of Buddhist diversity, *An Introduction to Buddhism* by Peter Harvey is an excellent and thorough survey of various Buddhist traditions.

Theravada Buddhism

Theravada, the "Tradition of the Elders," is the oldest and most conservative branch of Buddhism. One might think of the Theravada branch as "old school Buddhism," as among the three it holds most closely to the practice, emphasis and teachings of the early Buddhist community. Central to this branch of Buddhism is the community of monks. (Nuns are also an essential part of the tradition, but a history of blatant patriarchy has left them as second-class Buddhists in many ways.) Those who desire actively to pursue a Buddhist lifestyle and explore Buddhist teaching typically must do so as monks or nuns. With an emphasis on the attainment of wisdom, study of the sutras, and meditation, the path to enlightenment is almost exclusively reserved for those who dedicate themselves to the religious life full-time. It is worth pointing out, however, that it is common for Theravada Buddhists to become monks or nuns for a limited period of time. The decision to join a monastery does not imply a lifelong commitment.

For the laity, the path to enlightenment may not be one that they spend much time contemplating. This does not mean they are uninterested or inactive within the Buddhist community. Prayers, offerings, and support of the monks accrue positive karmic benefits. And while a religious hierarchy exists between the monks and the laity, both need one another. The laity work and support the monks in their daily needs, study and religious striving; the monks then offer their services to the community in return. This takes the form of encouraging good works, overseeing festivals and conducting funerals, among other social and religious functions.

The practice of meditation and seeking to escape *samsara* are generally reserved for the monks. In truth, many among the full-time religious seekers themselves are not so concerned with awakening and nirvana, but with living a contented life and setting oneself up for a good rebirth. The path to enlightenment, then, is not an immediate concern for many of those in the Theravada tradition, as it is regarded as a journey that takes many lifetimes to accomplish.

This most conservative branch of Buddhism is found today primarily in Sri Lanka and the countries of southeast Asia (Thailand, Burma, Laos, Cambodia), although less so in Vietnam because of the influence of Chinese Mahayana Buddhism, which we will consider next.

Martial artists may be aware of the association of this school of Buddhism with Muay Thai. While the Thai boxers—and their counterparts in neighboring countries—are unlikely to spend long hours in meditation, the pre-fight rituals of *wai khru* and *ram muay* are an important part of the history and culture of the art. In these rituals the fighter expresses appreciation to his teachers and may petition the Buddha to protect him in the fight. The *mong kon* (headband) he wears may be blessed or inscribed with prayers by Buddhist monks and wrapped in silk thread. Here, one can clearly see the popular Theravada mindset, which focuses on personal well-being rather than the way of religious awakening.

Mahayana Buddhism

The Mahayana traditions, beliefs and practices differ from the Theravada in quite a number of respects, but there is one underlying current which helps explain their divergence. The Mahayana tradition makes the regular practice of Buddhism accessible to the masses, hence its name. The word "Mahayana" is usually translated into English as "The Great Vehicle." The image behind the name is that of a large ferry boat which has room for many people, a vehicle which will help transport them across the river—a common metaphor for the journey to enlightenment. Buddhism is not supposed to be the sole privilege of the religious elite, the learned and wise. Mahayana opened up the practice of the faith to countless more people.

While this branch of Buddhism began in India, it flourished in China. A religious tradition less concerned with abstract philosophical reasoning appealed to the practical Chinese, as did the teaching that one could remain a responsible householder—committed to family and work—and still excel in religious discipline and faith. And so the dominant schools of Buddhism throughout China, and later Korea and Japan, developed within the tradition of Mahayana Buddhism.

If Theravada practice emphasizes wisdom on the path to enlightenment, Mahayana stresses compassion (each of these traditions places great importance on both, but there exists a discernible difference in emphasis). Given the Mahayana school's orientation toward making Buddhism a religion to be actively practiced by the people, this should not really surprise us. Not everyone has the mental capacity, time, resources and drive to study and internalize the profound teachings of Buddhism; everyone can practice compassion. Acts of selflessness and generosity come to play a central role in understanding the life of the Buddha as well as one's own religious discipline. According to Akira Hirakawa, "The Mahayana tradition maintains that a person must save himself by saving others."*

* As in Michael Molloy, *Experiencing the World's Religions* (Mountain View, CA: Mayfield Publishing Company, 1999), 123.

The emphasis on compassion in Mahayana Buddhism manifests itself in a very interesting way with its adoption and development of the idea of the *bodhisattva*. The paragon of compassion, the *bodhisattva* is an individual who delays or foregoes full enlightenment in order to assist others on their way. Thus, we see here a conscious move toward directing attention and compassion to others. Buddhists must struggle to avoid focusing exclusively on their own salvation, leaving practitioners completely curved in on themselves. The *bodhisattva* tradition is a response to this, helping adherents turn their attention to others.

The compassionate *bodhisattvas* can be historical flesh and blood individuals, but they are very often legendary figures who currently abide in some heavenly realm. They may be called upon by the devout for assistance with all manner of difficulties, from the spiritual to the mundane. Heavenly *bodhisattvas*, then, end up playing a role in Buddhism not all that different from the saints in Roman Catholicism. Obviously, different figures play more prominent roles than others. One of the most influential has been Avalokitasvara, who changed gender and appeared as the *bodhisattva* of compassion, Guanyin in China and then Kannon in Japan.

Mahayana also played a large role in the multiplication of buddhas in the tradition. While Siddhartha, known as Shakyamuni Buddha, was the historical Awakened One, there are human histories other than our own; we exist in only one eon of time. Over countless billions of years in many universes, there were certainly other buddhas. As fully enlightened beings, brimming with the fullness of compassion, they may make themselves available to us during our times of need. While some of these play secondary roles to the historical Buddha, certain traditions in Mahayana place other buddhas at the center of their fidelity, relegating Shakyamuni Buddha to an insignificant role. One example in Japan is Tendai Buddhism, with its devotion to the great cosmic Buddha Dainichi.

Similarly, consider the largest Buddhist sects in Japan today, the Pure Land schools. Both *Jōdo-shū* and *Jōdo Shin-shū* are Japanese expressions of the Mahayana Pure Land sect that developed in China. Legend speaks of the fifth century monk Tan-luan, whose vision launched this immensely popular Buddhist tradition. Adherents devote themselves completely to Amitābha Buddha (Amida Butsu in Japanese), the great compassionate Buddha of the Pure Land. For those who trust in and devote themselves to this Buddha, in his great compassion he will guarantee them rebirth in the Pure Land—a wondrous place of bliss and peace from which the attainment of enlightenment is far less difficult than it is in this world.

The Japanese monk Shinran (1173–1262) developed this school of thought further, insisting that our good works and merit in this lifetime are meaningless when compared to the great saving power of Amida Butsu. All that is necessary is faith and the sincere recitation of the Nembutsu: "*Namu Amida Butsu*" ("Homage to Amida Buddha"). Interestingly (like Martin Luther in Germany), Shinran insisted that even the saving faith itself is due to the grace of the savior. His school, *Jōdo Shin-shū*, or True Pure Land Sect, is the largest in Japan today.

During both the fifteenth century and the period of Japanese imperialism, there were a considerable number of *Jōdo* Buddhist soldiers who took up arms and eagerly fought to the death, trusting that they would be reborn in the Pure Land. General Hayashi Senjūrō (1876–1943) described what he saw during the Russo-Japanese War, after a battle during which hundreds of soldiers were left stranded, dying on an open battlefield. "Many of these casualties were severely wounded and in great pain, but not a single one cried out for help. Instead, they recited the name of Amida Buddha in chorus, even as they died."*

Buddhist scholar and priest Ōsuga Shūdō (1876–1962) further explained the role of this faith among Japanese military men at the turn of the century:

* Brian A. Victoria, *Zen at War* (New York: Weatherhill, 1997), 31.

> Reciting the name of Amida Buddha makes it possible to march onto the battlefield firm in the belief that death will bring rebirth in paradise. Being prepared for death, one can fight strenuously, knowing that it is a just fight, a fight employing the compassionate mind of the Buddha, the fight of a loyal subject. Truly, what could be more fortunate than knowing that, should you die, a welcome awaits in the Pure Land.*

Vajrayana Buddhism

The Vajrayana, or "Diamond Vehicle," branch of Buddhism also developed in India, as we saw with Theravada and Mahayana, before spreading out to other areas of the world. In the case of this third tradition, Tibet and Japan became the primary loci of its later development. While both the Tibetan and Japanese expressions of this esoteric form of Buddhism fall within this same branch, and share common scriptures and practices, it is interesting to note that the former is often associated with a radical emphasis on peace while the latter is often associated with various warrior traditions, although we should be wary of overgeneralizations.

Vajrayana traditions draw much of their inspiration from the *Tantras*, a set of scriptures with their roots in the Hindu tradition of India. For this reason, one often finds reference to the "Tantric Buddhism" practiced by adherents of these traditions. Most westerners, when they hear the word "tantric," think first of sexuality. It is true that there are tantric "sexo-yogic" practices, where male and female participants come together for sexual congress without the spilling of semen. However, tantric sex is a small part of the larger picture, albeit a more interesting one for many people. In a nutshell, the *Tantras* provide tools for accelerating one's path toward enlightenment. By making use of resources within oneself and throughout the universe, the long, arduous road to awakening can be traveled more quickly. This discipline, then, makes the prospect of reaching buddhahood in this lifetime a real possibility. Through the use of mantras (oral

* Ibid., 31f.

chants), *mudras* (choreographed hand gestures), mandalas (ritual diagrams), and various meditative practices, the Vajrayana faithful tap into energy and resources that provide great assistance to the seeker.

Very often, Shakyamuni Buddha is of minor importance in this practice, as other cosmic buddhas have come to the fore. Visualization of these buddhas, along with various *bodhisattvas* and deities, constitute an essential role in the meditative practices of these Buddhists. This visualization is complemented with *mudras* that represent these figures, and chanted "seed syllables" which bring one into synchronization with their power. Those who are able to establish connection and unity with these divine figures may then draw upon their spiritual resources to assist them in their own journey.

The teachings and practices of this tradition, however, are not simply made available to anyone who comes knocking; it is an esoteric practice, for the initiated alone. Adherents of Vajrayana Buddhism explain that such tools are not for raw novices or the self-guided. This may sound suspicious to many, and not much in keeping with the egalitarian spirit of the Buddha. However, this careful and deliberate conveyance of knowledge has been compared to raising children. Just as I do not hand my young sons power tools, so should those who are not mature enough for the doctrines and practices of this tradition be protected from their power and potential for misuse. The secrets of Vajrayana Buddhism are then provided to the faithful through one's spiritual teacher or guide at different stages of one's development. For this reason, it is a religious discipline of secrecy and initiation. In addition, the practices—especially in Tibetan Buddhism, which co-opted elements of the native Bon-Po religion—are often described by scholars as various forms of "magic." Through the proper ritual incantations, gestures and secret knowledge, those within the tradition reap the benefits of forces outside the realm of normal human experience.

In Tibet, Vajrayana Buddhism is the dominant form of the religion, and the tradition of the world's most famous Buddhist, the

Dalai Lama. Actually, Tenzin Gyatsu (1935–) is the fourteenth individual to hold this title, in a lineage dating back to the fifteenth century. This Nobel Peace Prize winner, who went into exile when the Chinese annexed Tibet, has inspired people around the world, of all religions, primarily because of his emphasis on peace. While it would be an error to conclude that all Tibetan Buddhists have favored non-violence—as there were those who took up arms against the Chinese—the teaching of *ahimsa* is particularly strong in the Tibetan tradition.

Westerners are often taken with Tibetan Buddhism—although it is worth noting that there are different schools of Vajrayana in Tibet. Whether it is the aesthetic of its practice, the emphasis on peace, the mystique found in the "Wisdom of the East," or the plight of the Tibetans, there is a great deal of lip service paid to this tradition. Much of this, however, is shallow commentary. To be certain, there is a great deal to admire, but few westerners look beyond the attractive veneer that is on display around the world. Vajrayana is a tremendous source of religious insight and practice, but there is much that is not easily accessible to those looking in from the outside, and we do the tradition no favor when we romanticize the little we do know. For those looking for depth on this subject, consider the two volumes by Reginald A. Ray, *Indestructible Truth: The Living Spirituality of Tibetan Buddhism* and *Secret of the Vajra World: The Tantric Buddhism of Tibet.*

Vajrayana Buddhism also found a home and fertile soil for development in Japan. The most famous Japanese teacher and monk of this tradition was Kukai (773–830), better known by his posthumous title of Kobo Daishi. After traveling to China to study Buddhism, and discovering the esoteric *Mahavairocana* sutra, he returned and established his famous monastery on Mount Koya in 816. It was he who founded the Shingon school of Buddhism, one of the most influential, and still today one of the largest schools of Buddhism in Japan.

As is the case with Tibetan Buddhism, the historical Buddha

remains part of the tradition, but is associated with a more simple form of the dharma. The more profound teachings of the faith are associated with the great cosmic Buddha Mahavairocana, or Dainichi in Japanese. In the words of Kobo Daishi, the teaching of the historical Buddha is "exoteric; it is apparent, simplified, and adapted to the needs of the time and the capacity of the listeners." The doctrines of Dainichi, on the other hand, are called "Esoteric; it is secret and profound and contains the final truth."* Here again we see that the teachings of this tradition are guarded carefully and only provided to those who have been initiated into the sect.

Japanese practitioners learn the same esoteric means toward the attainment of complete enlightenment in this lifetime: mantras, *mudras,* and meditation involving visualization techniques. When these are used in conjunction with the mandalas (diagrams that represent both the macrocosm of the universe with its various Buddhas and the microcosm of one's true nature), unification with the guiding agents takes place and allows for the individual's awakening.

One of the more popular esoteric sects that developed out of Shingon was Shugendo, a spiritual discipline familiar to certain students of Japanese martial arts. Combining elements of esoteric Buddhism with Daoist magic and Shinto shamanism, the Shugendo tradition became one in which adepts undergo feats of physical endurance combined with the secret rites of Vajrayana Buddhism. While the concept of attaining buddhahood within this lifetime remains, there is a great deal of emphasis on the supernatural abilities which are fostered through these disciplines. Historically, the *yamabushi*—literally, those who lie in the mountains—pursued this path in solitude during the winter months. Enduring the bitter cold, they practiced austerities such as standing under waterfalls or being suspended upside down over the precipice of a cliff. The warmer months brought them down to the villages in order to assist the common people through their abilities as healers or exorcists. (Please note that the

* Robert Ellwood, *Introducing Japanese Religion* (New York: Routledge, 2008) , 92.

suffix "bushi" is a transliteration of a different kanji character than the more familiar "bushi" we associate with the "bushido" of the samurai. Many *yamabushi* were trained in fighting and were formidable warriors, but it is incorrect to translate the name as "mountain warrior.")

While the *yamabushi* enjoyed their glory days long ago, during the Tokugawa period (1603–1868), they have not exactly disappeared. Men still return to the mountains for winter retreats filled with physical asceticism, ritual and a rejuvenation of their spiritual and masculine energies before returning to the mundane life of modern Japan.

There is also considerable interest in Shugendo on the part of contemporary practitioners of ninjutsu. The secretive nature of both disciplines does make for a fitting match. Unfortunately, this is not the place to explore this spiritual discipline in depth, or its implication for the martial techniques of this style. Fans of martial arts movies, however, will recall the portrayal of Frank Dux in the movie *Bloodsport*, complete with depictions of our hero in meditation displaying *mudras* and learning the secret *dim mak* techniques of his "*shidoshi*."

A bit more within mainstream martial arts, Morihei Ueshiba (1883–1969), the founder of aikido, was influenced by Vajrayana Buddhism as well. He was sent to study at a Shingon temple in Wakayama prefecture at the age of seven. While he would later convert to Omoto-kyo, which might be described as an apocalyptic Buddhist cult, the influences of various religious traditions are found in his training, teaching and philosophy. The use of sacred words or "seed syllables" in Japan arose from the Shinto practice of reciting *kotodama*. Shingon Buddhism also made use of this practice, believing that such ritual vocalizations brought a type of divine power to ordinary world. This led to their use in martial applications, involving *kiai*. Ueshiba was trained in this tradition and "was deeply committed to this practice."* While not studied and practiced by all *aikidoka*, it continues to have a role in the training of some. We should also

* Michael L. Raposa, *Meditation and the Martial Arts* (Charlottesville: University of Virginia Press, 2003), 19.

note that other Japanese martial arts have incorporated *kotodama* into their *kiai* as well. And so there still exists an esoteric relationship between Vajarayana Buddhism and various Japanese martial arts.

Zen Buddhism

As we can see from the brief descriptions above, both historical and contemporary Buddhism developed to a point where a great deal of spiritual practice centered on power, magic, incantations, rituals, rites and ceremonies conducted by religious authorities, be they human or heavenly. It is hard to avoid the suggestion that this bears little resemblance to the teaching and practice of Siddhartha Gautama. In fact, the school of Zen finds its foundation and strength in this observation and critique. Recognizing that the historical Buddha achieved enlightenment by meditating, the Zen tradition made a conscious move back to basics, with a profound emphasis on meditation. In fact, the Sanskrit word for meditation—found in the seveth step of the eightfold path—is *dhyana*, pronounced "Ch'an" in China, "Son" in Korea, and "Zen" in Japan.

In this section we will take a quick look at this school of Mahayana Buddhism, with a focus on its practice in Japan. Certain themes treated in this brief introduction to Zen will be delved into more deeply in later chapters, as we consider the history and contemporary relevance of Zen Buddhism to the study of martial arts.

Origins

According to legend, this school of Buddhism can trace its roots back to the Buddha himself and his famous Flower Sermon. Legend has it that the Buddha wished to communicate a teaching to his disciples that could not be expressed in words. He held up a single flower, a lotus plucked from muddy water. While others conjectured about the meaning of this gesture in vain, Mahakashyapa smiled at the Buddha, indicating that he had understood. We see in this story a fundamental principle of Zen. It is "not reliant on the written word, [but] a special transmission separate from the scriptures." It was this same Mahakashyapa who became the first patriarch of the tradition.

Far more familiar to many readers of this book is the 28th patriarch, a man named Bodhidharma. The dates of his life and work in China vary, but the majority of scholars place him in China in the late fifth century. Known by various names (e.g., Dharma, Damo, Ta-mo), his face can be seen around Japan with remarkable frequency today, from the plentiful Daruma dolls for sale in department stores to paintings of his stern countenance that adorn the walls of more than a few karate dojos. As we saw with Shakyamuni Buddha, there is a great deal of myth mingled with history in the telling of his story, and scholars continue to debate what is fact and what is fiction.

According to most accounts, he arrived in China from India with the living message of Buddha, rather than the dead faith of books and letters. (Interestingly, there is some evidence that he may have actually come from Iran rather than India, but the legend is more compelling when he shares the same homeland as the Buddha himself.*) In addition to chastising Emperor Wu-ti for his self-serving benevolence and sailing across the Yangtze River on a single reed, his remarkable skill in meditation made him quite famous as well. He spent nine years meditating in his cave outside the Shaolin monastery, situated beneath Mount Shaoshi in the Song mountain range. It is from this peak that the monastery was likely named, *Shao-lin*, the grove below Mt. Shaoshi.

There, in his profound meditation, he was able to hear ants scream. He even cut off his eyelids to keep from falling asleep. It was from these eyelids, cast on the cave floor, that China's first tea plants grew. His gaze was so intense, we are told, that it bored holes in the wall of the stone cave. It is also said that he sat for so long that his legs withered and fell off. This last legend does compete with the one that concerns us here, in which he gets up and sets about developing

* Jeffrey L. Broughton, T*he Bodhidharma Anthology: The Earliest Records of Zen* (Berkeley: University of California Press, 1990), 53f.

an exercise program. It seems that the monks at the temple could not endure his demanding meditative practices, and so he allegedly penned the *Sinews Transformation Classic* (Yijin jing) and *Marrow Cleansing Classic* (Xisui jing), although we now know they were written centuries later. These exercises, as the story goes, formed the basis for the resulting martial schools of Shaolin *gun fa* (staff fighting) and *quan fa* (unarmed combat). In reality, the *Sinews Transformation Classic*, the more influential of the two, was written roughly one thousand years after the life of Bodhidharma. The preface is a forged document, alleging to have been written by the famous general Li Jing (571–649), in which Bodhidharma's authorship is asserted and Li's victories are credited to his reliance on the text.

The legends continue to describe how Bodhidharma lived to the ripe old age of 150. There are even stories relating how, after his supposed death, he was seen walking back to India wearing one sandal. When his coffin was unearthed, it was empty… except for one sandal! These fantastic stories actually betray the influence of Daoism on the Bodhidharma story, rather than Buddhist hagiography. The Daoists were the ones who believed that men and women of great spiritual and physical discipline could achieve tremendous longevity, or even immortality. And so here we see an early melding of Ch'an Buddhism and Daoism, as both traditions looked on this man as a religious hero. In fact, it was the Daoists who were the first to claim that Bodhidharma had taught physical exercise. As early as the eleventh century, Daoist literature attributed embryonic breathing to Bodhidharma.* The Shaolin monks, interestingly enough, had credited the mythic Vajrapāni as the source of their fighting systems. It was only around the eighteenth century that the Buddhists adopted the Bodhidharma myth as their own.†

It is highly unlikely that Bodhidharma was a trained fighter, despite other legends that he had studied the Indian martial art of

* Meir Shahar, *The Shaolin Monastery: History, Religion, and the Chinese Martial Arts* (Honolulu: University of Hawai'i Press, 2008), 172.

† Ibid.

kalarippayattu. What is trustworthy, however, is that the Shaolin Monastery did function as a school and repository of various disciplines of martial arts. The different styles of martial arts that were taught there, however, were very often developed elsewhere. There is no evidence that the Shaolin monks' early military exploits during the Tang Dynasty (618–907) were carried out with a style of fighting original or unique to the monastery. It is true, however, that Shaolin's system of staff fighting during the Ming Dynasty (1368–1644) was legendary and highly regarded, and likely a distinct style that evolved on the premises. The unarmed combat for which the temple became so famous was significantly influenced by Daoist *daoyin,* a precursor of qigong. Meir Shahar, who has written the essential book on the subject, *The Shaolin Monastery,* argues, "[T]he foundations of late imperial bare-handed styles such as Shaolin Quan… were laid during the late Ming and the early Qing by the integration of Ming hand combat with an ancient gymnastic tradition that had largely evolved within a Daoist context."* He goes on to point out, "By the late nineteenth century, Buddhist monks at the Shaolin Temple were practicing gymnastic methods that had been recorded in Daoist scriptures, that had evolved in Daoist circles, and that had been attributed to Daoist immortals."† Ch'an Buddhism, then, had little to do with the development of the countless schools of martial arts developing throughout China and even within Shaolin itself. Moreover, Shahar presents compelling evidence that no modern martial art can claim for itself a foundation at the Shaolin temple prior to the twentieth century. Sufficient evidence simply does not exist.

From the perspective of a modern scientific viewpoint, the supernatural stories of Bodhidharma are easy to discard. In truth, scholars today also cast serious doubt on nearly the entire story. Bodhidharma may have never even entered the Shaolin Temple. As we have seen, stories about him teaching an early form of qigong are rather dubious and coincide with the creation of the *Muscle Change Classic*

---

* Ibid., 155.

† Ibid., 160.

in the seventeenth century. Accounts of him teaching actual martial arts appear to be a product of the twentieth century. According to Stanley E. Henning, it was a popular novel, first published in 1904, that started the myth.* If he is right, Liu E's *Travels of Lao Can* is the source of this remarkable legend. We do know that quite a number of books appeared in the early decades of the twentieth century which developed the story of Bodhidharma as the founder of Shaolin martial arts. Even today, the story is perpetuated by those who have uncritically accepted the account, or who are trying to tie their martial tradition to this great legendary figure in order to romanticize or legitimize their fighting systems.

Henning's article takes issue with the work of a few "seemingly scholarly practitioners," including this author, who "unquestioningly recite chapter and verse of the Bodhidharma story." I believe that in this Henning confuses the telling of the story with its acceptance as historical fact. Credible authors make some effort to communicate that the historicity of the story is not to be trusted. I do not believe, however, that the Bodhidharma story should be discussed only for the purpose of deconstructing it. While an accurate rendering of history is extremely important, we should remember that we are talking about a religious and cultural figure. It is a western tendency to separate fact from fiction for the sake of truth, which can cause the value of legend, myth and tradition to be overlooked. In the words of D. T. Suzuki, "Sometimes so-called facts are not so important. But what scholars call imaginations or legends, they are more important in the study of human nature."† A cultural icon like Bodhidharma, who represents the unity of physical and spiritual disciplines, communicates something of great value to practitioners today who strive for the same harmony in their lives and training. There is no need to cleanse karate dojos around the world of their images of Bodhidharma,

* Stanley E. Henning, "The Imaginary World of Buddhism and East Asian Martial Arts," Classical Fighting Arts Vol. 2, no. 12, 37-40.

† *A Zen Life: D. T. Suzuki*, DVD, produced by Michael Goldberg (Japan Inter-Culture Foundation, 2006).

although supplementing them with the occasional history lesson may be a good idea.

Teaching

Let us return to a discussion of the religious discipline with which Bodhidharma is intimately connected. Ch'an Buddhism developed in China, taking on a more distinctly Chinese character. In this process, certain themes were stressed more heavily than we find in other Buddhist traditions. One that is extremely important is the correct understanding of the self. To understand what the self is, and what it is not, is to be enlightened. Earlier we considered how there is no Self, *per se,* in Buddhist thought—at least in the sense of the Hindu notion of *atman*. However, assent to this claim is not enough; it is the existential understanding and appropriation of this belief that the Buddhist desires to achieve. Moreover, while it is easy to repeat that I have no Self, I must simultaneously recognize that I am indeed something. I do exist. Jeffrey K. Mann, father and husband, teacher, neighbor, friend, antagonist and curmudgeon is truly here (at the time of this writing). I am not merely a figment of your imagination. I have reality, as do you. But what are we? If I am illusion, it is not a visual hallucination. The illusion must be in my mental conception of what I truly am. The illusion is that I have a static, fixed reality. It might be said that Zen Buddhists strive to understand the two competing—yet not contradictory—statements: The self exists; the Self does not exist.

The Zen emphasis on the reality of self, or no-self, is illustrated very well in the story of Hui-neng (638–713). In the singular event of his response to a poem written on a wall, he demonstrated his superior understanding of the dharma and his worthiness to become the sixth patriarch of the Ch'an tradition. The story goes that the senior monk at the monastery wrote the following poem:

> The body is a Bodhi tree, the mind a standing mirror bright. At all times polish it diligently, and let no dust alight.

In response, Hui-neng, the illiterate kitchen-worker, asked a passing monk to write his reply:

> Bodhi is no tree, nor is the mind a standing mirror bright. Since all is originally empty, where does the dust alight?

The inclination of human beings is to believe in a concrete self or soul, that our very selves have some fixed reality. The Buddhists believe that no such thing exists, and Zen teachers insist that you face that reality. In so doing, they intend much more than a metaphysical statement about human nature. If Zen only offered this observation as an objective truth claim, we might discuss it in philosophy classes and then be done with it. The relevance of this claim lies in its power to transform human existence, to enable a person to live fully as a human being.

Too much of life is lived in the past or the future. Our lives are expressions of our thoughts: "I was happy before." "I did that when I was younger." "I am going to be this." "I want to have those." In reality, there is only "I" during this fleeting moment. The "I" of yesterday is not what I am today. I have already changed. The past is over and does not remain. The "I" of tomorrow is not only unknown, is not only without guarantee, but is also not what "I" am at this moment. How then does it make sense for us to live our lives in the past or the future, as so many of us do? To be fully human means to be living presently. When I live as the person I was yesterday or may be tomorrow, thinking they are the same thing, I fail to live as the only thing I can be, the person I am presently.

One of the more difficult concepts to grasp in Buddhist teaching, this idea is constantly misconstrued in the West. Young Americans may declare, "Live in the now!" and proceed to engage in endlessly irresponsible behavior. We all love the phrase "Carpe diem!" and may think that Buddhism is encouraging us to set off on exciting adventures, stand up to authorities, or scale Half-Dome in Yosemite National Park. Being present in the moment means something much more profound, however, to the Buddhist. It does not preclude reflecting on the past. It certainly does not eradicate our responsibility toward ourselves and others in the future. It means being fully present in the moment. It means being entirely in the moment when a person is speaking to you, not off planning your weekend activities in your mind. It demands attending to the task at hand, not being caught reliving last weekend's moment of glory while steadily becoming less aware of your current undertaking. Existing in the moment requires that my practice of *kata* is not spent thinking about how others will view me at the next *shiai* or seminar. It means that, while sparring, my mind is not stuck on my last encounter with this person. I exist now.

None of this is to say that we should never consider or ponder the past. Similarly, planning for the future is an important and essential aspect of human thriving. The question is, are these thoughts a result of a decision to consider the past and future that you are presently making, or are you being caught by the past and future. Are you addicted to living in the past? Are you obsessed with your happiness in the future? Are you incapable of being fully present?

Zen philosophy about the true nature of self is not unique within Buddhism, but it very often receives an emphasis not found in other schools. In fact, one criticism of the Zen tradition is that it places far more emphasis on this spiritual insight than on matters of right conduct, an observation we will discuss in greater detail later in the book. This intense focus on no-self, found especially in Rinzai Zen, can understandbly give one pause. Some even within the Zen community worry that this tremendous emphasis on the personal quest for self-understanding can overshadow ethical responsibilities. The Order of Interbeing, established by Vietnamese monk Thich Naht Hanh (1926–), is one example of the Zen *sangha* making a conscious effort to supplement this teaching with considerable emphasis on the importance of compassion, the life of "engaged Buddhism."

Overcoming the false sense of self carries with it a trait that is the desire of all human beings, not least soldiers: overcoming the fear of death. When you come to understand that you do not exist as you might imagine, that you have no soul and that you only exist in this moment, death loses it fearfulness; for what is lost? When you extinguish the desire to hold on to your possessions, you have made a good beginning in Buddhism. However, when you eradicate all craving, even for your very life, you are making true progress. While we struggle to avoid death, as is natural to all living beings, we strive to recognize that death is inevitable. When it approaches, you may then face it with the equanimity and composure sought by the samurai, whether death comes through natural means, an enemy, or one's own hand.

Many religions teach principles that lead their adherents to overcome the fear of death, and most traditions have stories of those who went fearlessly to the executioner for the sake of their convictions. In this regard, Zen Buddhism is no different. What does differentiate it from Islam, Christianity, or Pure Land Buddhism is that death is not seen as a portal to another realm for the righteous. Death is a natural and necessary function of the universe; its sting is a result of our craving for an identity which we cannot hold and do not truly have. Our lives are but a gentle wind that quickly passes.

The story of Chinese monk Wuxue Zuyuan (1226–1286), better known in Japan by his posthumous title Bukko Zenji, is a wonderful illustration of this overcoming. At a time when the Mongols were invading his homeland, seeking to uproot the Southern Sung Dynasty, Bukko took refuge in a temple. When the enemy soldiers entered the grounds, they found him seated in the lotus position and prepared to dispatch him. To their surprise, he recited a poem he had just finished:

> In heaven and earth, no crack to hide;
> Joy to know the man is void and the things too are void.
> Splendid the great Mongolian longsword,
> Its lightning flash cuts the spring breeze.

The enemy soldiers were so impressed with his courage and calm, we are told, that they left him alone.

For one to recognize and exist in a way that is devoid of false-self is far from easy. Lifelong habits and human inclinations make it quite difficult to accept that I exist without a static self or soul. Applying that belief in daily life and being truly present at every moment is extraordinarily demanding. For this reason, Zen Buddhism places great emphasis on cultivating the discipline, concentration, and insight to do this through extensive use of meditation. While meditation will be treated in greater depth later on, a few words here may be helpful.

As indicated above, the very name "Zen" means meditation. And while meditative practices are undertaken while walking, working, or drawing the string of a bow, the primary method in Zen Buddhism is *zazen*, or seated meditation.

There are two fundamental objectives in Zen meditation. We might call them concentration and insight. With regard to the former, the practitioner seeks to develop the mental discipline to control his own mind. Meditation makes this progress possible. To descibe in brief:

To develop *concentration*, one spends time in seated meditation. The primary type of meditation in Zen Buddhism is called "the mindfulness or awareness of in-and-out breathing." This type of *zazen* may be practiced from a number of different seated positions. *Seiza* is the position of choice in most dojos, as it is more conducive to self-defense (and easier to achieve) than the lotus position. When visiting a *zendō*, however, most of your time will be spent in a cross legged position (Burmese, half-lotus, or full-lotus position). Posture is tremendously important, as is the position of the hands. While Rinzai and Sōtō Zen practitioners may vary in the placement of their hands, the most common position for *zazen* is known as the "cosmic mudra," where the left hand is placed inside the right, palms up, with the thumbs lightly touching one another. While practicing in a dojo, however, one usually finds *budōka* with their hands on their thighs. Eyes should be slightly open, but not focused on any one thing.

Once in a proper position, the beginner focuses on breathing. As air is slowly brought in through the nose, down into the abdomen, and then out through the nose again, one's attention is given entirely to this simple physical act. Air is brought into the body; air is expelled from the body. One is not thinking about the others in the room, the sweat on one's brow, the physical discomfort from sitting still, although one is aware of the existence of all of them. Attention is on the breath. Zen Master Shunryu Suzuki explained, "If you think, 'I breathe,' the 'I' is extra."* Concentration is on the breath, not the one breathing. This is, of course, remarkably difficult (especially for those of us with Type A personalities and the attention span of an 8-year-old). Ideas, thoughts, and distractions constantly bombard our conscious minds. This is not a bad thing, but these mental disruptions are not to divert one from concentrating on breathing. We allow those thoughts to come into consciousness and then pass out of view. We are not to dwell on them, or fret when they appear; rather, we renew our efforts to be attentive to our breathing.

NiOsho Dai-En Bennage, abbess of Mt. Equity Zendo, offered the following analogy, which I have found quite helpful: Imagine that your small child has run ahead of you and crossed a railroad track right before a locomotive arrived. Now the two of you are separated by the passing train. As you stand on your side of the track, you are focusing intently on the child while the boxcars fly by. You do not look at the cars, but you are aware of them, looking through them, as much as possible, at the object of your attention. Similarly, Tenshin Giryu (Tanouye) Roshi (1938–2003) spoke of being able to "see through one's thoughts as one looks through a propeller."†

The practitioner is likely to find this type of meditation quite difficult. (The reader is certainly invited to put down the book and try it for a few minutes.) However, through diligent practice, one finds oneself able to be more present with the breath and less captured

* Shunryu Suzuki, 29.

† As in Kenneth Kushner, *One Arrow, One Life: Zen, Archery, Enlightenment*, (Rutland, VT: Tuttle Publishing, 2000), 43.

by thoughts and perceptions of one's environment. One begins to master the mind. And, as we shall see, this is both a means of working toward nirvana and the experience of nirvana itself.

The development of *insight* in Zen often takes place through meditation on a *kōan*: a riddle, statement, or conundrum which the seeker strives to understand. The use of *kōan* is typically associated with Rinzai Zen, although its practice is found in the history of Sōtō Zen as well. A meaningful examination of *kōan* practice is beyond the scope of the book, but I highly recommend Philip Kapleau's *Three Pillars of Zen* and Trevor Leggett's *Zen and the Ways* to anyone who wishes to learn more about this fascinating method of religious discipline.

Briefly, the nature of the *kōan* is not a puzzle that one answers through the use of logic, but a problem that forces one to move beyond typical discursive thought in order to understand the spirit of the enigma. The most famous *kōan* in the West is the sound of one hand clapping. (The smart-ass response often given by my students, slapping the palm with the finger-tips of the same hand, would certainly guarantee a painful correction from many Zen masters in Japan.)

The *kōan* that most disciples of Rinzai Zen are familiar with, however, is known as Jōshū's *mu*. The story is about a disciple who asked Jōshū (778–897), the Chinese Ch'an master, whether a dog has the Buddha-nature. Jōshū replied with a firm "*Mu*!" (*Mu* expresses the negative, suggesting a response of "no.") The *kōan* given to students of Zen still today may be, "What is *mu*?" The disciple may first tackle the problem from a logical angle, trying to explain the answer from a philosophical perspective. "Jōshū said *mu* because dogs do not have the capacity for self-realization." "*Mu* is not about the dog's nature, but the idea that any being can 'have' a Buddha nature." Such answers may be correct, from an objective Buddhist perspective, but if given to one's roshi during *dokusan* (one's Zen master during an individual interview), the seeker will be sent back to work on the *kōan*. The disciple will be told not to engage in philosophical speculation, but to concentrate entirely on *mu* and to understand what *mu* is.

The *kōan* is said to foster both concentration and insight in the practitioner. The time spent on a *kōan* is not usually measured in days, but months and often in years. It is to become an all-consuming task to understand the problem of one hand clapping, *mu,* a goose in a bottle, or your face before your ancestors were born. In fact, it is often compared to swallowing a red-hot iron ball, of which you cannot rid yourself. However, when the moment of enlightenment comes, in an instant, everything changes. Those who have had this experience describe a great opening of perspective, as if the truth had been right before their eyes the entire time without their perceiving it. This moment of satori, or sudden enlightenment, cannot be communicated directly, nor can the answer to *mu*. The excited practitioner may then enter the next *dokusan* and when asked "What is *mu*?" reply by seizing the baton from the roshi's hand or simply raise a finger.

The answer, like the initial question, is likely something an outsider cannot understand, appearing nonsensical. It may be a phrase that appears completely out of context or a physical act, perhaps embracing or even striking the roshi. Meditating on a *kōan* is then not a test of cleverness or intelligence, but a means of grasping the nature of reality. For an individual to appropriate these teachings about the self and the world which Buddhism offers, it is not sufficient to read and recite what the Buddha taught. It must be experienced. Rinzai Buddhism helps the disciple do this by means of the *kōan*.

If this type of indirect communication appears strange, it is certainly not exclusive to Zen. Consider the story of Jesus when asked "Who is my neighbor?" His answer provides neither definition nor differentiation, but a parable about a man who gets mugged. In fact, not so different from many Zen masters, Jesus often communicates this way, telling his interlocutors that the kingdom of heaven is like a woman searching for a coin or a man buying a field. What these religious teachers understood is that life-transforming truth is not communicated directly and comprehended by logic, but by challenging the listener to immerse herself in the question and experience the answer existentially. To be certain, Zen masters have often taught this way with deeply cryptic and intense methodologies, but the method itself is not unique.

We often hold a stereotype of the Zen master speaking in incomprehensible language and disciplining his students with extreme severity, beating them silly from time to time. Of course, a stereotype is not falsehood, but an oversimplification of the truth. To be sure, there have been teachers of this stripe, some very famous ones, in fact. At the same time, there are many teachers who are far more direct and less severe than their idiosyncratic counterparts. Human nature being what it is, however, we prefer to read about and share stories of the most peculiar of these teachers and so the stereotype is further embedded in our minds and cultures. It is not my intention to skip these stories, or replace them with less entertaining ones, but simply to warn the reader that what is offered here is only one part of the picture.

Such stories of indirect communication abound in Zen literature, tales of conduct between teachers and students that are, shall we say, a bit surprising to western readers. One can read of a great many encounters where a student was struck, his nose twisted, thrown off a terrace, or shouted at. Readers interested in learning more about the subject should consult D. T. Suzuki's *The Zen Doctrine of No-Mind*(86ff). At times these accounts are comical, other times they are bewildering, especially when the violence leads to enlightenment, but we need to realize that they are far from being nonsensical.

One story that illustrates this involves Ch'an master Lin-chi I-hsüan, (Rinzai Gigen in Japanese, d. 866), founder of the Lin-chi/Rinzai school. On one occasion, he was approached and asked about the nature of Buddhist teaching. The master rose from his seat, grabbed the man by his robe and struck him across the face. Standing there in shock, the questioner was asked by the teacher's disciples why he did not bow to the master in appreciation for the answer to his question. As he was preparing to bow, he suddenly had his breakthrough, or *satori*, and understood both the lesson and the nature of Buddhist teaching.

The master could have responded to the question with a lecture on the dharma, or stories about the life of the Buddha. However, if one wants to understand the nature of Buddhist teaching, an objective presentation of philosophy will not communicate what Buddhism is. The Zen tradition is, again, "not reliant on the written word, a special transmission separate from the scriptures; direct pointing at one's mind, seeing one's nature, becoming a Buddha." And so, a logical explanation of the tradition cannot communicate what Buddhism is. The practice of Zen means to exist in the present, not ponder abstract questions about human nature, religion, philosophy, and the like. The only way that Lin-chi could communicate this to his interlocutor was to draw him out of his abstract thinking and bring him into the present. And nothing brings one into the present more than a strike to the face.

Understanding this helps one also make sense of the *kyosaku*, sometimes known as the *keisaku*. This implement, familiar to all practitioners of Zen, is a large flat wooden stick with which practitioners are struck on their backs or shoulders during meditation. Translated as the "warning stick" or "encouragement stick," it is used to revive those who become weary or distracted while sitting. The force with which it is wielded varies. I have been struck with a smaller one that barely left an impression as well as by a larger one from an able handler who was clearly determined to bring me into the present. In some contexts its use is only by request of the one being struck. In others, it is at the discretion of the *ino*, or *jikijitsu*, who wields it. Typically, anyone visiting a *zendō* will not be struck without requesting so. I advise anyone visiting Konzenji in Naha, however, not to request the *kyosaku* if they have any reservations about being struck with significant force.

I should probably add that it's not surprising that westerners will make jokes about the "Zen whacking stick." It is, after all, a strange and surprising custom to outsiders. It is important to remember, though, that the *kyosaku* is part of the Zen religious practice and is sacrosanct to its adherents. Japanese visitors to a Roman Catholic Church who make jokes about eating Christ's body, an equally strange notion to them, would be demonstrating very poor manners. Likewise, we should remember to treat others' customs respectfully, even when they seem odd to us. I mention this, not from a position of superior cultural sensitivity, but as one who needed to be corrected on this point and would like to spare others the same embarrassment.

Returning to our quick overview of Zen practice, at times the conduct of Zen roshi seems overly harsh and even mean-spirited. While I am sure there were a few sadistic teachers over the centuries, it is a mistake to view all such severe behavior as uncaring—quite the opposite. Extreme measures are often required to bring a person out of his state of delusion and self-destruction, and it is not compassion that leads one to coddle another and thereby fail to help him. The sometimes brutal behavior of the teacher is truly a type of "tough love."

During my first experience of *zazen* in Okinawa, one of the senior men from the temple was quietly walking behind the row of seated neophytes, correcting our posture. Having seen the poor posture of some of the others around me, I was fairly confident that I needed only a small correction if anything. I was wrong. The gentleman came up behind me, placed one hand gently on my shoulder, and with the other smacked me in the lower back with such force that I immediately shot up into a posture I did not know I was capable of attaining. With a look of shock and disbelief, and a bit of pain in my eyes, I glanced over and saw him smiling warmly at me before moving on to the next person. I remember thinking that he could have gently positioned my body into the right position. Perhaps, but ever since then, when I sit in meditation, I think of that afternoon seated in *zazen* at the Budōkan, and I strive to recreate the posture he forcefully produced. Had he done so gently, I would have long forgotten what he was trying to teach me. As it is, I do not think I will ever forget.

Chapter Three

The Warriors' Zen

Part One: Initial Attraction

"The atmosphere of the classical bujutsu is that of Zen. To engage in such classical training is to learn the mode of Zen. It follows naturally that the characteristics of Zen must also permeate the classical budo forms; and those who do not appreciate Zen will not understand budo." –Donn F. Draeger

The Introduction of Zen to Japan

The above quote from martial arts historian Donn F. Draeger (1922–1982) is about the intimate and essential connection between Japanese martial traditions and Zen. While he has overstated their relationship, it is clear that Zen and Japanese fighting arts have a long and intertwined history. Certainly for the student of *budō* to understand the history and contemporary practice of her art, knowledge of Zen is of enormous help. So, let us begin by taking a look at the interconnection of these two remarkable disciplines, and at what it is that has brought seemingly disparate philosophies together.

Buddhism initially made its way to Japan through Korea. In the middle of the sixth century, a Korean king sent an image of the Buddha, along with Buddhist scriptures, to Prince Shotoku (573–621) in Japan. Whereas the Buddha is worshipped throughout East Asia, the Korean sovereign explained, perhaps the Japanese would like to get on board as well.

According to the apocryphal tale, the Japanese were unsure about this spiritual and religious advice, concerned as they were with how the local *kami,* or deities, would regard the competition. Eminently reasonable, they decided to test the proposal. One individual was instructed to venerate the Buddha; the others would watch and see what would happen. When the test subject's house burned down, the others determined that the Korean king had given rather poor advice; the *kami* were angry. The image was thereupon thrown in a river. What happened next, however, was even more shocking. An epidemic in the land broke out almost immediately. Clearly the Buddha was not a figure to be cast aside so lightly. It is from this point that we can trace the curious relationship of Shinto and Buddhism in Japan, struggling to exist side by side and make sense of one another.* For the most part, mutual respect and coexistence have been the norm, along with a great deal of co-mingling of traditions.

Beyond the entertainment value of this story, there was a very practical matter that Prince Shotoku recognized: a new faith with a single central figure could unite the Japanese. Shinto's many provincial *kami* contributed to the division of clans throughout the Japanese mainland. A unifying religion was desirable. As Korea's gifts were soon supplemented by the import of Buddhist scriptures from China, it was clear that Japan offered fertile soil for this millennium-old religion that was slowly making its way Eastward.

The emergence of Zen in Japan would have to wait several centuries, however. According to historian Winston L. King, Zen had existed in Japan since the seventh century, quietly minding its position under the umbrella of Tendai Buddhism.† It finally made it mark on Japanese culture, however, in the mid thirteenth century, thanks to a man named Eisai (1141–1215). It was he, known as the "founder" of Zen in Japan, who traveled to China in the late twelfth century. He returned in 1191 and proceeded to share his new religious discipline with the military government. Initially, Zen was found primarily in Kyoto, where numerous other Buddhist schools were located. As the proverbial new kid on the block, the Zen school had to watch itself around the larger and more senior schools. However, this was not a problem in the city of Kamakura, the seat of the Hōjō government.

---

* Ellwood, 78.

† Winston L. King, *Zen and the Way of the Sword: Arming the Samurai Psyche* (New York: Oxford University Press, 1993), 27.

The militaristic Hōjō regime was on the rise as the Minamoto family declined. The former attributed this to the elegant and effeminate nature (read "weakness") of Minamoto culture. The Hōjō comprised a strict, no-nonsense martial government, and this new school of Zen appealed to them, for reasons we will discuss below. It was not long before the heads of the Hōjō administration embraced Zen. The first in the family to undertake serious Zen discipline was Tokiyori (1227–1263), the fifth regent in the Kamakura Shogunate, who, it is said, mastered it.

The Hōjō family's preference for Zen then filtered down to samurai throughout different regions of Japan. The dissemination of Zen was extensive enough to foster a saying during the Kamakura period (1185–1333), "Tendai is for the imperial court, Shingon for the nobility, Zen for the warrior class, and Pure Land for the masses."* It is worth pointing out that the samurai were at this time interested in the relevance of Zen to their daily lives, which is to say that their interest and understanding of Zen were governed by the application of this religious discipline to their work as samurai; they had no interest in retreating from the world and the responsibilities laid upon them by virtue of their place in society.

Transplanting Zen from China into Kamakura was not without its difficulties. The members of the warrior caste, men and women, who began to undertake serious study of Zen had a problem; they knew little if any Chinese. Therefore they could not read or study the literature and scriptures that had been brought to Japan by men like Eisai and Dōgen (1200–1253), the founder of Sōtō Zen in Japan. Visiting Chinese teachers could not engage in the subtle conversations and interviews which were so much a part of the tradition. Zen in Kamakura needed to change.

The all important *dokusan*, the interview between master and student, could not use classical Chinese references anymore; teachers needed to address events in Japanese culture. Also, these exchanges

* Ibid, 30.

came to be conducted with very few words. These very short lessons were then known as "one-word" Zen. Teachers who could not explain the history and context of certain *kōan* adapted to their situations and created various new *kōan* on the instant; these related to the samurai's life and experience, thereby earning the name *Shikin*-Zen, or "On-the-instant Zen." The short and pithy remarks which Zen was known for were only reinforced by this change. Additionally, *kōan* specifically for samurai were developed (e.g., "Wielding the spear with empty hands"), often utilizing incidents from the lives of early warrior-disciples.

While this linguistic handicap suggests an impediment on the part of the samurai to learning the dharma, they were at the same time perceived to have a distinct advantage over others who undertook Zen discipline. The samurai, because their lives were regularly on the line, threw themselves into the study and practice of Zen with much more rigor and determination. While the monk believed himself to have decades to pursue the life of Zen, the warrior might have only one more day. Due to the fact that he counted on—and hoped for—death in battle at any time, he pursued Zen with a far greater sense of urgency. For this reason, Hakuin (1686–1769) remarked that what a samurai could accomplish in Zen in a few days would take a monk a hundred days to do.*

When Japan later entered the peace of the Tokugawa shogunate (1603–1868), the samurai had more time for learning. As a result, they were able to study the Chinese classics. Eventually, the use of the classical *kōan* was reestablished and the warrior *kōan* fell out of use. Unfortunately, the roughly three hundred *kōan* of this "Warrior Zen" were lost, leaving us today with the sad loss of a tradition. Trevor Leggett's excellent book *Zen and the Ways* provides a good introduction to this history, along with an intriguing appendix on the subject by Imai Fukuzan. However, it should be noted that questions regarding the historicity of these warrior *kōan* are starting to be raised.

---

* Trevor Leggett, *Zen and the Ways* (Boston: Routledge & Kegan Paul, 1978), 36.

With the rise of the Ashikaga shogunate, during the Muromachi period (1336–1573), even greater attention came to be paid to the beneficial relationship between Zen and the samurai's life and work. A number of the shoguns of this period became enamored with Zen and its relationship to samurai culture, to the point that they became what King called "addicts." This affinity reached its apex under shoguns Ashikaga Yoshimitsu (1358–1408) and Ashikaga Yoshimasa (1443–1490). The majority of generals under their leadership followed their example by taking up the practice of Zen themselves.

Additionally, the influence of Zen was strong in the schools of *bujutsu* that were taking form at that time. Kami-idzumi Ise no Kami Hidetsuna (d. 1577) founded his school of swordsmanship, *Shinkage-ryu,* on the basis of what the Shinto *kami* Kashima allegedly taught him. However, we can clearly see Zen philosophy in its teaching. On the final certificate that is given to those who have mastered the art, there is nothing but a circle—a famous Zen image which often represents a mirror free of dust or imperfection, which reflects perfectly the world around it. In this image we find the Zen concept of *mushin,* which we will return to in Chapter 6. Additionally, formerly secret documents of *Shinkage-ryu* teach the following about the philosophy of the school:

> Into a soul (*kokoro*) absolutely free from
> Thoughts and emotions,
> Even the Tiger finds no room to insert
> Its fierce claws...
> Some think that striking is to strike:
> But striking is not to strike, nor is killing to kill.
> He who strikes and he who is struck—
> They are both no more than a dream that
> Has no reality."*

The student of swordsmanship may wonder what this poem has to do with helping one become a superior swordsman. However, as

* Daisetz T. Suzuki, *Zen and Japanese Culture* (Princeton: Princeton University Press, 1959), 123.

we shall see with many of the schools of swordsmanship through Japanese history, training the mind is as important as training the body. Overcoming disrupting thoughts and emotional distraction, and responding to a situation without time-consuming deliberation, are traits essential to victory in battle, and it is through the study of Zen that many have learned how to acheive them.

The Attraction

As we have seen, the samurai found much to admire in the school of Buddhism known as Zen. King went so far as to call it "love at first sight" and cited a saying similar to one mentioned above, "Though other groups favor Pure Land or Shingon Buddhism, Zen is the religion of the warrior."* And so we must ask, why the attraction? What was it about this minimalist school of Buddhism, so concerned with seated meditation, that attracted warriors whose lives were consumed with discipline, service and violence? Anyone who suggests that Zen offered escape from their demanding lives could not be further from the truth.

However, before we look at the particulars of Zen as they relate to the work of the samurai, we must first consider why they were interested in a new religion at all. Confucianism already provided them with a meaningful philosophy that taught ethics and their place in society. Shinto gave them and their families access to the benefits and graces of the spirits that inhabit the Japanese islands. In what ways might Buddhist belief and ritual add anything to the mix?

To begin with, we in the West often think of religious communities as pleasant, supportive environments where the faithful come together for fellowship and singing in a welcoming and relaxed atmosphere. And this trend has only increased in recent decades. The religious practices of the Japanese, however, have a very different tone. While one finds hardship and rigor in the history of Jewish, Christian and Muslim practice in the West, there is little to match the intensity of the Japanese.

* King, 4.

Consider the *kaihogyo* practiced by the monks at Mount Hiei. This pilgrimage around the mountain, which involves devotions at a series of shrines along the way, requires participants to "run a course of increasing length for one hundred days a year over seven years; in the seventh year the daily run is 84 km or 52.5 miles."* It is furthermore worth noting that the priests and monks who undertake this discipline do so while wearing straw sandals and maintaining a vegetarian diet.

While this practice is extreme, a large number of other contemporary religious practices in Japan also require great physical and mental training and fortitude. Walking on hot coals, chanting under a frigid waterfall, massive tugs-of-war, walking pilgrimages that last for months—these are not casual undertakings. Before visiting Okinawa, I always need to practice sitting for extended periods in the half-lotus position, in preparation for *zazen* at Kozenji Zendo. I doubt that anyone first needs to get in shape in order to come and participate in worship at my Lutheran church in Pennsylvania.

Japanese religion is profoundly tactile and kinesthetic. For warriors who might shun traditions focused on emotion or academic disputation, the rigor and demand in many Japanese traditions could be appreciated, as they make one stronger and more disciplined. Zen in particular teaches a rejection of quaint and gentle religion. Suzuki Shōsan, a samurai who retired to the life of a Zen monk, castigated some of his contemporaries for forgetting this. "In learning the Buddhist Law (Zen) in recent years, many people seem to have forgotten that Zen includes high spirits of bravery and great power. Therefore, those who learn the Buddhist Law become so tender-hearted, admirable-looking, desireless, and good-natured that they somehow tend to lose the will to react to any unfavorable stimulus as angrily as if saying, 'Damn it!'"†

Beyond being a religion that favors the testosterone-laden, what

Robert Ellwood, 100.

Omori Sogen, *An Introduction to Zen Training*, trans. Dogen Hosokawa and Roy Yoshimoto (Rutland, VT: Tuttle Publishing, 2001), 99.

was is about Zen that drew the attention and admiration of the samurai? Yagyū Munenori (1571–1646) pointed to two primary aspects of Zen which were seen as invaluable by Japan's warrior class: In discussing the relationship between the disciplines of the warrior and the monk, he saw a great deal of common ground. "The martial arts are in accordance with the Buddhist Dharma, and have many points in common with Zen. These include in particular an aversion to attachment and aversion to being detained by things."* These two traits have been considered essential in Japan for one to reach the highest state of excellence in the various martial disciplines, indeed in every Japanese Way or art form.

To these we will add: the freedom to act, a preference for action over rumination, physical and mental discipline, and simplicity of life. While each of these themes will be treated separately, the reader should surely see the interconnection of them all.

Overcoming Attachment

From the beginning of our discussion of Buddhism, it is clear that mental attachment must be avoided. The importance of this cannot be overstated. While visiting Kozenji, I noticed that the first thing one sees upon entering is a large calligraphy immediately inside the door, facing those who enter, with the words, "Do not be attached to any one thing."

Those who take this advice seriously may think about overcoming attachment to money, possessions, or health. For the Japanese warrior something more immediate could be at stake; his very life could be required of him at any moment. Overcoming attachment to his own existence was not something abstract or to be pondered in his declining years. How firmly he would cling to his very existence was a daily concern.

Moreover, overcoming attachment to his own life was not only about spiritual maturity. The samurai realized that overcoming this

---

* Yagyu Munenori, *The Life-Giving Sword*, trans. William Scott Wilson (New York: Kodansha, 2003), 127f.

distraction made him a better fighter. King stated this quite decisively when he wrote, "But be it repeated: the main value of Zen practice in meditation for the samurai was the psychological conditioning of his combat skills at the moment of decisive action when life was at stake. Certainly the main goal of his superiors in sending him to a Zen monastery for training was not to produce a Buddhist saint, but to maximize his effectiveness as a fighter."* If one is in fear for his life, he cannot commit fully to battle. He will hesitate; he will second-guess himself. What is needed is the courage and instantaneous action found in those who have overcome their fear of death. D. T. Suzuki explained, "When there is the slightest feeling of death or of attachment to life, the mind loses its 'fluidity.' The fluidity is nonhindrance."†

Suzuki and others have explained that Zen's capacity to handle the problem of attachment and conquer the fear of death held a great attraction for the samurai. Also, the samurai were not simply warriors who *might* die in battle, like warriors in any nation or land. The samurai were part of a culture that *expected* them to die in battle, *expected* them to end their own lives if honor was at stake, *expected* them to die in the service of their lord, even apart from the context of battle. The samurai, whose very life existed "to serve," was *expected* to give his life in service. At the beginning of the Hagakure, a manual on the life and duties of the samurai, Yamamoto Tsunetomo (1659–1719) explains, "The Way of the Samurai is found in death."‡ Admittedly, Tsunetomo was a bit over the top in his views, exaggerating the ethos of the samurai. In any case, the members of the warrior caste were told to meditate on their mortality and impending demise at all times, so they would be ready at a moment's notice to die with dignity. According to Daidōji Yūzan Shigesuki (1639–1730), in The Code of the Samurai, "One who is a samurai must before all

---

* King, 178.

† Suzuki, *Zen and Japanese Culture,* 144.

‡ Yamamoto Tsunetomo, *Hagakure,* trans. William Scott Wilson (New York: Kodansha, 2002), 23.

things keep constantly in mind, by day and by night, from the morning when he takes up his chopsticks to eat his New Year's breakfast to Old Year's night when he pays his yearly bills, the fact that he has to die. That is his chief business."*

To this we might add Yamamoto Tsunetomo's advice:

> Meditation on inevitable death should be performed daily. Every day when one's body and mind are at peace, one should meditate upon being ripped apart by arrows, rifles, spears and swords, being carried away by surging waves, being thrown into the midst of a great fire, being struck by lightning, being shaken to death by a great earthquake, falling from thousand-foot cliffs, dying of disease or committing seppuku at the death of one's master. And every day without fail one should consider himself as dead.†

Again, the purpose of such fearlessness was not simply an honorable death, but more effective living. All other things being equal, those without fear of death will be superior on the battlefield. When faced with an opponent equally skilled with the sword, the slightest hesitation will likely lead to your head or limb taking leave of your torso. Any craving for one's life or attachment to this world, manifested in hesitation, could be the samurai's worst enemy. If attachment to this life is overcome through the discipline and study of Zen, one may live, fight and serve another day. It was Zen, many believed, that equipped one best for such an attitude. Speaking of the benefits of Buddhism for the *bushi*, Inazo Nitobe (1862–1933) wrote in his influential *Bushido: The Soul of Japan*, "It furnished a sense of calm trust in Fate, a quiet submission to the inevitable, that stoic composure in sight of danger or calamity, that disdain of life and friendliness with death."‡

At the same time, it is worth noting that overcoming the fear of death can manifest itself in reckless behavior. It should prevent

* As in King, 126.

† Yamamoto 172.

‡ Inazo Nitobe, *Bushido: The Soul of Japan* (Rutland, VT: Tuttle Publshing, 1969), 11.

self-defeating hesitation, not encourage carelessness. Such a state of mind must be accompanied with the strong desire to serve a greater cause if one is to avoid wild, inattentive, or thoughtless behavior on the battlefield. Even then, one must be attentive to whether one's actions actually serve the greater good or are simply reckless abandon. It was exactly this lack of critique that led to such counter-productive tactics during World War II as banzai charges. As King explained, "[M]ost of the banzai charges were merely man-wasting futilities."* In general, however, overcoming the fear of death is to be desired. As one American combat veteran expressed to me, "Those who are selfless are superior on the battlefield." It was precisely this selflessness that the samurai ascribed to in their lives of service, and overcoming the fear of death was one essential component they required of themselves.

Interestingly, while Buddhism helped the samurai achieve a proper state of mind regarding death, it was the samurai's constant and necessary acknowledgement of his own mortality which made it easier to undertake and understand Zen. According to Suzuki Shōsan, "Now the life of the samurai is especially one in which birth-death (*samsara*) cannot but be comprehended. And when one does understand birth-death, inevitably the Way [of Buddha] is there."† Overcoming attachment to this life was perceived as an absolute necessity for the samurai. The discipline of Zen assisted in this pursuit, and the fact that the samurai were already concerned about such a matter made them greater adepts of Zen.

Not to be Detained

The second benefit Munenori mentioned was the ability to avoid being detained by conscious thoughts and other mental distractions. This cleary relates to the first of Zen's benefits. The problem that so often presents itself to those in battle is hesitation. While there is certainly room for prudence, if one is detained at the point

---

King, 206.

As in King, 185.

in time when decisive action is required, the results can be disastrous. This is obviously a factor in any kind of fighting, but in the context of two men standing several feet apart, razor sharp *katana* in hand, a hesitation of only a few milliseconds could be decisive. One's actions should never be detained by conscious deliberation when the moment to act has come. When the decision to fight has been made, mental reflection only detains the fighter. In the heat of battle, conscious thoughtfulness only creates hesitancy. In the *Tengugeijutsu,* written by Tamba under the pen-name Chissai in 1739, the following question is posed and answered:

> Question: Why do the Buddhists reject conscious thinking as bad? Answer: Conscious thoughts are like the ordinary soldiers; when the general is entangled in material things and becomes confused and weak, he loses his authority. Then the soldiers under him do not avail themselves of his knowledge but look to themselves alone, and pursue their private plans. And as each one is working for himself, the camp is in disorder, with riots and affrays, and in the end the army meets a disastrous defeat.*

If there is no conscious thought, one might ask, how then does one make decisions in the midst of the fight? Certainly a thoughtless berserker is not the model for effective combat engagement. This question is important, and one that we shall return to in more depth in later chapters. For the moment, we may say that the individual relies on her training when thrust into a life-and-death struggle. Taisen Deshimaru (1914–1982), a Rinzai Zen roshi with a thorough knowledge martial arts, expressed it this way. "How does one choose the technique of attack? There is no choosing. It happens unconsciously, automatically, naturally. There can be no thought, because if there is a thought there is a time of thought and that means a flaw."† This is not to say that one acts without conscious awareness and control over what one is doing. This is a very common mistake when trying

* As in Leggett, *Zen and the Ways,* 197.

† Taisen Deshimaru, *The Zen Way to the Martial Arts* (New York: Compass, 1982), 32.

to understand the mindfulness that was being encouraged. If one is oblivious to the techniques being implemented in a fight, that is a mindset quite apart from what Deshimaru and others described. Again, we will return to this in later chapters.

The mental pause to be avoided is the disruptive conscious thought that interferes with the free flow of mental activity so necessary in battle. Imagine a warrior posed to strike down his opponent. Whether before or in the midst of his attack, if he thinks, "If this technique does not work, I am in big trouble," he delays and inhibits his attack in a miniscule but significant way. His thought is correct; it does not represent flawed logic. However, conscious thought at that time only detains his action. He must control his mind if he is to reach the apex of his ability as a warrior. D. T. Suzuki explained, "When there is no obstruction of whatever kind, the swordsman's movements are like flashes of lightening or like the mirror reflecting images."*

While the samurai recognized the value of Zen discipline for minimizing or eradicating the mental disruptions that compromised their effectiveness in battle, they also understood that they could exploit such a weakness in others. While they disciplined themselves in order to avoid falling victim to such a *suki,* or interval of broken mindfulness, they looked for it in others. Looking into the eyes of their opponents, they waited for a sign that the enemy had become mentally distracted—perhaps with a momentary reflection on the possibility of his death, or perhaps by pondering his strategy. That was the precise moment when success was most likely. During that *suki* the opposing warrior was most vulnerable to attack and could be cut down. Deshimaru offered this advice, "Think-first-then-strike is not the right way. You must seize upon *suki,* opportunity. Opportunity is most important, and thinking cannot create it. Only consciousness can seize upon the opportunity for action, the empty space in which one must act."†

---

* Suzuki, *Zen and Japanese Culture,* 159.

† Deshimaru, 32.

Not long ago there was a commercial on Japanese television that depicted two samurai, swords drawn in their respective *kamae* (fighting stance), poised to strike one another down. Suddenly, one of the two men shuts his eyes tightly and sneezes. The scene ends with the other samurai bringing his sword down on his hapless opponent. The commercial ends with a spokesman advising the viewers to purchase a certain cold medicine; one should always be at one's best. The first time I saw this commercial I was riding the Yamanote train line and burst out laughing—a bit of a social *faux pas* in Japan. The commercial was, of course, aiming for humor, but it accurately reflected the approach the samurai might take in a duel. Of course, one was looking for a *suki* somewhat less obvious than a thunderous sneeze. Any indication that betrays that one's opponent has been detained by conscious deliberation, or some mental break, represents the moment of his greatest vulnerability.

Freedom to Act

To reiterate, the eradication of conscious thought or deliberation does not mean that one responds merely on the basis of habit, training and instinct. The mind needs to be fluid and responsive, not slavishly subject to training routines. At the same time, the importance of such regular training is not thereby vitiated. The martial artist must develop the tools necessary for one's craft, and initially this requires that fundamental techniques be drilled continuously. However, at the highest level of one's training, there must be freedom of action, not thoughtless reaction. The individual sitting in *zazen* is not entering a state of obliviousness, but is fully present in the moment. Developing the ability to sit in this way takes great effort, but it fosters the mindfulness that permits one to maintain clarity of thought, and therefore freedom of action. In the midst of a physical struggle, this is of paramount importance.

An individual who finds herself in a self-defense situation may panic but will fall back on her training and effectively execute some good techniques. This is good. However, retaining conscious lucidity, with the freedom to act as the situation unfolds, is superior. If I am subject to aggression and can only respond from habit, using throwing techniques without conscious awareness of what I am doing, I may respond with unnecessary force. Even if I am successful in defending myself, I may do greater injury to my attacker than is morally or legally justifiable. The result could find me sitting in prison while my children grow up without a father, seeing my life-savings handed over to my attacker's family in a civil settlement. I recall reading an account by a former military man who was attacked by a kid with a knife. He responded according to his training, disarmed the teenager, seized the knife, and barely caught himself before stabbing the boy in the eye. Again, falling back on one's training in a moment of panic is good; the freedom of mind and action which *zazen* can inculcate is better.

In another example, from the Tokugawa period in Japanese history, students from a certain jujutsu school were being mysteriously murdered. All the bodies showed the same signs: no evidence of a struggle and the same stab wound in the torso. This appeared quite strange, as the victims were proficient enough in their art to have at least put up a good fight before succumbing to a superior opponent. It was eventually determined that the assailant had counted on the victims' habitual response to a particular attack. He had approached the jujutsu men with a short sword, held at his waist with his left hand. When in range, he apparently pulled the sword from its scabbard and raised it over his head, ready to bring it down on his victim. The victimes instinctively responded with the appropriate defense. However, what they did not perceive was that the attacker had reversed the position of the sword from the beginning. When he held it at his waist, the tip of the sword was forward, not back. What he raised over his head was not the sword, but the scabbard. With the victim's attention on the raised scabbard, the short sword that was still held at the waist was plunged into his body.* Admittedly a devi-

* Leggett, *Zen and the Ways*, 138f.

ous and dastardly strategy, one can see that it relied on the opponent's conditioned response. It could only be countered by one with considerable presence-of-mind and freedom of response—precisely the mindfulness practiced in Zen meditation.

The next example is a bit more encouraging. There was a young man with only one arm who dreamed of excelling at judo. While he was indeed quite good, given his handicap, he wanted to be able to compete against and defeat his two-armed opponents. Try as he might, this proved too difficult of a task. His teacher then took it upon himself to train the boy in secret for an upcoming tournament. He had the boy work on just two variations of the same throw, *hizaguruma*. Over and over, he practiced only this throw, without anyone knowing of his training. When in class with other students, he worked only on defense. The teacher, like the assailant in the previous example, was predicting and relying on the habitual response of the boys' opponents. As it turns out, the standard defense against *hizaguruma*, which the boy was perfecting, is to grab hold of the opponent's arm. At the *shiai*, the boy was able to execute the throws, winning round after round, and eventually winning the tournament, because his opponents always relied on their habitual defense of grabbing an arm… which was not there.* Of course such a trick can only work for time, for as soon as opponents catch on to what is happening, they can counter the move. However, in combat or contexts like the judo tournament, such a strategy is most effective. Only an individual with remarkable perception, who is freely responding to his environment, can be effective against such an attack.

Commenting on this interplay of habit and freedom, Trevor Leggett (from whose book the above examples are drawn), explains, "As a matter of fact, it is very easy to defeat a man who simply executes his techniques as a reflex. One can control his body through them. One sets off a reflex in him, and then waits with the counter."† In what may

* Ibid., 210ff.

† Ibid., 125.

be counterintuitive, he goes on to explain that it is the raw beginner who poses a greater challenge to a martial arts practitioner than one with more experience. The practitioner with some experience acts predictably. He uses techniques that his opponent has responded to many times before. "This is one reason why an expert finds it much easier to defeat a man who has trained for a year than an absolute beginner."*

Leggett recounts a contest between a friend who was a senior kendo practitioner and himself, a senior *judōka*. Neither had any experience in the other's discipline, but wanted to see what would happen if they challenged one another in their respective arts. In the judo contest, the *kendōka* simply launched himself "like a torpedo" at Leggett's legs, in a very unconventional, haphazard attack. Of course Leggett's years of training in judo never required him to defend against such a chaotic, random attempt, and so Leggett was taken down, but immediately took control and ended up on top of his friend. In the Kendo contest, Leggett simply jumped at his opponent with a wild strike, holding the *shinai* in one hand—an equally unsystematic and chance attack. He succeeded in grazing the *kendōka's* head, although not sufficiently to have merited a point in kendo, surprising his friend just as he had been surprised. Not being bound by the parameters set by the school's curriculum, both men's freedom of mind and action made them rather formidable opponents. Moreover, the habitual responses to standard attacks, formed by each through years of training, were not triggered by the unconventional attacker. Of course, it is foolish to conclude that studying either discipline is a waste of time, and that relying on slapdash techniques is beneficial. We must remember that both men had developed tremendous use of their bodies through their respective disciplines. Still, one can see the importance of developing a mind that is free in its movement.

* Ibid., 126.

Action Over Rumination

While certain schools of religion encourage practitioners to spend time in philosophical reflection, considering questions of metaphysics, ethics, or the afterlife, Zen eschews such rumination and book learning. Zen has long been a tradition which emphasizes action, not navel-gazing. Even during the long hours spent in seated meditation, the mind is neither absent nor lost pondering abstract problems. Even silent, unmoving *zazen* is characterized by one living and being present in the moment, a type of motionless action.

Long suspicious of scholars, bookworms and philosophers, the samurai found in their Zen masters men who were focused on the moment at hand. D. T. Suzuki explained:

> This was indeed the kind of spirit Zen cultivated among its warrior followers. Zen did not necessarily argue with them about immortality of the soul or righteousness or the divine way of ethical conduct, but it simply urged going ahead with whatever conclusion rational or irrational a man has arrived at. Philosophy may safely be left with intellectual minds; Zen wants to act, and the most effective act, once the mind is made up, is to go on without looking backward. In this respect, Zen is indeed the religion of the samurai warrior.*

In contrast with other schools of Buddhism that can be far more cerebral, Zen has preferred a course more existential. The influence of Daoism is certainly a factor in this emphasis, dating back to its early years in China. In Japan, there was the precedent of both Daoism and Shinto which may have encouraged this direction in Zen. According to King, "Zen joined forces with Taoist-Shinto roots of Japanese culture rather than with the intellectual tradition of Buddhism. For the warriors of Japan, visceral reactions were much more important than ideas; hence they found Zen most congenial."† Draeger also described the influence of the Wang Yang-ming school of

* Suzuki, *Zen and Japanese Culture,* 84.

† King, 43.

Confucianism, known as *Oyomei* in Japan, which "stressed reliance upon intuition and moral sense rather than upon intellect." In contrast to the school of *Chu Hsi*, *Oyomei* sought to unite knowledge and action through self-discipline. "Like Zen, both the system and its methods of spiritual cultivation are simple and direct, qualities that gave it a powerful appeal to warriors."* The culture of the Japanese warrior placed far greater importance on intuition and action, engaging life from the gut. Zen was the natural fit for such an individual. King continued, "Truth was existential, not intellectual; its realization and practice were visceral, not cerebral. This character of Zen then put it well within the range of samurai awareness and emotional compatibility."†

It is worth pointing out, however, that even within Zen itself, there can be the tendency to over-intellectualize the discipline. The Kyoto School of philosophy, highly influenced by Zen, is sometimes accused of this. Also, not long ago I had a chance to sit and talk with Sogen Sakiyama Roshi, abbot of Kozenji. (Some *karateka* will recognize him as a student of Chojun Miyagi, founder of goju-ryu, and later the Zen master of Shoshin Nagamine, founder of Matsubayashi-ryu, among many of the most senior karate instructors in Okinawa still today.) I asked him, "What mistake do most *gaijin* [i.e., foreigners] make when trying to understand Zen?" He replied that many foreigners think Zen is only about thought. He explained that they explore many books about Zen, but do not have the experience of sitting. They first read and then only later may sit *zazen*. This is a mistake. He later remarked that in Japan, it is the other way around. Practitioners are first told to sit, and only much later will the theory behind sitting be explained to them. (Personally, I think both ends of the spectrum are problematic. Certainly a middle way is preferable.)

---

* Donn F. Draeger, *Classical Budo: The Martial Arts and Ways of Japan* (Boston: Weatherhill, 1973), 23.

† King, 163.

Physical and Mental Discipline

The samurai were men of action, at least during the periods of history we have discussed so far. (We shall discuss the peace of the Tokugawa era a bit later.) As such, they were attracted to rigorous activities and discipline. The life of the academic was not one which they found appealing. According to Nitobe, "A typical samurai calls a literary savant a book-smelling sot."* Tsunetomo often takes this derision of academics a step further, "Recently, people who are called 'clever' adorn themselves with superficial wisdom and only deceive others. For this reason they are inferior to dull-witted folks. A dull-witted person is direct."† Or again, a quote which holds a place of honor on my office door, "Furthermore, scholars and their like are men who with wit and speech hide their own true cowardice and greed."‡

Training in Zen, however, requires great physical and mental rigor. This likely appealed to the hyper-masculine samurai culture. Disciplining one's own mind, bringing it under control, developing it with attention toward effectiveness in battle, and eradicating mental weakness are all undertakings that resonate with the desires and needs of men of action. Scouring manuscripts in an archive, debating the finer points of philosophy, or scribing long treatises also require great mental effort, but are perceived to have much less value for the professional warrior.

The idea of sitting may not sound like rigorous physical discipline to those who have not practiced *zazen*. An hour spent sitting in a *zendō*, however, is likely to change such an impression. To begin with, posture is of the utmost importance. Most people who give meditation a try, especially westerners, do not have the flexibility and strength to position themselves correctly. Even if they sit in a half-lotus position, rather than the full-lotus, keeping their knees on the ground may prove too much for them. While such a position expresses an ideal physical posture, and is conducive to great health,

---

* Nitobe, 17.

† Tsunetomo, 31

‡ Ibid., 50.

most people cannot maintain it for more than a few minutes. Add to this the breathing that is taught and practiced. Again, it is difficult to perform correctly but carries with it enormous physical benefits. Details of such posture and breathing will be provided in chapter 5. For the moment, it is sufficient to point out the significant physical demands which *zazen* places on the one sitting, even aside from the mental discipline. (Think back to the legend of Bodhidharma and his early disciples.)

During my first time sitting in formal meditation, the other greenhorns and I discovered just how difficult sitting can be. We only sat for three twenty-minute periods, with *kinhin,* or walking meditation, separating the second and third. The room was full of *karateka* who had traveled to Okinawa for training and were attending this program on Zen during one afternoon. By the third session, I recall my hip flexors twitching so strongly that my knees were visibly shaking. My back and shoulders were painfully stiff, and one of my feet had fallen asleep. (It is worth pointing out that some of this was due to incorrect posture on my part.) Many of us who accepted the *kyosaku,* the large, flat stick with which those sitting may be struck to assist their mindfulness, were quite surprised that we were not given a sharp slap but a tremendous blow. I recall being sure I would have two long bruises down my back. (I did not.) One teenage boy sat up after being struck with tears in his eyes. The signal for the end of *zazen,* the final bell, as it were, was greeted with quite a few sighs and groans from the participants. Strong athletic karate practitioners were unable to stand, requiring assistance from those seated on either side. Not one of us left with anything less than respect for the physical rigors of *zazen.*

What I came to realize later was that we were given a beginner's introduction to seated meditation. While there are temples where less rigorous sitting is common, much of the tradition is far more demanding. Trevor Leggett describes a Zen *sesshin,* a kind of retreat for those who are willing to push themselves both physically and mentally for an extended period of time:

> A Zen training week is severe. Very little sleep is allowed; some temples allow none at all during the training week at the beginning of December called *Rohatsu,* which ends on the anniversary of Buddha's illumination. The pupils cannot make their replies [to their Zen master] casually; in a traditional training hall there is quite a lot of beating of those who are slack in their efforts. A real master brings his students to a state where they feel their very life depends on the right answer. This is a duplication of the Buddha's resolve: "Either I will solve the problem, or I will fall dead on this meditation seat."*

Simplicity

"Zen discipline is simple, direct, self-reliant, self-denying; its ascetic tendency goes well with the fighting spirit."† So claimed D. T. Suzuki, and it is hard to disagree. Here we may briefly treat the attraction which simplicity held for the samurai. When we speak of simplicity in regard to Zen, it should be clear that we do not mean that the concepts and ideas found in Zen are simplistic or simple to comprehend and appropriate. Those who decide to dedicate their lives to Zen discipline can count on years or decades of rigorous training before a major realization is reached. At the same time, we may say that in other ways Zen is very simple. Zen does not require advanced studies in religion or philosophy. It does not require its disciple to own a massive library or purchase secret teaching. In many ways Zen is a simple concept, and those who achieve *satori,* or awakening, sometimes remark that once their eyes were opened, perceiving existence correctly became crystal clear, and they wondered why they had not seen it all along.

We have previously discussed how the samurai favored a religious discipline set apart from the academic and effeminate life of the imperial capital. In Zen, not only did they find an attractive school of thought, but attractive schools as well. The very aesthetic of the

---

* Leggett, *Zen and the Ways,* 14.

† Suzuki, *Zen and Japanese Culture,* 62.

zendō held great appeal to the samurai class. Simplicity, austerity, rustic and irregular surroundings, the ideals of *sabi* and *wabi,* were the hallmarks of teachers of both Zen and *budō*. This spartan ideal still exists in Japan, as Zen has penetrated into a great many of the Japanese cultural traditions. During the periods of history we are discussing here, when military campaigns and arduous travel were the norm, the minimalism of the Zen temple could be appreciated.

This simplicity, again, should not be misunderstood to mean simplistic. The sparse design of a *zendō,* dojo, or tea room, is meticulously organized and arranged. There is great thought and effort expended in making the aesthetic appealing. Minimalism does not mean, simply, having little stuff. In architecture, décor, conduct and endeavor, the plainness and effortlessness involved demand great skill. In the various Japanese art forms, or Ways, outsiders may think something very basic is being practiced. However, *shodō* is not simply writing; *chadō* is not simply serving tea; *zazen* is not simply sitting; *kyūdō* is not simply shooting an arrow. Likewise, creating the simple environment of the *zendō* and practicing its associated activities are extremely rigorous. Ellwood hits the nail on the head when he writes, "The match [between Zen and the samurai] was right: on the one hand the discipline of Zen, including ability to endure pain and privation, went well with the warrior's spirit; on the other, the austere but elegant arts of Zen suited the rising warrior's aspiration to refinement."* To "refinement" we might also add maturity, spirituality and a unified life. Before we move on, I would be remiss if I did not point out that for the student of Zen who pursues the activities discussed above, it is eventually realized that *shodō* is simply writing, *chadō* is simply serving tea, *zazen* is simply sitting, and *kyūdō* is simply shooting an arrow. Fully to comprehend and appropriate this observation is the task of a lifetime, so we shall leave it at that for now as we continue our attempt to understand the warrior's Zen.

---

* Ellwood, 133.

Chapter Four

The Warriors' Zen

Part Two: An Established Relationship

"I do not know the way to defeat others, but the way to defeat myself." –Yagyū Munenori

From War to Peace

The previous chapter laid out how the samurai were introduced to Zen and some of the reasons they found it so appealing. This chapter will continue our brief survey of Japanese history, up through the early twentieth century. Here we will undertake a closer examination of what this curious relationship between religion and the way of the warrior entails.

The sixteenth century in Japan was one of significant bloodshed. The Ashikaga shogunate, established in 1336, transitioned into what is called the Sengoku Period or "Warring States Period" by the middle of the fifteenth century. As centralized government crumbled, power was held in the hands of the local *daimyo*, or feudal lords, who engaged in battle after battle, campaign and campaign, war after war, in the pursuit of power, land and honor. As the name suggests, it was a time characterized by great violence. The immense suffering of people during such periods is regrettable and should not be glamorized. At the same time, there is room to appreciate the development of the military strategy, practice and skill that necessity demands during such times. What is inefficient will be weeded out. What is effective will survive and be further developed. And what is promising will be explored with great vigor.

The martial schools of this time period had ample opportunity to test themselves and evolve, as continual warfare was the norm

For our purposes, it is worth noting that these schools did not focus on physical skills alone, but emphasized mental development as well, as technical ability alone could never be sufficient. Within the Hōzōin School of spearmanship, founded by Buddhist monk Hōzōin Kakuzenbō In'ei (1521–1607), it was taught, "In the knightly arts, first see that you yourself are right, and after that think of defeating an opponent."* Zen was a philosophy—if we can call it that—that was relied on consistently for this purpose.

Leggett points out an interesting fact about most of the scrolls which taught martial ways at this time. While the technical explication of the art made up at least 80 percent of the material, the remaining "theoretical presentation… is overwhelmingly in terms of Zen."† One could also find elements of Shingon Buddhism and Daoism, primarily in the jujutsu schools, and increasing Confucian principles later in the eighteenth century, but the primary approach to mental or spiritual development came through the language and principles of Zen.

Leggett cites a number of examples from the Ittō School (or "One-sword school") of the later sixteenth century which reflect Zen principles as they relate to combat effectiveness:

> "Master Chokai says: If you try to use going-into-action and waiting with the idea that they are two distinct things which you can do, then you cannot attain to what is meant by not making technique primary."
> "In our school it is recommended to have the 'posture of no posture', so that there is no difference between the external and internal."
> "There is a posture, but when the mind is not fixed in one, that is called the posture of no posture."
> "If there is an idea of some hoped-for gain behind the technique, how will the technique be able to adapt to unexpected circumstances?"‡

* Leggett, *Zen and the Ways*, 165.
† Ibid., 182
‡ Ibid., 171ff.

It is often suggested that Zen became wedded to *budō* during the Tokugawa period of peace, when the samurai had the time and luxury to pursue such discipline for the sake of personal improvement, quite apart from the demands placed on them during periods of armed conflict. The material above is evidence to the contrary, as the role of Zen in the lives of samurai during the Warring States Period was significant. We will see additional examples below from samurai whose lives bridged these eras of war and peace. It is true that the word "Zen" does not appear with much regularity. It is the word *dō* which is generally used instead. Even today, the Japanese prefer to speak of *dō*, or way. However, I believe that it was Zen more than any other school of thought that determined the Japanese understanding of the various arts as vehicles to explore and understand the *dō*.

As we enter the seventeenth century, and mark the all important transition into the Tokugawa Shogunate, or Edo Period (1603–1868), the Japanese warriors were transitioning from the apex of martial experience, science and tested effectiveness into an era of peace during which the warrior ways came to be practiced and perceived in a new light. Warfare ceased. Contests between different *ryūha*, or styles, were banned, as was the practice of roaming the countryside, *à la* Miyamoto Musashi, looking for worthy opponents with whom to test one's skill. Leadership in the various schools became predominantly hereditary and the practice of *kenjutsu* focused on constant repetition of *kata*.

At this time, there were roughly two million samurai in Japan, or approximately 8 percent of the population.* While their fighting skills were no longer required on the battlefield, and bureaucratic duties began to consume their time, they were first and foremost members of the military caste. They were not about to abandon their identity as warriors. And so, training in the martial disciplines continued, albeit with a far greater emphasis on the development of self through the pursuit of perfection in these arts. The primary aim of

* King, 92.

armed and unarmed training was less about battlefield readiness and more about *shugyō,* austere mental and physical discipline.

Three remarkable works were written during this epic transition in Japanese history that have guided subsequent generations down to our own day. Their titles in English will be familiar to many readers of this book: Takuan Sōhō's *The Unfettered Mind,* Miyamoto Musashi's *The Book of Five Rings* and Yagyū Munenori's *The Life-Giving Sword.* Written by men whose time bridged the Warring States Period and the Tokugawa peace, they were able to reflect the pinnacle of Japanese martial effectiveness and at the same time communicate a philosophy of martial practice that guided the samurai through their efforts to maintain the ways of the warrior at a time when warriors were not often needed. It is these three remarkable works that we will now consider in turn.

Takuan Sōhō and The Unfettered Mind

The first written of the three, Zen priest Takuan Sōhō (1573–1645) penned this work around the year 1632. The title of the primary work in this collection is *Fudōchi Shinmyōroku,* translated, "The Mysterious Record of Immovable Wisdom." Considering how many martial artists have turned to the pages of this book for direction, it may be surprising to note that Takuan was not a warrior. He was a monk. While born into a samurai family, he joined the Jōdō sect of Buddhism at the age of ten. Four years later he began practicing within the Rinzai tradition of Zen. By the age of thirty-five, he was the abbot of Daitokuji, one of the larger Zen temples in Kyoto. *The Unfettered Mind* was then not a military manual or book of technical instruction on swordsmanship, but rather Takuan's reflections on the relevance of Zen thought and practice for one who practices the discipline of the sword. The book was written to Yagyū Munenori, head of the Yagyū Shinkage school and personal instructor in the art of the sword to two shoguns. The fact that it was so prized by its recipient, and is today a highly regarded classic, speaks to the great value Sōhō's words have had for those pursuing the martial ways.

The main thrust of the work is the common concern that both Zen practitioners and swordsman share: one must overcome the tendency of the mind to stop. For the one practicing *zazen*, it is very easy for the mind to attach to a thought, concept, memory, category, or desire and therefore proceed to… stop. This does not mean that the person stops thinking, but that the mind has ceased to exist freely in the moment and has become fixated at some point. It has become "hung up," one might say. In Zen circles, it is discussed how this tendency leads us to dualistic thinking, which clouds the correct perception of ourselves and this world. One must overcome this inclination and predisposition, through long and diligent practice, if one hopes to overcome attachment and live unhindered in the moment. "In Buddhism we abhor this stopping and the mind remaining with one thing or another. We call this stopping *affliction*."*

For the swordsman, as with all people, this penchant for mental fixation is likewise a problem. However, the swordsman is not so concerned with pursuing enlightenment as with keeping his head on the battlefield. When one's thoughts attach to fear, glory, or strategy, the mind stops. A mind that has stopped, that is so "afflicted," cannot respond freely and effectively to its environment in the moment. When faced with a skilled opponent whose *katana* is raised overhead, any mental fixation, stoppage, or affliction is likely to be disastrous. "The Right Mind is the mind that does not remain in one place. It is the mind that stretches throughout the entire body and self. The Confused Mind is the mind that, thinking something over, congeals in one place."†

In confronting an opponent, it is not enough to avoid thinking about the past or the future, pain or glory, death or victory. One should not fixate on the opponent himself. One's thinking should not stop with the opponent's sword, his stance, or his movement. It should not stop with your own *kamae* or the *mai-ai* separating you.

---

* Takuan Sōhō, *The Unfettered Mind: Writings from a Zen Master to a Master Swordsman*, trans. William Scott Wilson (New York: Kodansha, 2002), 38f.

† Ibid., 47.

When your opponent attacks, your mind should not stop with that one attack. "[I]f you think of meeting that sword just as it is, your mind will stop at the sword in just that position, your own movements will be undone, and you will be cut down by your opponent. This is what *stopping* means."*

The ultimate state of mind that Takuan described, what he called "immovable wisdom," is not simply a result of controlling one's mind. This is an important first step, but the mind that does not stop is something more than a mind that is merely controlled. "Bringing the mind under control is a thing done only in the beginning. If one remains this way all through life, in the end he will never reach the highest level. In fact, he will not rise above the lowest."† It is not my intention to explore here the full concept of "immovable wisdom," but rather to offer, in this brief section, a glimpse of something more profound, which I hope may encourage you to read the works of Takuan and others.

Miyamoto Musashi and The Book of Five Rings

If Takuan approached the art of swordsmanship from the perspective of an outsider, Miyamoto Musashi (1584–1645) was the quintessential insider. A veteran of countless duels who allegedly killed fifty-three men early in his life, he wrote *Gorin no sho*, or *The Book of Five Rings* as a letter to his student Terao Magaonojō shortly before his own death. In contrast to *The Unfettered Mind*, this work conveyed much more of the technical expertise and strategy of a skilled and experienced swordsman. This is clearly the work of an expert practitioner. At the same time, it is through the lens of Zen that one can make the most sense of Musashi's practical instruction.

In the section entitled "Posture in Combat," Musashi teaches not only the mechanics of proper posture, but its philosophy as well. Echoing the Zen teaching of the "original mind" or "everyday mind," he advises his readers, "In all the martial arts, it is essential to make

* Ibid., 28f.

† Ibid., 57.

the everyday stance the combat stance and the combat stance the everyday stance."* What is true in the stance is reflected in the mind. Engaging in combat should be undertaken with the same mind as when one reaches for a glass of water or signs one's name. When everyday posture and stance are of the same nature as one's position in fighting, both body and mind may be properly attuned without the hindrance of transitioning from one mode of thought to another.

As an example of using the "everyday mind" in a martial context, my jujutsu instructor Jeff Ramsey recently told me a story about his participation in an international jujutsu competition in 1999. He was competing in the semifinals against a rather formidable opponent. The first round was not going well. At the end of the round, he realized that the essential problem was, as we often say, that his head was not in the game. And so he made a psychological shift, so to speak. He imagined himself in the everyday context of his employment. It is important to note that my teacher's occupation is not as mundane as many of ours. His job, in "stop loss security," involved detaining shoplifters at a large retail establishment. As such, he imagined himself during the second-round of the competition in his everyday—yet still quite serious—context of detaining a thief. Thus, instead of trying to compete within a mentally unfamiliar context, he made the shift to his own "everyday mind" and ultimately won the semifinal round.

For most of us, our everyday frame of mind revolves around activities that are a little less violent, e.g., punching buttons on a keyboard, driving a car, brushing our teeth. And so existing in that state of mind while engaged in a fight is a psychological jump of some distance, considerably more than the one my jujutsu instructor made. However, through mindful discipline and meditative practice, such mental control can be cultivated and developed.

In the same way that we have seen that one should cultivate immovable wisdom, mindfulness that does not stop, and freedom in

---

* Miyamoto Musashi, *The Book of Five Rings* (New York: Bantam Books, 1982), 37.

the movement of one's everyday mind, so victory may be attained through disrupting such possibilities in one's opponents. "One must irritate the stance of the other side, by designing strategies which the opponent would never foresee, by confusing, upsetting, or frightening the opponent, or by agitating him so as to break his rhythm."* One does not defeat one's enemies by virtue of superior technique alone, but when one attains and maintains superior fluidity of thought.

Musashi uses the word *Heihō* in this work to refer to the path sought by the expert swordsman. The word has the connotation of a path to enlightenment, but Musashi is primarily concerned with this path as a road to victory. "In *Heihō,* one may generally consider the spirit of the other person to be the subject of the point of concentration [as opposed to the sword, eyes, etc.]." Your fight is not with the opponent's sword, but with his spirit. The victor is the one with the indomitable spirit. He who conquers the other's spirit will conquer his body as well.

Throughout this remarkable little book, the connection between Zen and swordsmanship does indeed exist, even when not clear to the reader. However, Musashi's appreciation of Zen appears limited to its usefulness in helping one become a superior killing machine. There is no ethic, compassion, or broader concern for development as a complete human being. Others are nothing more than opponents or enemies. Zen has been reduced here to a tool that one may use in order to kill more consistently and effectively.

Yagyū Munenori and The Life-Giving Sword

The third major treatise on the subject that appeared at this time was *Heiho Kadensho,* written around 1632 by Yagyū Munenori (1571–1646). Often translated as *The Life-Giving Sword,* or sometimes *The Book of Clan Traditions on the Martial Arts,* this work holds a middle ground when compared with the two above. A great swordsman himself, founder of the Yagyū Shinkage school, he was also an

* Ibid., 98.

enthusiastic pupil of Takuan (and recipient of the monk's writing, discussed above). As such, his work discusses both the technical and philosophical aspects of the art.

Unlike Musashi, Munenori was more concerned with how the study of the Way could make one a better swordsman *and* a better human being. His life was caught up in the politics of the day, serving in a position of authority both at the local level and in the service of the shogun within the Tokugawa government. Effective skills with a blade are important, but a nation will be in peril if its leaders are fighters alone. In the Foreword to his translation of this work, William Scott Wilson explains, "Munenori saw in the practice of the sword a Way to forge and temper the student into a total human being."*

As such, *The Life-Giving Sword* offers readers technical advice on the use of the sword and how to fight more effectively. In keeping with Musashi, there is advice about how to disrupt the mental state of your opponent. "If your opponent brandishes his sword and establishes a broad rhythm, you should brandish your sword with a short rhythm. If you opponent establishes a short rhythm, you should use a broad rhythm. This, too, is understood as using a rhythm to keep your opponent out of rhythm."†

Likewise, Takuan's emphasis on the mind not stopping is echoed here as well. When engaged in combat, one's mind should not stop after the initial strike. Even if a significant blow is landed, the mind must not stop. "The frame of mind indicated with this phrase is: if you strike with your sword and think, 'I've struck!' the mind that thinks I've struck!' will stop right there, just as it is. Because your mind does not return from the place you struck, you will be distracted, struck by the second blow of your opponent, and your initiative will be brought to nothing. With your opponent's second blow, you will be defeated."‡ (I cannot help but think that the following advice has

---

* Yagyu Munenori, *The Life-Giving Sword*, trans. William Scott Wilson (New York: Kodansha, 2003), 11.

† Ibid., 84.

‡ Ibid., 109f.

special relevance for those training in sport *budō* today.) It is interesting to note that the later principle in Japanese martial arts of *ikken hissatsu*, or "one strike, one kill," is not the principle Munenori works from, most likely due to his direct experience with actual combat. This stands in contrast to the idealized notion of warfare during much of Tokugawa Japan… and still today.

Clearly, one cannot simply decide to circumvent "the mind stopping." I cannot say to my mind, "OK, next time don't stop until I tell you." Too often, our mental focus is narrowly trained on one object, and when that object is reached, our mind stops. Of course, time does not stop when the object is reached, and so a fluidly thinking mind is of significant benefit. As an example, years ago I was the second-string wide receiver on my high-school football team. The only reason I was second-string was because our team was too small to have a third-string. After my only season on the team, I reflected on the difference between our star receiver, Les Lewis, and me. Aside from his greater athletic ability and knowledge of the game, he was remarkable for the flexibility of his thinking. When I ran a route and looked for the pass, I could concentrate on only one thing—the ball coming into my hands. If I caught the ball, I had no idea at that moment of the location of other players, the sidelines, or the end zone. If the ball slipped from my fingertips, I considered the play over and stopped. Les, on the other hand, did not let his focus become so narrow or allow his mind to stop. If the plan was interrupted, he simply adapted. On one occasion, he leapt for a high pass and was able to get a hand on the ball, but before he could bring it in, he was hit from below by a defender. Seemingly nonplussed, he fell to the ground on his back, watched for the falling ball, reached out and pulled it in for a reception. It was his mental acuity that made him such a remarkable player.

Munenori was one who understood that mental sharpness is of utmost importance for the one engaged in combat. For him, this involved the connection between Zen and *budō*. We saw in the previous chapter the traits he believed "martial arts" and "Buddhist dharma" hold in common. As a result of his tutelage under Takuan, he held a deeper and more nuanced appreciation of the benefits and importance of what Zen offers the entire human being. In what could be seen as a rebuke of men like Musashi, he wrote:

> To think only of winning is sickness. To think only of using the martial arts is sickness. To think only of demonstrating the result of one's training is sickness, as is thinking only of making an attack or waiting for one. To think in a fixated way only of expelling such sickness is also sickness. Whatever remains absolutely in the mind should be considered sickness. As these various sicknesses are all present in the mind, you must put your mind in order and expel them.*

In regard to the three authors mentioned above, we may say that they conveyed the importance and influence of Zen in Japanese martial culture at a time when such claims could still be made on the basis of experience. Once we enter the era of peace during the Tokugawa regime, much of the writing on military strategy, effectiveness and honor could only be conjecture. With Takuan, Musashi and Munenori we find three remarkable figures with the credentials to speak of the mind of the warrior on the basis of experience. Their commentary and advice provided a great deal of guidance in the coming centuries as the ways of the warrior adapted to an age of political calm.

Tokugawa Japan

The period known as the Tokugawa era (1603–1868) began with a great deal of violence, intrigue, betrayal and bloodshed. A time of villains, heroes, and tales of valor, the early Tokugawa years were tailor-made for epic histories and romantic legends. They are still being told today. Of course, history is rarely as simple, or romantic, as our telling of it.

---

* Ibid., 89.

This period of warfare came to a close around the year 1615 when the Tokugawa shogun destroyed the final Toyotomi stronghold in Osaka. What followed was 250 years of relative peace, stability and isolation thanks to an effective feudal hierarchy under samurai control. The religious milieu of the time saw an increase in the influence of neo-Confucian thought, along with Shinto, although the Tokugawa authorities officially practiced Pure Land Buddhism. The growth in neo-Confucian ideals and ethics magnified the Japanese appreciation for loyalty and service, thereby romanticizing the lives of the samurai of old and establishing an ideal to which Tokugawa samurai ascribed. Honor, fearlessness and valor on the battlefield are, of course, much easier to espouse when no one is actually called upon to go there. Master swordsmen did arise and teach their arts, often in connection with Zen thought, but they were men teaching a martial art at a time when lethal conflicts were officially outlawed.*

It should not be surprising that during the peace of Tokugawa, when life and death combat became exceedingly rare, the *bushi* were concerned about losing their edge. If you only train with bamboo or wooden swords, knowing you will not lose your life in physical contests, how can you be sure you have the mettle to engage in genuine combat? (This same question is often asked, as it should be, by contemporary martial artists pondering their abilities outside the safety of the dojo.) Physical training within the safety of a school can only go so far in creating what we like to call "the real world." During the Tokugawa period, there were those who believed their physical practice needed—more than before—to be supplemented with mental discipline. The eighteenth century martial artist and military scientist Adachi Masahiro (f. c. 1780–1800) explained, "Now at the present time there is no warfare going on, so there's no trying out combat with real swords, and consequently there's no way to know how strong or weak our minds will be, or how excited or calm, where real swords are used. Nevertheless, when you train your mind under

* King, 181.

ordinary circumstances, your mind will be calm and unafraid even with real swords."* Zen was a means of such training.

Bujutsu and Budō

At a time when life-and-death struggles ceased to be situations faced by most samurai, martial arts were bound to change. There is a tendency to think of the pre-Tokugawa period as the time of "*bujutsu*," while the Tokugawa peace ushered in the age of "*budō*." This is not entirely incorrect, but it is an oversimplification of Japanese history. As a starting point, we should consider Draeger's definitions of these terms. "The *bujutsu* are combative systems designed by and for warriors to promote self-protection and group solidarity. The *budo* are spiritual systems, not necessarily designed by warriors or for warriors, for self-perfection of the individual."† *Bujutsu* did not cease to exist with the Tokugawa peace; these practical disciplines still exist today. Furthermore, we have seen above in the writings of men like Yagyū Munenori that warriors designed *bujutsu* arts that also stressed the personal development of character in its practitioners.

Karl Friday, in an excellent article on this subject, presents a compelling argument that the sword arts of Japanese *bushi* before the Tokugawa era were not truly about practical fighting technique, as we often imagine. From the beginning, the schools of swordsmanship taught self-cultivation over and above realistic combat. He argues, "[T]hese arts were never meant to be straightforward tools of war—that, rather, visions of martial art as a vehicle to broad personal education shaped and characterized this phenomenon from its nascence."‡ Practical combat at this time focused on missile

* *Training the Samurai Mind: A Bushido Sourcebook*, Ed. and Trans. Thomas Cleary (Boston: Shambhala, 2008), 187f.

† Donn F. Draeger, *Classical Bujutsu: The Martial Arts and Ways of Japan* (Boston: Weatherhill, 1973), 19. I would add that the definition would be better served by adding "the pursuit of" before "self-perfection."

‡ Karl Friday, "Off the Warpath: Military Science and *Budō* in the Evolutions of *Ryūha Budgei*," *Budo Perspectives*, Ed. Alexander Bennett (Auckland, New Zealand: Kendo World Publications, 2005), 250.

weapons (e.g. arrows, rocks, bullets) rather than swords. The former accounted for roughly 75 percent of fatalities throughout this period, as opposed to 5 percent that could be credited to the sword. Practical martial skills therefore revolved around archery rather than *kenjutsu*. Those studying the sword within a particular *ryūha*, therefore, were not doing so for purely practical reasons. These men, "even during the Sengoku period, had more in common with Olympic marksmanship competitors—training with specialized weapons to develop esoteric levels of skill under particular conditions—than with Marine riflemen. They also had as much—perhaps more—in common with Tokugawa period and modern martial artists than with the ordinary warriors of their own day."*

Bearing this in mind, *bujutsu* and *budō* are helpful terms as long as we remember that they often point us to degrees of emphasis more than distinct arts or disciplines. Generally speaking, though, Draeger was right when he wrote of this transition, "It was an age in which the desire for self-protection gave way to one of self-perfection."† A distinct change did take place and we may call what was born a "*budō* culture."

Although living in an age of peace, the Japanese people did not de-emphasize the martial arts; they found a new appreciation and respect for them. Their approval of these arts lay, not simply in their effectiveness, but their potential to inculcate excellence in the person who practiced them. In this vein, the brutally effective firearm, adopted from the West, was shunned in favor of another weapon that required skill on the part of its wielder. Noted Japanese historian Edwin Reischauer explained:

> In a land at peace the samurai could turn their backs on distasteful firearms and resume their traditional love affair with the sword. Schools of swordsmanship flourished. However, as the chance to use swords in actual combat diminished, martial skills were gradually

* Ibid., 256.

† Ibid., 50.

> becoming martial arts, and these increasingly came to emphasize the importance of inner self-control and the character-building qualities of swordsmanship rather than its untested military efficacy. A whole mystique of the sword grew up which was more akin to philosophy than to warfare.*

So, what was this *dō* that came to be suffixed to *bu*? The word is the Japanese translation of the Chinese *dao*, a word commonly translated into English as "way." The reader will recall that Zen Buddhism was greatly influenced by Daoism in China, and this principle is essential in understanding the discipline of the Zen practitioner. What is sought in *budō* is not merely a particular skill, the ability to win in a fight, or the maintenance of an historical art form. It is a way of life. The student who disciplines herself for years while learning the *kihon* of aikido, to use a modern art as an example, is not simply developing the ability to apply an *ikkyo* against a non-compliant partner, or how to employ *ukemi*. She is becoming a person of industriousness, diligence, respect, with a great attention to detail. She becomes a person who can control her attachment to things in this world, her emotions, her very life. Draeger expressed it by writing, "The Tao as dō was therefore understood by the Japanese to be a 'way' or 'road' to follow in life. That way is endless and profound. It is long, steep and filled with numerous technical difficulties. It is to be traveled as a means of self-cultivation, and it leads ultimately to self-perfection."†

With some reluctance to criticize Mr. Draeger, whom I hold in high regard, ultimately reaching self-perfection is not the goal, perhaps not even a possibility. His earlier mention of the *dō* as "endless and profound" does greater justice to the Japanese understanding of this road we may travel. In the words of Taisen Deshimaru Roshi, "[T]he *dojo* is not like a university. In Budo… you have to practice until you die."‡ As an example, I have often heard Morio Higaonna

---

* As in King, 113.

† Draeger, Classical Budo, 24.

‡ Deshimaru, 14.

Sensei, 10th *dan* in goju-ryu, tell his students that he is still learning, still working to improve. He has not arrived at the end, nor do I suspect he will ever claim to have reached such a point, despite the fact that he is regarded as being at the pinnacle of his art.

Put simply, the *dō* is the path that one follows in cultivating oneself and living in harmony with others. While the methods of treading and studying the path vary, as one may undertake calligraphy, flower arranging, or martial arts, what is learned and internalized in that discipline is for the sake of one's entire life, not simply the time spent within the particular discipline. For many, the *dō* has been understood through the lens of Zen Buddhism.

I would be remiss in my duties if I left the reader with the impression that all *bushi* were practitioners, or at least advocates, of Zen. They were not. Yagyū Munenori's famous nephew, Hyōgonosuke, a tremendous swordsman, taught and practiced *kenjutsu* without philosophical or psychological theory, but rather focused on technique alone.* There were also plenty of men in the samurai class who looked at the Zen tradition with suspicion or disdain. The Confucian scholar Saito Totsudo (1797–1865) was one example of a man who thought that Zen was an impediment to a strong Japan. He wrote, "Study of the heart may seem like Zen study, but Zen is a path studied by people who wither in mountain forests; even if they settled their minds they are far from the principles of social norms."† There were certainly those who believed the *dō* is to be found in neo-Confucianism rather than Zen.

Shugyō

During the time I lived in Japan, I struggled to understand the motivations, values and worldview of the Japanese people. More than any concept I examined, it was the principle of *shugyō* that provided

* Cf. Uozumi Takashi, "Research of Miyamoto Musashi's *Gorin no sho*—From the Perspective of Japanese Intellectual History," *Budo Perspectives*, Ed. Alexander Bennett (Auckland, New Zealand: Kendo World Publications, 2005), 45-67.

† As in Cleary, 243.

me with the most insight. And it was in the Tokugawa era when this social practice was developed. *Shugyō* is a tricky word to define. At a basic level, it is a mental and physical discipline one undertakes for the sake of self-cultivation. The word comes to us originally from its use in Buddhist training, although it does not carry a distinct religious connotation today. In Zen circles, much the same meaning is captured in the word *kūfu*, which may be translated, "employing oneself assiduously to discover the way to the objective."*

Within Japanese culture there exists a special appreciation for an individual's practice of a specific discipline. This may take the form of the study of a musical instrument, *shodō* (calligraphy), *chadō* (the tea ceremony), *ikebana* (flower arranging), or gardening. I have even been told that the attentiveness taken to house-cleaning is considered a valuable discipline of *shugyō*. (This helps explain the importance of the community cleaning the Buddhist temple together after meditation.) Of course there has long been an appreciation for various *budō* as *shugyō* as well. In all such practices, one devotes oneself to the task with great attention to detail. Excellence is found not only in the physical discipline, but the mindfulness with which one undertakes one's work. *Shugyō* is thus both a mental and physical undertaking. Furthermore, as one matures in such a practice, both physical skill and mental acuity are enhanced. However, in the end, it is not the quality of music, beauty of flowers, or the arrow hitting the target that is sought, but the improvement of the self which comes through diligent effort in the chosen discipline.

In a manner of speaking, the particular activity is but a means to a greater end. The mind which sheds distraction, disruption and craving through years of severe practice—whether wielding a sword or a brush—becomes better able to engage life in all manner of activity. Patience, present-ness and attention to detail in one area of life may

* D. T. Suzuki, *Zen and Japanese Culture*, 157. Richard B. Pilgrim provides an excellent definition of Shugyō as, "an absolutely dedicated and concentrated discipline of body and mind through some particular practice, with the purpose of breaking through to spiritual fulfillment." *Buddhism and the Arts of Japan* (Chambersburg, PA: Anima Books, 1981), 46.

be translated to ten thousand others. *Ichigei wa mangei ni tsūzuru*; one art corresponds to ten-thousand arts. Draeger explained, "Metaphysically speaking, the *dō* forms urge their advocates to seek an understanding of the whole of life through a segment of it, a sphere of personal activity in which the cadence of nature can be sensed and experienced. The *dō* forms thus involve transferring an attitude toward life from the particular to the universal and absolute."* While many commercial schools of martial arts today advertise the value of discipline, respect and patience for youngsters, serious practitioners recognize that this is a discipline for a lifetime.

Trevor Leggett refers to such disciplines as "fractional expressions of Zen"—a wonderful phrase. When engaged in *shugyō*, one may find in a particular practice a momentary experience of the mind being completely present, attentive to one's task, devoid of the false distinction between oneself and the world. For that moment one overcomes the illusory notion of selfhood and exists in union with all that exists. "They are fragmentary manifestations of Zen which depend only minimally on circumstances; to practice them means to be able to experience a breath from beyond, to have freedom for a time at least from the drabness and cramp of life, and to become able to recognize in a particular field the cosmic life, and give it play."†

Returning to Japanese history, one cannot be very surprised to find that the practice of martial arts throughout the Tokugawa Era underwent a substantial change. As mentioned above, *budō* became a discipline for self-improvement much more than self-defense. Attention to detail was emphasized more than functional use. It was unavoidable, therefore, that the focus of these arts should narrow. While the samurai in previous generations needed to study a plurality of *ryu*, or styles of martial arts (e.g., swordsmanship, grappling, horseback riding, tying up an enemy), these early mixed martial artists slowly disappeared as excellence was pursued in a focused art

---

* Draeger, Classical Budo, 25.

† Leggett, Zen and the Ways, 120.

form. The ancient art of combative archery eventually became *kyūdō*, where arrows are shot from a standing position at a target, equidistant in every dojo. Such a martial art provides exceptional possibilities as *shugyō*, but is rather limited in what it offers its practitioners in the way of warfare.

Today, one sees the same thing among *budōka* in Japan. Many *karateka* are exceptionally proficient with a small array of techniques while engaged in long-range fighting but are likely to be at a complete loss if forced into a grappling situation. *Kata* experts may have little or no understanding of the applications of the movements they have perfected. I have engaged in *randori* with Japanese *judōka* who were remarkably strong while standing, but unable to continue their art effectively on the ground. Foreigners are quick to criticize this one-dimensional training, but the disparaging comments often assume the Japanese study these arts for the same reasons as those who are doing the criticizing—a faulty assumption.

This shift from *bujutsu* to *budō*, self-defense to self-cultivation, also carries with it an admirable emphasis on martial arts as a means to foster peace, moral depth and integrity in its practitioners, and subsequently in society at large. At the same time, there have been those who have expressed the concern that the emphasis on "*dō*" has led to the neglect of "*jutsu*." That is to say, the practical martial applications and purposes of these ancient arts may be disregarded or forgotten by those who train a martial discipline as *shugyō*. While this need not be the case, it is impossible to deny that this has quite often taken place.

While Draeger clearly appreciated both *bujutsu* and *budō* (enough to write a book about each one), it is clear to the reader that he regrets the loss of military function in many of the samurai arts as they have been handed down to us. Foremost among these may be the narrowing of focus in many of these arts, a trend which minimizes their real world applicability. "A lack of combative is the outstanding characteristic of all budo entities. Combative balance is established and maintained by attaining expertise in a wide range of weapons and familiarity with other martial systems. But the effect of peace in the Edo period eventually eroded this sense of practical realism."* What is perceived as good for self-cultivation may detract from the breadth of training necessary for defending oneself and one's family in a world with manifold dangers.

Even within particular disciplines, training was modified to focus on the pursuit of perfection. Mention has already been made of the obvious difference between archery in a *kyūdōjo* and that performed from horseback against a moving target. In other arts too, the move from training outdoors on varied terrain to a polished wood floor represents another shift to which Draeger drew attention. Footwork, posture and movement will all change as *budōka* engage one another in the peculiar environment of a dojo. Lessons on how to move on uncertain landscapes will inevitably be lost.

Along with the changes mentioned above, the *intention* behind the training will manifest itself in its practice as well. Again, Draeger expressed his concern regarding one particular art. "The classical warrior's intention that fighting arts should be effective in combat was replaced by the satisfaction derived from their rhythmic form and aesthetic pleasure became the object of many systems of *jujutsu*"† While the reader may object to Draeger's reduction of *budō* practice to aesthetics, a concern I share, it is clear that one's objective in undertaking a martial art will play a significant role in the transmission of that art to the next generation. Concern about the precise position of a fist in chamber, to the centimeter, may indeed have martial value, but the focus on such subtleties to the neglect of more combat-oriented elements of training will shape the art and determine what is handed down to the next generation. While questions endure about how a martial art should be taught, there exists the very real concern for *budōka* that their art forms not lose sight of the forest for the trees, or that what is being taught is, after all, a martial art. Whether or not this shift is regrettable, natural, progressive, or regressive will

* Draeger, Classical Budo, 106.

† Draeger, Classical Bujutsu, 50.

be treated in the final chapter, as we look at the contemporary status of Japanese martial arts around the world.

In addition to the tension between *bujutsu* and *budō,* to which Draeger drew our attention (even if it is overstated), the increasing popularity of martial arts as sport had also begun, even before the twentieth century. In 1895, the *Dai Nihon Butoku Kai,* or *Butokukai,* was established and began making efforts to maintain what they perceived to be the traditional aspects of *budō* arts over against the increasing role which modern sports were beginning to play.* Competing goods of tradition, pragmatism, nationalism and spiritual development were already at play at this time. The dissolution of the *Butokukai* in 1945 by the Americans gave an edge to, but did not instigate *budō* as sport in the twentieth century.

From Peace to War

A detailed account of the rise and fall of Japanese militarism is well beyond the scope of this little book. One of the great turning points in Japanese history, however, was the day that the Tokugawa era ended and the Meiji Restoration began. On November 9, 1867, the fifteenth Tokugawa Shogun, Tokugawa Yoshinobu (1837–1913), returned authority to the emperor. Power returned to the imperial palace and increasingly extended into the modern Japanese military, as the samurai were disbanded. It was decided that Japan would become a modern nation, and the vestiges of feudalism should be relegated to the history books. This was a time, of course, that has served as fodder for countless romantic novels and movies. And it is true that the proud samurai class did not simply turn in their swords, cut off their topknots, and get to work in the new industrialized nation. The pride, legacy and tradition of such a social class do not disappear overnight. Even today, I have found many Japanese who wear their family's samurai heritage as a badge of honor.

---

* Cf. Suzuki Sadami, "Twentieth Century *Budō* and Mystic Experience," *Budo Perspectives,* Ed. Alexander Bennett (Auckland, New Zealand: Kendo World Publications, 2005), 15-44.

The effect of this official abolition of the samurai on *budō* and *bujutsu* was not their dissolution but extension throughout Japanese society. Swordsmanship could no longer be limited to the warrior class, and money was to be made teaching both traditional and practical disciplines. There was resistance to this casting of pearls before swine. However, both the financial and military advantage of a trained citizenry ensured the popularization of *budō*, albeit it with a few alterations:

> During the nineteenth century, kendo, despite opposition, became popular among commoners. So widespread was its practice that the rules governing its methods were standardized, and its already only quasi-martial nature was diluted still further by the confinement of its techniques to prescribed postures and actions. The progress of trainees could be compared by having them compete safely against one another and by scoring their strikes, thrusts, and other technical matters. Thus it was that the original basis of kendo as a spiritual discipline—a classical budo form—veered into a new direction and increasingly took on the character of a sport.*

Again, a detailed discussion of martial sport will have to wait, but an historic shift was already taking place that had profound effects on the future of *budō*. It is important to note, however, that standardization and reduction of an arts' martial focus need not be correlated with a shift toward sport. Consider the discipline of *iaidō*—developed in the twentieth century, highly ritualized and with a narrow curriculum—which still exists quite apart from the realm of sport (at least until it was warped and disfigured by westerners in their "Extreme!" martial arts displays).

As the Japanese military machine began rolling through east and southeast Asia and into the Pacific, the training of soldiers necessarily focused on firearms, artillery, aircraft and naval vessels. As with other modern nations, these skills were supplemented with hand-to-hand training. Traditional Japanese *bujutsu*, along with the recent

* Draeger, *Classical Budo*, 83f.

discovery of Okinawan karate, made their way into the training of Japanese officers and soldiers. With all Japanese citizens being eligible, obligated and directed to serve as the new warrior class, training in traditional and modern warfare was mandated for all serving in the military.

While there was a return to the practical focus of *bujutsu,* this was combined with the need to teach students quickly. Gichin Funakoshi's shotokan was more attractive to those entrusted with training raw recruits than Morihei Ueshiba's aikido. The fundamentals of the former could be communicated and practiced more quickly than aikido's gentle harmonizing of energy.

In addition to the physical, mental training played a significant part as well. The legacy of samurai who had cultivated their spirit so as to reach their full potential as fighters was not lost on the military hierarchy. Zen teachers, meditation and language all made their way into the training of Japan's modern military. This should not surprise the reader, as the value of a disciplined mind among warriors had long been appreciated by Japanese practitioners of *bujutsu* and *budō*. However, the use—or misuse—of principles and teachings of Zen in order to create unquestioning, unflinching, uncritical soldiers continues to be a concern for Buddhists and scholars today, a theme we shall return to in chapter 7.

Chapter Five

Meditation

"The heart of Zen discipline is zazen. Remove the heart and a mere corpse remains." –Philip Kapleau

What is Zazen?

The mental acuity that many of the samurai desired, which men like Yagyū Munenori described, is obviously worth cultivating. That takes work. One does not simply decide to avoid attachments or stop fearing death. As discussed in chapter 2, the primary discipline followed in the Zen tradition is *zazen,* or seated meditation. It is true that adherents of other religious schools prescribe other meditative practices for martial artists. Michael L. Raposa's *Meditation and the Martial Arts* offers a fine introduction to additional meditative studies, in particular aikido. However, our focus here is on Zen meditation. In this chapter we will take a more in-depth, yet still introductory, look at the practice of *zazen,* along with qualities that are fostered through this rigorous mental and physical undertaking.

Our brief examination of the practice of *zazen* here will not consider further the use of *kōan*; hopefully, the material and suggestions in chapter 2 will give you a useful basis. Rather, we will focus on a meditation of mindfulness, beginning with awareness of the breath. As a starting point, the following description of *zazen* by Dōgen, founder of Sōtō Zen, can help orient us as we begin our look at a practice which is both fundamentally simple and at the same time frustratingly elusive. He writes in the *Shōbōgenzō,* "What is *zazen*? It is being wholly in the instant, beyond all the existences of the universe, achieving Buddhahood and living there. *Zazen* is only that:

beyond Buddhists and non-Buddhists, experiencing the very heart of the experience of the Buddha."*

Hopefully this quote will not prompt the reader to put down this book and walk away, sure that it is all getting too esoteric. What Dōgen is saying is that *zazen* is not about sitting a certain way, or thinking about certain things, but being present in the moment. Being present is not about labels we wear, religious beliefs we hold, or how we understand the world. *Zazen* is the same present-ness with the world that Siddhartha Gautama experienced 2500 years ago. We need to begin this chapter by understanding that Zen is not about doctrines, dogmas and teachings, but about experience. And it is in seated meditation that this experience is possible. Dōgen insisted, "You should stop pursuing words and letters and learn to withdraw and reflect on yourself."† The irony of writing a book about this is inescapable, of course. However, some orientation and clarification can be helpful, as long as they are not understood to be the essence of Zen. Signposts on a mountain trail may be an imposition on the natural scenery, but they can be helpful nonetheless. Bearing that in mind, for those who will want to look further than what is presented here, I know of no better books on Zen meditation (especially for martial artists) than Shunryu Suzuki's *Zen Mind, Beginner's Mind* and Omori Sogen's *An Introduction to Zen Training*—two rather different books by two rather different roshi. Interested readers will find a wealth of valuable information and insight in them.

Posture

Proper posture is of the utmost importance in *zazen*. I mentioned in chapter 2 my posture-correcting experience during my first visit to Okinawa. Since that time my seated posture has improved substantially, but I am still corrected most times I visit Kozenji. (The day they stop correcting me will be the day that either I finally get it

* As in Deshimaru, 54.

† Yūhō Yokoi, *Zen Master Dōgen: An Introduction with Selected Writings* (New York: Weatherhill, 1976), 46.

right, or they simply give up on me. Chances are it will be the latter, while I will imagine that it is the former.) While most of us will never achieve the impressive carriage of a senior practitioner, who appears to sit as nobly and immovable as a mountain, we can certainly progress from where we are. For the novice, a few words of instruction may be helpful.

To begin with, *zazen* is not practiced while sitting on the floor. One sits on a cushion, known as a *zafu*. Moreover, the *zafu* should not be used like a seat cushion; do not sit on top of it. If you sit for any length of time in *zazen* with your knees up in the air, your hip flexors will quickly fatigue, leaving your knees trembling furiously. The proper way to sit is forward on the front third of the cushion, so that your knees are on the floor. You will then be in contact with the ground at three points. This will also increase the angle between your legs and torso, facilitating fuller breathing.

Ideally your legs should be placed in the full-lotus position (*kongo-za*). However, this is difficult for many people, and so the half-lotus is often used. Here, one foot is up on the opposite thigh, while the other is placed on the ground (*kissho-za* when the right foot is up; *goma-za* when the left is up). There is also the quarter-lotus position, where one foot is on the opposite calf. For those who cannot manage this position, the Burmese position (*agura*, in Japanese) is also used, where the legs are simply crossed. Alternatively, one can sit in *seiza* ("proper sitting"), with the feet tucked under the rear end. This may also be practiced with the use of a *seiza* bench. And finally, for those whose physical constitution will not permit any of these positions, sitting in a chair is permissible in some meditation halls.

I should point out that while most teachers of Zen are happy to work with you, helping you find a seated position which you can manage, you may be "encouraged" to practice with a posture you find more difficult. My first time sitting for a full hour, I decided to adopt the more comfortable *agura*. It was not long, however, before one *sempai* came by and told me to get that foot up on my right knee. I obliged. The hour was trying, but I was able to make it. Incidentally, I never sat in anything less than a half-lotus again.

It has long been believed that correct posture will manifest itself in a properly focused mind.* While seated, it is important to keep the ears, shoulders and hips in a vertical line with one another. The natural curve of the lower back is maintained, but the spine should not lean to either side. Shoulders should be relaxed—something I find easier said than done. The back of the head should be raised toward the ceiling, which will also bring the chin in slightly. "When your chin is tilted up, you have no strength in your posture; you are probably dreaming."† The tip of the tongue may be gently placed behind the front upper teeth.

The hands are placed together in what is called the Cosmic Mudra. Here, the left hand sits on top of the right, both palms facing up, so that the fingers overlap. The thumbs are held lightly together, with just enough contact to maintain a piece of paper between them. The hands are then placed on top of the soles of your upturned feet, if you are in the full lotus, or else comfortably in front of the *tanden*, roughly three finger widths below your navel.

Of course, providing a helpful written account of proper posture is rather difficult. Even with pictures, it is difficult to capture the spirit and attitude of proper bearing in *zazen*. Finding a knowledgeable guide to correct your posture is invaluable. I have also found the following three reminders helpful during my own meditation, when I want to perform a mental check of where I am. Taisen Deshimaru instructed his students:

- Let your posture be full of energy; otherwise it is like flat beer in a bottle opened the night before.
- You must be like a general on horseback in front of his army.
- Your posture must be that of a lion or tiger, not a sleeping pig.‡

* Philip Kapleau, *The Three Pillars of Zen: Teaching, Practice, and Enlightenment* (New York: Doubleday, 1980), 21f.

† Shunryu Suzuki, *Zen*, 26.

‡ Deshimaru, 69.

Maintaining such a posture has tremendous benefits for the health of the mind and body. It allows for deep and proper breathing and counteracts the destructive effects on our skeletal and muscular systems through our daily hunching and slouching. It is also quite difficult. Initially, legs may fall asleep and the back may cramp. Remaining still for extended periods of time can cause the strongest athlete to grow faint. I have seen strong, young karate men fall over when trying to stand up after *zazen*. Nevertheless, fidgeting and adjusting one's position during meditation are strictly forbidden. It is far better to be helped to your feet after sitting than to disrupt others while trying to make yourself comfortable. Curiously, I have found that while I exhibit various physical tics in my everyday life, they rarely appear during *zazen*.

Regarding the importance of being still, I was once told of a group of Italian *karateka* who visited a Japanese monastery some years ago. During *zazen*, many were moving and fussing considerably. The roshi asked one woman why she was moving. When she replied that the posture was painful, he angrily replied, "And do you stop your karate practice when it is painful?!" Personally, I would much prefer to discipline my mind and body through the aching stillness of *zazen* than face such a disapproving question.

One's eyes should be half-way open during *zazen*, gazing at a spot on the floor roughly three feet to the front. They should not be focused on the spot, but holding a general awareness of what is there. Do be mindful, however, that your head is not tilted down at the same angle as your eyes. While there are, of course, other meditative practices where one's eyes are closed or focused on an object, in Zen this is typically not the case. Passive consciousness of one's surroundings is expressed both by one's mind and one's eyes. In the *Zazenron*, written by Daikaku Zenji (1213–1278), we are told, "One with the eyes open sees things at a distance, the attention is distracted forcibly and the heart thrown into confusion. When the eyes are closed there is a fall into darkness, and no clarity in the heart. When the eyes are half open the thought does not rush about, body and mind are at one."* In *zazen,* we are not to be detached from the world, alone in our own minds, nor have our mind caught by any one thing. Our eyes express this.

I often find my eyesight glazing over during *zazen,* so that while my eyes are not closed, I no longer see what is in front of me. This is also a mistake, and usually an indication that I have mentally retreated into my own mind and am no longer present, so to speak, in the room. Also, after a period of time spent in meditation, it is often the case that my eyes have trouble focusing again. The unfocused gaze of *zazen* does not immediately switch off and return to normal eyesight. If the world looks a little blurry after meditation, this is completely natural and should not be cause for concern. Proper focus will return shortly.

Breath

If proper posture is vital in meditation, then proper breathing is indispensable. Mindfulness of breath is the gateway to true *zazen*. There are, however, a variety of approaches to breathing that are taught in Zen schools and monasteries. The rhythm of breathing varies from *zendō* to *zendō* as well. Some teach that the exhalation should be long and smooth. There are visualizations of the breath moving through the body that are also recommended for some. This is, obviously, not the place to delve into various breathing techniques and their relative merits. Rather, unless under the direction of a qualified teacher, I encourage anyone to follow the direction I received at Mt. Equity Zendo: breathe naturally. That is to say, do not artificially lengthen or shorten your breaths, nor attempt to create a rhythm that is contrary to your body's natural impulses. Visualization can be helpful, but these techniques should be understood as "training wheels." They are not essential aspects of seated meditation. (I am not too proud to admit that I still need training wheels.)

---

* As in Leggett, *Zen and the Ways*, 45. To this we may add Omori Sogen's observation, "While it may seem easier to unite your spirit with your eyes closed, that would become detached *zazen* and not living *zazen*." *An Introduction to Zen Training*, 39.

This should not be understood to mean, however, that there is no difference between our breathing during *zazen* and, say, while watching television. One important aspect of breathing is the idea of breathing into and with the *tanden* or *hara*,* what the Chinese call the *dantian*. It is comparable to the *manipura* in Indian thought. The *tanden* is believed to be the physiological center of the human body, roughly three finger widths below and two finger widths in from the navel. I assume this is based on a typical lean Asian physique, and so well-fed westerners may need to rely on other directions to find their center. More than our physiological center, this is believed to be the seat of our being and the energy which enlivens the body. Hirokazu Kanazawa (1931–), Shotokan judan, explains, "We use the word *hara* or the belly where 'ki' or the intrinsic energy resides and we use this energy to drive us to be more spiritual."†

During *zazen*, one may breathe with the mental image of the air descending all the way to the *tanden*, where it circles in our physical and spiritual center, before being exhaled. Of course, the air we breathe does not descend this far in our bodies. Our lungs do not reach our *tanden*. However, this visualization allows for the proper breathing and mental focus during meditation. And while we are mindful of our *tanden*, placing our mind and strength there, there is the common mistake of forcing too much of our energy and attention to this area. Omori Sogen Roshi explains, "[T]here is the tendency for people to think that 'to sit' means 'to put strength in the lower abdomen.' Though they are mistaken, a considerable number of people think that unless they fill the lower abdomen with strength,

---

* The Japanese word *hara* refers to the abdomen or belly in general. It is common word, such that a child might complain that her *hara* hurts, or a boxing fan might yell at the TV for his favorite pugilist to hit the other in the *hara*. *Tanden* refers to the more precise point, discussed above, where it is believed that *ki* may be focused.

† Interview with Hirokazu Kanazawa, http://www.youtube.com/watch?v=iKDdXBOJDBo. It may be important to note that Kanazawa's mention of "ki" should not bring to mind some superhuman energy that allows one to perform superhuman feats. Rather, it is a kind of cultural shorthand for the various energies that quicken the body.

it is impossible to sit in Zen meditation. They strain the lower abdomen to the limit thinking it is *zazen*."*

Of course, placing the mind in the *tanden* is not as easy as the decision to do so. It is likely to take years for a serious practitioner to understand what this means. I have caught glimpses in my own seated and active meditation. At the same time, the effort can be undertaken and progress can be made. When one is able to embrace life from the gut, so to speak, to get out of one's head and live viscerally in the world, then we find authentic living. This is not to say that Zen favors emotion over intellect, or is distrustful of thought, but that there is a danger in living life from an objective distance, intellectualizing one's very existence. Doing so does not create the mental stability we desire, but the exact opposite. We may easily become caught in our thinking when we retreat from the world of experience into our own heads. Philip Kapleau Roshi (1912–2004) corrected this misperception. "Thus, one who functions from his hara, is not easily disturbed. He is, moreover, able to act quickly and decisively in an emergency owing to the fact that his mind, anchored in his hara, does not waver."†

This unwavering mind, as we have seen, may benefit us all in crucial ways. The mind "anchored" in this way during *zazen* may then keep its moorings when we leave our cushion and proceed about our business. In the various Japanese *dō*-disciplines, such a mind is sought, facilitated and cultivated. Kapleau continued, "Masters of the traditional Japanese arts are all accomplished in thinking and acting from the *hara*—they would not merit the title 'master' if they were not."‡ Moving from the *tanden* is thus central to mastery of various art forms. For those engaged in the practice of *budō*, it is easy to see that such ability may not only enhance one's performance of the art, but keep one alive. Adachi Masahiro was a martial artist and teacher of military science. Influenced by both Zen and Daoism in

---

* Sogen, *An Introduction to Zen Training*, 58.

† Kapleau, 16.

‡ Ibid.

his development of "The Divine Warrior" school of martial arts in Kyoto, he taught, "The basic mind, making both principle and technique its own, being single-minded and certain, opens an eye through the navel, so it is not thrown into confusion in emergencies."* It is this concept that can help us understand certain cryptic comments by *budō* teachers, like the following from Euen Herrigel's *kyūdō sensei*, Awa Kenzo: "Aim at the target with your belly."†

It may appear that this activity we are describing, being seated on a cushion, breathing deeply in a natural rhythm, would cause both the rate of one's breathing and one's heart-rate to subside. The former is true, the latter is not. When one is consciously breathing, sitting still, without the normal impediments we create through bad posture, the number of breaths per minute is likely to decrease. However, one's heart rate is likely to increase to a small degree. This is not a cause for concern, but a natural result of *zazen*. We are also likely to find that our heartbeat is far more easily felt as we sit quietly. I often notice this myself and come to wonder how it is that I am oblivious to it during the rest of the day. This also is normal.

Mind

"To think 'I will not think'—
This, too, is something in one's thoughts.
Simply do not think
About not thinking at all."‡

It is well known that Zen meditation involves the overcoming of thought. What this means, however, is not always clear. Indeed, misunderstandings of "no-thought" abound. As we will see, not thinking is not about shutting off one's mind. To the contrary, it is about achieving a state of mind that remains fluid, flexible and aware.

---

* As in Cleary, 187.

† As in Stevens, 41. Likewise, Yagyu Munenori advises, "The mind should be thoroughly concentrated below the waist and the *ch'I* should not be driven too precipitously." (76)

‡ An old poem cited approvingly by Takuan, 50.

Those beginning *zazen* are generally taught first to count their breaths, a practice that may find its origin in Tendai Buddhism.* It is as simple as counting each inhalation and exhalation, from one to ten, and then beginning again. When I say "simple," I mean in theory, not necessarily in practice. As we sit and breathe, and begin counting our breaths, our attention should only be on our breath. When we reach ten, we simply begin again. There is no mental catalog of how many times we have reached ten, but only counting.

Each count should fill the breath. That is to say, we do not finish the breath and then say a quick "one" in our head. The count lives throughout the breath. Typical of his intense Rinzai practice, Omori Sogen advised us, "We should count our breaths, 'one, two….' with all our might, as if trying to penetrate the earth."†

What makes this practice so difficult is that one's attention should *only* be on the breath. Our mind should not become attached to any other thought. This is where we begin to see the value and demands of *zazen*. As I sit, even in a most serene environment, my mind will be stimulated with thoughts. This is not a bad thing. However, in *zazen* I must keep my mind from dwelling on or being caught by those thoughts. Those thoughts should not put down roots. They come into mental view, we acknowledge and are aware of them, and then they pass by. Like gazing into a large aquarium, we may see the fish swim by, but we do not allow our focus and attention to become attached to any single one of them.

Invariably we will be caught by some mental construct, image, or idea. When this happens, we should simply acknowledge that it happened and continue in our counting. If we have been caught for a longer time, it is better to start counting again at one, rather than try to remember where our counting left off. In my own case, my mental activity usually runs along the lines of the following:

* Omori Sogen, *An Introduction to Zen Training*, 46f.

† Ibid., 51.

> One... two... three... is my posture correct?... four... maybe I should stretch more next time before sitting... five... but it sure is better than it used to be... six... I remember seeing some people sitting who had really bad posture, mine is a lot better than theirs. Oh crap! What number was I on? Oh well. One... two... three... after this I need to hurry to karate practice, I don't want to be late... four... what should we do today? Hmmm, we should probably do some kakie and pad work. Whoops! Five... six... seven... eight... good grief! I've been here a couple minutes, I think, and still haven't reached ten. Did I do nine yet or not? I don't know. One...

Now surely there are those for whom counting breaths is an easier task, right from the start. For others it is immensely difficult. That is OK. *Zazen* is not competition. As I practice my deeply flawed meditation, I learn a great deal more about myself. I also start catching my wandering mind more quickly. I improve. I find myself existing in *zazen* rather than it being something that I do. I am able to make sense of Shunryu Suzuki's teaching, "If you think, 'I breathe,' the 'I' is extra. There is no you to say 'I.' What we call 'I' is just a swinging door which moves when we inhale and when we exhale."*

For those who do make progress, counting every complete breath may give way to counting only exhalations, or sometimes only inhalations. One may then stop counting all together. However, those of us with competitive natures must be careful that we do not throw away our "training wheels" too early. We might never get rid of them at all. According to Omori Sogen, "You can become enlightened splendidly by counting breaths. It is better to do it this way than to say '*Mu*' only with the tip of your nose."† Craving a more advanced practice of meditation is a sure sign you are not ready. Counting breaths is sufficient for a lifetime.

As we spend more time in meditation, we will face distractions and diversions of our mindfulness. Very often, we become aware of

---

* Shunryu Suzuki, 29.

† As in Hosokawa Dogen, *Omori Sogen: The Art of a Zen Master* (New York: Kegan Paul International, 1999), 121.

the thoughts that steal our attention and become frustrated, wanting angrily to cast them out of our minds. It is important that we not become irritated with these thoughts and attachments. They will come. Let them go. Shunryu Suzuki advised us, "If you want to obtain perfect calmness in your *zazen*, you should not be bothered by the various images you find in your mind. Let them come, and let them go."* When we become aggravated, we create a new duality between where we are and where we think we should be. This is craving. Rather, I can acknowledge that this mind is easily distracted, and then proceed with my meditation.

We must likewise be careful that we do not try to turn off our minds. *Zazen* is not about having an inactive mind, existing in a state of obliviousness. It is quite the opposite. I mindfully exist in this instant, in this place; I am not "zoning out." Shunryu Suzuki, once again, offered excellent advice, "Do not try to stop your mind, but leave everything as it is. Then things will not stay in your mind so long. Things will come as they come and go as they go. Then eventually your clear, empty mind will last fairly long."† As I mentioned before, there are times that I catch myself reaching a kind of obliviousness. I find that my eyesight has dimmed so that I am not seeing the floor in front of me and my mind is no longer present with me in my sitting. At those times I need to come back into the room, mentally speaking. "Even in wrong practice, when you realize it and continue, there is right practice."‡

As this quote suggests, we make progress. It is not a question of how good my meditation is. It is the discipline of sitting; improvement will happen. The Buddha is said to have advised his half-brother Nanda, "In order to obtain gold, one must wash away the dirt—first the big clods and then, to cleanse it further, the smaller ones, until finally one retains pure particles of gold. Just so, in order to obtain liberation, one must discipline the mind and wash away from it first

* Shunryu Suzuki, 32.

† Ibid., 128.

‡ Ibid., 73.

the big clods of one's faults and then, to purify it further, the smaller ones until finally one retains pure particles of Dharma."* While this is a helpful metaphor, it must be remembered that we don't scrub our minds, craving what we will be after years of meditation. We sit today, and that is all. At the same time, it is true that our minds are cleansed.

So, we see that our sitting should not be filled with frustration, dissatisfaction and annoyance when our *zazen* is not up to our expectations for ourselves. There are times of meditation during which I realize how detached and distracted I am, not even close to what *zazen* should be, and a slight smile plays on my lips as I realize how poor I am at this discipline. I suppose it is not too different from laughing at myself if I slip and fall, or when I absent-mindedly and unintentionally switch from one *kata* to another—as long as no one important is watching at the moment. At those times when I am particularly distracted, I have the most to gain by a renewed commitment to mental discipline.

When the physical pain of sitting is not disturbing me, there are times when *zazen* can be a pleasant experience, even one of enjoyment. Although we get pleasure from such moments, we need to remember that such sensations are not the goal of zazen, and can be a distraction to true practice. Again, Shunryu Suzuki provided essential counsel. "Actually, when your practice is involved in a feeling of joy, it is not in very good shape either. Of course this is not poor practice, but compared to the true practice it is not so good."†

True *zazen* is not a pleasant escape from our daily lives. It is discipline. Meditation that is not rigorous in its mindfulness is what Omori Sogen calls "empty *zazen*." Such easy sitting "will be of no use no matter how long, how often, or for how many days we may sit during sesshin. It is far better to sit earnestly even for five minutes."‡ So, those who find their *zazen* to be painful, difficult, distracted and

* From the 2nd century C.E. poet, Aśvaghosa, as in Strong, 134.

† Shunryu Suzuki, 73.

‡ Omori Sogen *Zen Training*, 74.

mentally exhausting can appreciate that they are not wasting their time.

Benefits?

One might ask, what benefits come from the discipline of *zazen*? Clearly it is not a practice for the purpose of enjoying some quiet time. Omori Sogen made the point, "[I]f Zen is only calming the spirit, would it not be more expedient to take tranquilizers or drink alcohol and pleasantly fall asleep than to sit for a long time enduring the pain in your legs?"* This difficult practice must serve a purpose greater than itself. To be sure, there are indeed specific aims to which we can point. Philip Kapleau's teacher, Haku'un Yasutani (1885–1973) offered three: "1) development of the power of concentration (*joriki*), 2) satori-awakening (*kensho-godo*) and 3) actualization of the Supreme Way in our daily lives (*mujodo no taigen*)."†

In regard to the second aim listed above, not everyone who practices *zazen* does so with an eye to enlightenment. We saw this earlier in the case of the samurai. Indeed, not every person who sits believes that *satori*, or *kenshō*, is even real. Historically, most martial artists who have undertaken Zen have not done so with the intent of reaching enlightenment. Unlike western religions, which focus on the *telos* (i.e. final goal) of eternity with God, most practitioners of eastern religions do not concern themselves with reaching Enlightenment. There are indeed those who do, including *budōka*, but this is not always the aim of the one practicing *zazen*. Since a proper treatment of *satori* is beyond the scope of this book, I recommend Kapleau's *Three Pillars of Zen* as a good place to start.

What Yasutani calls "actualization of the Supreme Way" connects strongly to the development of moral character, an essential aspect of Buddhism. The experience and expression of the *dō* in one's life is certainly cultivated in Buddhist disciplines, and certainly in *zazen*. This subject will be dealt with in detail in chapter 7. For the time

---

* Ibid., 17.

† As in Kapleau, 49.

being, I will address his first "aim" of *zazen,* that of concentration, or *joriki.*

Those who can control their minds, who can develop the "now-muscle" in their brains, exist in the instant and overcome attachment to thoughts and distractions; such people will live a more authentic life. This allows us to be the people we currently are, not who we were before or hope to be in the future. "That is why we practice *zazen*: to clear our mind of what is related to something else."* In *zazen* we cultivate through concentration the ability to exist as authentic human beings at the moment. We are not caught by others' expectations or our own. When we eat, we eat. When we lie down, we lie down. When we draw a bow, we draw a bow. This is what is called *ichigyo-zammai,* or one-act concentration. We attend to that which is at hand and are not caught up in that which is not currently relevant. "In the midst of noise and change, your mind will be quiet and stable."†

The advantages of such concentration should be apparent (and applicable!) to us all. Whether writing an annual report, driving home a nail, or listening to a friend, a quiet and stable mind that can attend to the task at hand is of the utmost importance.

Once again, it requires no great effort to see the relevance for martial artists. A strong mind while sitting will be a strong mind while standing; a strong mind while standing will be a strong mind while fighting. A great deal of noise is made in the martial arts community today about mental readiness for self-defense in "the real world." All of our physical training, in whatever form it takes (*kata, embu, randori,* MMA cage fighting), can only be a simulation of a real life event. *Zazen* allows one to develop the mental stability that is absolutely necessary when one's life is on the line. Adachi Masahiro's remark during The Tokugawa peace is worth repeating here, "Now at the present time there is no warfare going on, so there's no trying out combat with real swords, and consequently there's no way to know

* Shunryu Suzuki, 88.

† Ibid., 58.

how strong or weak our minds will be, or how excited or calm, where real swords are used. Nevertheless, when you train your mind under ordinary circumstances, your mind will be calm and unafraid even with real swords."*

Through the discipline of *zazen,* we overcome external and internal distractions, even the very notion of self. The Japanese believed that when this reaches its apex the highest level of fighting proficiency is reached. One who acts in this way is fit to be called a *meijin*—a genius or master. According to D. T. Suzuki, "The man emptied of all thoughts, all emotions originating from fear, all sense of insecurity, all desire to win, is not conscious of using the sword; both man and sword turn into instruments in the hands, as it were, of the unconscious, and it is this unconscious that achieves the wonders of creativity. It is here that swordplay becomes an art."† Stories in martial arts lore abound of the man who, while having no training with a sword, achieved this mental acuteness and was able to rout a trained samurai. Whether they were masters of Zen‡ or of the tea ceremony,§ their concentration and mindfulness allowed them to overcome their military-trained adversaries. While of dubious authenticity, they point to the great esteem in which the Japanese held the training of the mind.

This clarity of thought is the same as the awareness fostered in *zazen.* We should not, however, confuse this with automatic reaction. Speaking of this mindfulness *zazen,* or *shikan-taza,* Yasutani taught:

> Compared with an unskilled swordsman a master uses his sword effortlessly. But this was not always the case, for there was a time when he had to strain himself to the utmost, owing to his imperfect technique, to preserve his life. It is no different with *shikan-taza.* In the beginning tension is unavoidable, but with experience this tense *zazen* ripens into relaxed yet fully attentive sitting. And just as

* As in Cleary, 178f.

† D. T. Suzuki, *Zen and Japanese Culture,* 146.

‡ Ibid., 204.

§ Ibid., 189.

> a master swordsman in an emergency unsheathes his sword effortlessly and attacks single-mindedly, just so that *shikan-taza* adept sits without strain, alert and mindful.*

The mind fostered in *zazen* is the same mind we should have in training or fighting.

We have discussed the advantages of this facility of *joriki*, or concentration, when practicing martial arts, or any undertaking in life. It appears that there are a great many obvious benefits that come as a result of the practice of *zazen*. Most people familiar with Zen would grant that claim. However, I was given a surprising answer to a question years ago which led me to consider that there may actually be no benefits to practicing *zazen*.

I was attending a blackbelt *gasshuku* in Coronado, California several years ago with Morio Higaonna Sensei. After training one day, we had the opportunity to sit and ask questions. Knowing of the seriousness with which he practices Zen, I asked him, "Sensei, if one can practice meditation while performing various art forms, *karatedō, shodō, chadō,* what is the benefit of doing seated meditation?" Without missing a beat he replied, "There is no benefit." And then he smiled and continued, "But still, do it."

It might be easy to conclude that he was encouraging seated meditation because it is the tradition, rather than because it has value. However, that would be to miss his point. To the contrary, he was telling us something far more profound about the practice of *zazen*. If we are looking for benefits, we are on the wrong track in two respects.

First, there is nothing additional that is being brought into the equation of our existence. We must understand that Buddhism does not provide access to something new or different. It does not offer us something we do not have. Buddhism cannot help you attain the Buddha-nature; it is already here. A "benefit" suggests the addition of something of value, but there is nothing to add.

---

* As in Kapleau, 57.

In his curiously named *Zen in the Martial Arts*, Joe Hyams stated, "Some martial artists achieve a state of awareness suggestive of a sixth sense; this is the total involvement in environment for which Zen practitioners aim."* Rather than the addition of a "sixth sense," the awareness fostered by meditation is aided by the subtraction of distraction and mental disturbance. If you are looking for something to add to who you are, look elsewhere than Zen. *Zazen* does not bring about any benefits. There is nothing to add to who we are. Higaonna Sensei was telling us that if we think that meditation—moving or otherwise—will provide us with something we do not presently have, we have misunderstood what Zen is. Living in accord with the Way does not require that anything be appended to who we are. We might even say that there is no secret ingredient.

The second danger in thinking of "benefits" as they pertain to *zazen* is related to the first. When we crave after something which we believe is not ours, we live in the future rather than the present and contribute to our own disappointment and despair. The *Vimalakīrti Sūtra,* known in Japan as *Yuima Kyō,* teaches, "Seeking the dharma consists in not seeking anything, not getting attached to anything; for when there is any seeking or attachment, from it grows every form of hindrance, moral and intellectual, and one will be inextricably involved in meshes of contradictions and alterations. Hence no end of illness in this life."† When we focus on benefits that come from *zazen* we are creating difficulties in both the present and for our futures. We must remove all ideas of progress, accomplishment, improvement and achievement from our practice. Omori Sogen insisted, "[I]t goes without saying that since time immemorial it has been forbidden to practice Zen as a means of accomplishing some purpose or other, for Zen should be without purposes and without acquisitions."‡

---

* Joe Hyams, *Zen in the Martial Arts* (New York: Jeremy P. Tarcher/Putnam, 1979), 97.

† As in D. T. Suzuki, *Zen and Japanese Culture,* 415.

‡ Omori Sogen, *Zen Training,* 119. To this we may add the advice of Shunryu Suzuki, "When you try to attain something, your mind starts to wander about somewhere else. When you do

At the same time, the more objective and intellectual thinkers may reply, "Yes, I understand your point. But at another level, surely we can speak of benefits. Are not improved health, posture, blood pressure and concentration benefits?" Of course. An objective response can be given, and is given by many Zen practitioners—although Higaonna Sensei's answer was the "correct" one, from a Zen point of view. Omori Sogen wrote of what is gained through meditation:

> You may wonder then, 'Why do Zen priests do *zazen*?' It is because in *samadhi* [i.e., concentration of the mind], there is *ji-zanmai* (*samadhi* limited to a particular field of activity) and *oo-zanmai* (the great *samadhi*). *Ji-zanmai* is the *samadhi* only when you are doing something.... *Oo-zanmai*, however, is the fundamental and best samadhi that is universal and can be experienced during *zazen*. In an instant, the mind, body, and breath become one, creating stability and *samadhi*. This *samadhi* can be used for anything and under any circumstances.*

We seek to practice the highest form of *samadhi*, or concentration, in *zazen*. When this meditation is practiced, we may more easily translate such mindfulness and concentration to our lives off of the cushion. So yes, we might say there are benefits to *zazen*; then again, we might not.

From a medical point of view, various forms of meditation have been shown to accentuate alpha activity in the brain. An increase in alpha rhythms, along with a subsequent reduction in beta rhythms, is correlated with greater relaxation and a reduction in stress. Studies have found a variety of disciplines and biofeedback techniques that make this possible, *zazen* being one. James Austin, a physician who has written a massive work on the subject, points out, "When

---

not try to attain anything, you have your own body and mind right here." (26f.) "But as long as you think you are practicing *zazen* for the sake of something, that is not true practice." (47) "Just remain on your cushion without expecting anything." (49)

* Hosokawa Dogen, 116.

patients who are severely and chronically anxious do learn to facilitate their alpha rhythms, they gain a global feeling of increased well being. The alpha increases even before their inner feelings show marked improvement."* Western science is continually discovering what our friends in the East have known for millennia: meditative exercises can facilitate mental and physical well being.

These increases in alpha activity are not limited to the time spent seated in meditation. They do not necessarily cease when the *zazen* practitioner leaves his cushion. Studies with Sōtō Zen monks demonstrate that increased alpha levels are maintained during walking meditation (*kinhin*). Moreover, those with greater experience in meditation displayed greater alpha activity than those with less experience, while a control group of graduate students with no meditative experience displayed no alpha activity during the same activity.† We should be careful to note that our brains do not exist in either an alpha or beta state. We do not move back and forth between them, and certainly not at a moment's notice. Various complementary wave activities are going on in our minds at the same time; we are talking here about ratios of activity. Moreover, increased alpha activity is not turned on like a light switch. Even advanced Zen practitioners may require fifty seconds to significantly alter their brainwaves.‡

Austin also discusses how alpha activity is associated with maintained attention to a subject. While increases in beta activity correlate with a shorter duration of intense focus, alpha waves increase during sustained vigilance.§ It appears to follow that these meditative exercises that foster alpha activity allow for more keen awareness. It is also quite fascinating—and relevant to martial artists—that while practitioners of other meditative disciplines habituated to stimuli in their environment during deep meditative practice, this was not the case with those practicing Zen meditation. In one experiment,

* James H. Austin, *Zen and the Brain* (Cambridge, The MIT Press, 1998), 85.

† Ibid., 88.

‡ Omori Sogen, *Zen Training*, 130.

§ Austin, 86.

recurring sound stimuli—either a "click" or the names of family members—were presented during meditation. Practitioners of Raja Yoga and Transcendental Meditation habituated to the sounds so that they eventually ceased to register in their conscious minds. The Sōtō Zen monks, however, demonstrated continual awareness of the sound, both on an EEG and in later interviews. "[T]he monks reported afterward that, though they clearly perceived each click stimulus, [it] did not appear to disturb them."* That is to say, they consciously perceived the sounds but did not become attached to them. This bears a striking resemblance to the passive awareness that is fostered by Zen adherents and described as *zanshin* by many in the martial arts community. (We will turn to the subject of *zanshin* in the next chapter.)

Of course we could go on at great length about the benefits of Zen and meditation in general. Hundreds of books and thousands of articles have been written about the physiological and psychological benefits of *zazen*. This is obviously not the place to explore them. What is imperative to remember, however, is that Zen is not about the time you spend on your cushion. In the words of Chinese Zen master Pen-hsien (941–1008), "If you really wish to get into the truth of Zen, get it while walking, while standing, while sleeping or sitting, while talking or remaining silent, or while engaged in all kinds of your daily work."†

* Ibid., 105.

† As in D. T. Suzuki, *The Zen Doctrine of No-Mind: The Significance of the Sūtra of Hui-neng* (Boston: Weisner Books, 1969), 110.

Chapter Six

Mushin and Mindfulness

*"*Mushin *means an empty mind which is in a state of total control and concentration... the mental attitude you need in your journey to find success in your life."* –Hirokazu Kanazawa

Mushin

Among martial artists, one of the most popular—and yet most misunderstood—concepts in Zen is *mushin,* usually translated as "no-mind." One can find the name "Mushin Dojo" above the door of shotokan, aikido, jujutsu and ninjutsu schools around the world. Clearly martial artists have great affinity for this concept, but what exactly is this principle of "no-mind?"

Joe Hyams recorded an alleged conversation with Bruce Lee about this subject. Lee is reported to have said, "If it was a real fight, I'm certain I would hurt my assailant badly, perhaps kill him. If that happened and I was forced to stand trial, I would plead that I had no responsibility for my action. I had responded to his attack without conscious awareness. 'It' killed him, not me." On the following page, Lee continued, "'It' is the state of mind that Japanese refer to as *mushin*."* The conversation continued with Lee explaining that it is only through constant practice that one reaches such a mindset, where actions are automatic.

If Hyams' account of this conversation is accurate, then I think we can say that Lee's understanding of Zen and its relationship to martial arts is vastly overrated. It would also appear that he understood very little about the law and avoiding jail time after getting in a fight. As we will see, *mushin* is not about automatic reaction or lack

* Hyams, 89.

of thought. As Kanazawa explains, where there is *mushin,* there is total control."

The mistaken idea of *mushin* as instinctive reaction is not surprising. For students of various *budō* arts, the initial stage of study involves a great deal of repetition. The *judōka* practices the *kuzushi* ("unbalancing") for *harai-goshi* hundreds of times. This is followed by the *tsukuri* ("fitting in") and *kake* ("execution"), all separately for the same throw. Then he puts the three parts together. He practices the throw with a compliant partner over and over. Next he attempts it during *randori* against a noncompliant partner, and eventually begins to pull off the throw successfully. And then, one day, he is grappling with another student, perhaps thinking of another throw, when the opportunity for *harai-goshi* presents itself. Without any thought, he executes it perfectly as an automatic reaction. It is a wonderful feeling, and he has certainly attained a level of proficiency that he did not have before. That must be, he concludes, what people call *mushin.* Unfortunately, he is wrong.

We find written descriptions of no-mind-ness that may reinforce this mistaken notion. Yagyū Munenori wrote, "If you can clear from your mind those things you have learned, they too will become nothing; and when you perform the techniques of the various Ways, the techniques will come easily regardless of what you have performed and without being contrary to it. When you perform an action you will be in harmony with what you have learned, without even being aware of it."* This certainly appears to be consistent with the experience of the *judōka* and his spontaneous *harai-goshi.* However, we would be hasty to conclude that Munenori is speaking of the same obliviousness that Lee spoke of. Trevor Leggett offers us a helpful corrective as he points out that the highest ideal is not a spontaneous response to one's environment. "The main thing to realize is, that it is not a question of established tricks simply going into action automatically as a sort of reflex." Uncritical reaction is not the apex of

* Yagyu Munenori, 74f.

achievement in *budō*. "It is the very reverse of mechanical repetition because it is creative."* If the ability to perceive, control and deviate from one's actions is lost, one has not mastered one's art. The mindfulness of *mushin* is a complete awareness without the fettering of conscious thought.

Mindfulness and no-mind may appear to be mutually contradictory. However, they are two sides of the same coin. Mindfulness in the context of Zen refers to being present in the moment, aware of one's actions and environment. Mindfulness means that while I am washing the dishes, I am fully aware of my actions, feeling the soapy water and dishes in my hands, not daydreaming about watching the game after the dishes are done. At the same time, I am not mentally caught up with my domestic chore so that I am unaware of what exists around me. My consciousness is free and open, not fixed on any action or category, not even my washing of dishes. I am mindful of myself at the same time I have no-mind. This principle is best understood through experience, as a mental state can only be described with words in a limited way. Like trying to describe the taste of cinnamon, words will not suffice; once you experience it, it is understood.

When we understand how *mushin* is consistent with mindfulness the love affair between the samurai and Zen becomes clearer. Recall the story of the unfortunate members of the Tokugawa era jujutsu school who were stabbed through the abdomen when they relied on their instinctive response to a raised sword, which turned out to be a decoy in the form of a scabbard. Leggett's words are worthy of repeating in this regard, "As a matter of fact, it is very easy to defeat a man who simply executes his techniques as a reflex. One can control his body through them. One sets off a reflex in him, and then waits with the counter.... This is one reason why an expert finds it much easier to defeat a man who has trained for a year than an absolute beginner."†

So, *mushin* is not unthinking reaction. How, then, can we best

* Leggett, *Zen and the Ways*, 118.

† Ibid., 125, 126.

describe this state of no-mind? Again, Leggett provides considerable help. He pointed to two characteristics: "(1) complete cutting off of the thought-streams; (2) freedom from unnecessary thoughts while engaged in some activity."* What is important to note is that he referred to thought-streams and unnecessary thoughts. One should not think that thoughts are not present. *Mushin* is not thoughtlessness, but a state of awareness without thoughts becoming carried away, caught up in a stream of consciousness.

D. T. Suzuki characterized the views of the great *kendōka* Takano Hiromasa in this way, "It means letting your natural faculties act in a consciousness free from thoughts, reflection or affections of any kind."† Here, "thoughts" are precluded from the description of this state of mind. However, one should note that they are listed here along with "reflection or affections" in a context that suggests being mentally caught. He described "consciousness" free from mental activity that hinders fluidity in thought. The one acting with an unthinking mechanical response does not do so consciously. Here, the person with no-mind acts consciously yet unrestrained by thought. There is no *suki*, the interval of broken mindfulness we discussed in chapter 3.

In relation to *zazen*, as discussed in the previous chapter, we find that the mind cultivated in meditation is the same mind one should have in martial training or combat. Michael Raposa's explanation of *mushin*, both for meditation and the martial arts, is excellent:

> One does not achieve such a state of consciousness by trying to drive all thoughts out of the mind or to obliterate the mind's contents. Instead, in calmness one links the mind to the breath, attentive to all thoughts and feelings as they move into and out of consciousness, watching them come and go, listening to them, but never with attachment and never with any specific expectation about what will appear next.‡

---

* Ibid., 22.

† D. T. Suzuki, *Zen and Japanese Culture*, 127.

‡ Raposa, 78.

The mindfulness of no-mind that is fostered in *zazen* is no different than the ideal state of mind while practicing *budō*. Several years ago, I attended a *gasshuku* in Coronado, California. Our training and instruction was under the watchful eye of Morio Higaonna Sensei. While I still stand in awe of the man, at that time I was equally intimidated as well. Among the seventy or so men and women on the floor, I tended to gravitate toward anonymity somewhere in the middle. However, Sensei decided to split the class into two, working with each group individually. The result was that when my group was called up to perform *kata*, I was standing front and center, with Sensei within arm's reach. (I am sure that many readers, with smiles on their faces, can easily think of a time when they were called on to perform their art in a situation that created similar anxiety.) However, as various fears bombarded me, I attempted to focus solely on the *kata*, the same way I focus on breathing during *zazen*. While I did not become unaware of Sensei's presence, my concentration was on the one task before me. This is, ideally, how one should practice *kata* at all times, and the type of attention that *zazen* cultivates in its practitioners.

The same benefits obviously extend to all manner of activity. Competitive athletes cannot afford to be distracted by fans, cameras, personal grudges and pride. Airline pilots must have tremendous powers of concentration during bad weather conditions. At other times it is our ego that distracts us from the tasks we pursue. Walpola Rahula explained:

> Mindfulness, or awareness, does not mean that you should think and be conscious 'I am doing this' or 'I am doing that.' No. Just the contrary. The moment you think 'I am doing this,' you become self-conscious, and then you do not live in the action, but you live in the idea 'I am,' and consequently your work too is spoilt. You should forget yourself completely, and lose yourself in what you do. The moment a speaker becomes self-conscious and thinks, 'I am addressing an audience,' his speech is disturbed and his trend of thought broken. But when he forgets himself in his speech, in

> his subject, then he is at his best, he speaks well and explains things clearly. All great work—artistic, poetic, intellectual, or spiritual—is produced at those moments when its creators are lost completely in their actions, when they forget themselves altogether, and are free from self-consciousness.*

So the archer does not think, "I am doing archery," but is mindful only of shooting the arrow. "If he is shooting, he just takes out his bow, puts an arrow to it, stretches the string, fixes his eyes on the target, and when he judges the adjustment to be right he lets the arrow go. He has no feeling of doing anything specifically good or bad, important or trivial."† Likewise, the painter is aware of her brush strokes but not of herself as painter. In the same way, the *karateka* may be in a state of *mushin* while practicing *kata, bunkai, kihon, makiwara* or *kumite.*

The incident in which I had to really focus on the *kata* movements in order to block the distraction of performance anxiety had a positive outcome. My *kata* went well. I needed no corrections from Sensei. Lest anyone think that I pretend to be a model of the enlightened *budōka,* however, the next day was a different story: While training on the beach with the others—this time safely tucked into the anonymous throng—I was swept away by thoughts of the beauty of the ocean, how we must have looked to passers-by, and what new material and stories I would bring home to my dojo. This time the result was not as positive. In the middle of *shisochin*–my strongest *kata* at the time—I became completely lost. While others were continuing, I could not for the life of me remember the next movement. The seconds ticked away while I remained motionless, frantically trying to remember how I had come to my current position and determine what came next.

Superior concentration is not something one pulls out of a hat from time to time, at a test, tournament, or demonstration. More-

---

* Rahula, 72.

† D. T. Suzuki, *Zen and Japanese Culture,* 147.

over, trying to think yourself into *mushin* is a waste of time. "[S]urely it would be like trying to wash off blood with blood, to get rid of thought by thought."* It is cultivated by long hours of discipline, not a conscious choice. And relying on a text will not allow you to understand the reality of *mushin*. Takuan Sōhō explained, "One may explain water, but the mouth will not become wet. One may expound fully on the nature of fire, but the mouth will not become hot."† However, whether sitting on a cushion or drawing a bow, we can be practicing. Whenever a martial artist practices his craft, he should strive to attain such a state of mindfulness. It is only through diligent training that one develops such mental strength. I stumbled across an excellent description of such training one day on the internet. Anthony Mirakian, reflecting on his days in Okinawa being taught by Meitoku Yagi Sensei, wrote:

> All of the students would line up. There was a complete silence. We would begin by going through all the Goju-ryu kata to Suparinpe [sic], one after the other. This practice was done very seriously, with tremendous concentration; the mind wasn't wandering, there was no wavering of the eyes. Once the student was training in the dojo, he had to be in command of his mind and in complete control of himself.

The misconception that *mushin,* either during meditation or in action, is characterized by one who has mentally checked out, is not that uncommon. It is an easy trap to fall into. In trying to help his students understand Zen properly, Omori Sogen distinguished between the state of no-thought and *kuku jaku jaku,* or "the state of quiet emptiness." Those who intend the former, but find themselves sitting peaceably in the latter are wasting their time. True *mushin* does not exist for the sake of one's time sitting, but must be carried into the battles of everyday existence.

---

* Leggett, *Zen and the Ways*, 24.

† Takuan, 42.

What good, after all, is obliviousness? And why on earth would the samurai be interested in a discipline that left them unaware of what was happening around them? Hyams told another story about visiting a Tae Kwon Do practitioner who was busy punching away at a *makiwara*. He found that the man did not react at all to Hyams' arrival. "His concentration was so complete that he was unaware he had visitors."* Of course, you and I do not know if the man was aware of Hyams or not. However, the idea that he was so singly focused as to be unaware of others entering the room is not only inconsistent with *mushin*, it is its opposite! Hyams thought this was desirable. Describing his own training, he wrote, "This [breathing] technique, which I had been taught as a prelude to aikido, is an aspect of Zen practice that makes one oblivious to external impressions."† This is not faithful to either Zen or aikido! Obliviousness and distraction are what get soldiers killed, whether in medieval Japan or the mountains of Tora Bora. Quite the opposite of what Hyams described, Yasutani taught his students, "This is the degree of alertness required: If you were sitting in one corner of a room during shikan-taza and a door on the other side was quietly opened half an inch, you would know instantly."‡

Kapleau compared the emptiness of *mushin* to the harmonies of a great symphony, a wonderful image that conveys clarity and intelligibility, not a void. *Mushin* does not leave us mentally unavailable, but quite the opposite. "Zazen that leads to self-realization is neither idle reverie nor vacant inaction but an intense inner struggle to gain control over the mind and then to use it, like a silent missile, to penetrate the barrier of the five senses and the discursive intellect."§

As far back as the *Platform Sutra*, the sixth Zen patriarch Huineng (638–713) warned us:

---

* Hyams, 101.

† Ibid., 70.

‡ Kapleau, 138

§ Ibid., 13.

> Deluded people who like to label things say that this meditation, this direct mind, is to sit unmoving, to cast aside error and let no thoughts occur. If this were so, their teaching would simply turn us into inanimate objects, and set up a barricade to the Way. But the Way should flow freely: why should we clog it like that? When the mind is not attached to events, then the Way flows freely; it is when the mind is attached that it gets all tangled up.*

The great masters of Japanese swordsmanship, like Yagyū Munenori, believed that this mental acuity must be developed for one to achieve the highest level of fighting proficiency. When the distractions of this world, the commotion in our minds, and even the fear of death are overcome, one reaches one's potential as a warrior. Without expectations, with full awareness and fluidity of thought, we overcome the barriers to success. "Action is accomplished with full insight into all principles, lightly throwing principles off and letting none remain in the mind. It is accomplished by keeping the mind empty, and by keeping it ordinary and nothing special. If you do not reach this level, it will be difficult to call yourself accomplished in the martial arts."†

This appreciation for the value of Zen training for soldiers and martial artists is no relic of the past. From the Japanese military's use of Zen in the twentieth century to the Buddhist chapel at the U.S. Air Force Academy, built in 2005, we find that those who understand the importance of mental preparedness among fighting men and women are able to appreciate what Zen has to offer.

Omori Sogen told the amusing story of the Chinese Zen master Toko Shin-etsu, who visited Japan during the Ming dynasty (1368–1644). On New Year's Day he found himself in the company of a certain Mitsukini, a Japanese lord who was one of his students. The Japanese lord offered a large cup, full to the brim with *sake,* to Toko. Immediately after receiving it, a gunshot rang out from the next

---

* As in Strong, 302.

† Munenori, 130.

room. Carefully watching his Chinese visitor's reaction, Mitsukini noticed that his guest showed no reaction at all. He then apologized, offering as an explanation, "It is customary to fire a gun in a warrior's house. Please excuse me."

When Lord Mitsukani's cup was next filled with *sake,* Master Toko unexpectedly let out a loud shout of "*Katz*!" whereupon his host jolted and spilled his drink. The teacher then offered his own apology, with apparent earnestness, "It is customary for Zen men to give a single shout of 'Katz!' Please excuse me."* This remarkable story, approximated under laboratory conditions by psychologist Paul Ekman, complete with gunshots, demonstrates an imperturbability of mind which would be the envy of anyone serving in the military, or, for that matter, anyone striving to keep family and self safe in the world today.

The key to understanding such a mental state is easily missed. Trying to make one's mind imperturbable is to miss the point. One does not remove thought with more thought. We do not exist in this instant when we struggle to attain something that is not currently ours. I cannot become immune to the terror I feel upon hearing a random gunshot by trying hard not to be scared. Rather, I simply need to exist as who I am right now. If random gunshots frighten me, then I simply need to acknowledge that I am frightened when one happens.

A man once asked Rinzai Master Bankei Ekaku (1622–1693) why he always became scared by loud noises, like thunder. The man inquired whether it indicated a lack of discipline and how he might proceed to overcome all fear. Bankei replied, "When you get frightened, just be as you are. If you take precautions, you'll be dualistic."†

I try to bear this advice in mind myself, in various contexts. There are times, before I speak publicly, that I can feel my blood pressure rising. When I perform *kata* in a competition, my heart rate increases significantly and I become quite nervous. In such instances, I wish I

---

* Omori Sogen, *Zen Training,* 90f.

† Ibid., 62.

could calm down. I even try to calm myself down, talking to myself (silently, of course), saying there is no need to be anxious. This rarely works. Rather, following the advice of Master Bankei, I am better served by acknowledging that I am apprehensive. I simply need to recognize "OK. I'm nervous. My heart rate is up. My blood pressure is higher than normal." And then I carry out what I intend to do, simply being with my anxiety, neither denying it nor craving to be free of it.

Is this nervousness a shortcoming, a weakness, a limitation? Sure. At the same time, I find that time spent in *zazen* does tend to reduce my various anxieties. I can also practice throughout the day, strengthening my mind wherever I find myself. I can follow the advice of Suzuki Shosan, "Use your mind strongly even when you walk down the street, such that you wouldn't even blink if someone unexpectedly thrust a lance at your nose. All warriors should employ such a state of mind all the time in everyday life."* Someday, perhaps I will be as even-keeled as Master Toko. Until then, I simply acknowledge the reality of my emotions when they appear. Aware that they are part of who I am today, I proceed to undertake the tasks I have before me.

Zanshin

The concept of *zanshin* is another that *budōka* often speak about. As with "*mushin*," one can find numerous Zanshin Dojos teaching martial arts around the world. Also, as is the case with *mushin*, there are those who misunderstand what this word means. Some teachers use the easy translation of "awareness." I have even seen it explained as being "hyper-aware." However, many people hear such a description and think that what is being spoken of is intense concentration—focusing one's entire mental energy on one thing like a laser beam. Such a practice is actually the opposite of *zanshin*.

In different arts, *zanshin* is invoked to address various concerns. In *kyūdō*, *zanshin* is cultivated to ensure that attention does not wane

---

* As in Cleary, 44.

after the arrow is released. The same idea is expressed by some Japanese baseball coaches to their pitchers. After the pitch, awareness must remain, as an inattentive pitcher might eat a ball if his attention fades after releasing the pitch. In kendo, one must likewise remain mentally engaged after a strike. While in aikido, *zanshin* is fostered so that attention is directed not only toward the one being thrown, but other potential opponents who may suddenly appear. In karate, *kata* are finished with *zanshin,* where the practitioner is aware of his surroundings.

While in some of these arts, attention or awareness may be directed primarily in one direction, we should not think that *zanshin* is about paying attention to one thing. The essential idea is of complete awareness of one's surroundings. As we saw above, the mind does not stop. The mind does not stop after the arrow is released, the ball thrown, the opponent struck, or the performance completed. Awareness remains and is mindful of its environment, 360 degrees.

Draeger translated *zanshin* as "alertness remaining-form" and explains that it signifies "physical form united with mental acuity and concentration."* This is good, but not the best introduction to the idea. If we look at the Japanese word itself, the kanji 残心 is literally translated as "the remaining mind." By itself, however, this translation offers little to those who do not already understand the concept. I find it helpful to begin by explaining *zanshin* as a state of passive alertness and awareness. If we begin with this description, we can begin to make more sense of what *zanshin* is about. Afterwards, the literal translations are more easily understood.

If we say that *zanshin* is a state of passive alertness and awareness, we begin by noting that it is not an action that a person does; it is not a verb. It is a state of mind, intimately related to *mushin,* as we will see. As such, I cannot simply decide to *zanshin*. It is not comparable to a stance or movement, where I can demonstrate it for students and have them copy me. After *kata,* I am told to be in a state of *zanshin.*

---

* Draeger, *Classical Bujutsu,* 62.

I can be shown what this looks like, but then I may only copy the external behavior of my teacher. As a state of mind, it is something that my instructor can talk about, explain,and model, but it cannot be reproduced by imitation. *Zanshin* is experienced existentially, not intellectually. Each individual must experience it for herself. The teacher can point the way, or function as a midwife, but the student must undergo the discipline to discover and foster it.

As a state of mind, we may experience *zanshin* at different levels. As beginners, we catch a glimpse into what it is about. Through diligent practice and effort, we may improve our alertness and calm our minds. At times we will be more successful, and other times we fall far short. Moreover, there are individuals whose psychological makeup is more conducive to this practice, and those for whom it is especially difficult. However, whether we are having more or less success with our efforts, we are striving toward that complete state of *zanshin* where only "the spirit remains." Even if we never achieve it perfectly, we learn to correct our mistakes more quickly.

Let us return to the word "passive." We might also use the words relaxed, calm, or serene to describe our awareness, yet each is only an approximation of the idea we are trying to express. Whichever word we use, the principle that is essential to understanding *zanshin* is that the mind is not concentrating on any one thing. Your mind is not focused intently on the enemy, but quite the opposite. It is not focused on anything, yet it is aware of everything it can perceive. This is reflected in one's face; it will be relaxed and calm yet observant. We are all familiar with fighters whose reddened and contorted faces convey their intense energy, their eyes glaring right into their opponents. This can be intimidating, but it is not a state of awareness. Contrast this with the face of a true master who projects tranquility and power simultaneously; there is nothing that escapes his notice and his mind is not clouded with emotion or distraction. (Granted, samurai would sometimes feign rage to intimidate a weak adversary, but they sought serenity behind the mask they projected to their enemies.)

In the words of D. T. Suzuki:

> While being trained in the art, the pupil is to be active and dynamic in every way. But in actual combat, his mind must be calm and not at all disturbed. He must feel as if nothing critical is happening.... His steps are securely on the ground, and his eyes are not glaringly fixed on the enemy.... His behavior is not in any way different from his everyday behavior. No change is taking place in his expression. Nothing betrays the fact that he is now engaged in a mortal fight.*

The alertness and awareness of *zanshin* are of a general sort. Awareness cannot be directed solely at one thing. While the *kyūdōka* may be facing the target, mindful awareness engages the entire dojo, not the target alone. In this calm state, one is aware of everything that stimulates the senses.

Morihei Ueshiba, founder of aikido, was sitting with a student one day, enjoying tea and conversation. Without looking around, he suddenly reached behind himself and picked up a young cockroach. After identifying what it was, he gently put it down and continued his tea. Whether legend or history, this story illustrates quite well the all-encompassing awareness that one strives for in *zanshin*. In contrast, as soon as I affix my attention to any one thing in particular, it becomes much more difficult to perceive anything other than the narrow object of my focus.

Consider the common military practice of creating a diversion (with obvious parallels in martial arts). If I want to attack my enemy from his right flank, I may create a diversion to his left. With his attention drawn to the left, he is less likely to notice me as I sneak in on the right. If he falls for the diversion, his thinking is focused in one direction which makes him less aware of the other, from where my attack is coming. Boxers and fencers obviously use feints to the same end.

Diversions, however, are not always created by the other guy.

* D. T. Suzuki, *Zen and Japanese Culture,* 185.

Whenever our attention is in one direction, we create our own diversion, one to which we ourselves succumb, thereby aiding our opponent. When sparring with my students, invariably I get hit when I think, "I'll wait until she throws that right punch, then I will do such-and-such." While my mind is on her right hand, she kicks me with her left leg. If, however, I could maintain a level of alert awareness where I do not mentally attach myself to any one thing, I would be far less susceptible to the effects of a diversion, feint, or over-strategizing.

If this is beginning to sound a lot like *mushin,* then I am doing my job. As we have seen in *mushin,* there is no conscious attention to any one physical perception or mental construct. The Buddhist nun walking through the forest perceives the birds chirping, the creek gurgling, the scent of honeysuckle, the color of leaves, and her own breathing and heartbeat, but she does not mentally attach herself to any one of them. Likewise, her mind does not fixate on thoughts of dinner or some philosophical problem (unless she so desires). She is completely alive in the present without clinging to the past, craving for the future, or holding to the fleeting present. So, the passive awareness of *zanshin* shares this mindfulness. In her typically succinct commentary, Dai-en Bennage expressed it to me this way: "*Zanshin* exists within *mushin.*"

Perfect awareness exists within the disciplined mind of the Zen practitioner. "When *mushin* or *munen* [no-thought] is attained, the mind moves from one object to another, flowing like a stream of water, filling every possible corner. For this reason the mind fulfills every function required of it. But when the flowing is stopped at one point, all the other points will get nothing of it, and the result will be a general stiffness and obduracy."*

This is the primary lesson that *kyūdō* student Eugen Herrigel struggled to learn under his archery master in Japan, the story of which he famously tells in *Zen in the Art of Archery.* Herrigel toiled for countless hours trying to overcome his natural tendency to make

* D. T. Suzuki, *Zen and Japanese Culture,* 111.

a conscious decision when to release the arrow from the drawn bow. He found that the decision is made at a non-conscious level. Students of *kyūdō* are also taught that they are to remain in a state of *zanshin* after the arrow is released. One does not "check out" mentally after the arrow flies. In *kyūdō* competition, such alertness is watched for and judged. Of course, one can mimic *zanshin* without truly experiencing it.

In competitive sport karate, participants competing in *kumite* are expected to display *zanshin* after scoring with a punch or kick. They are not to hit their opponent and then immediately look away, continuing a 5-second-long *kiai* while trotting around the mat. According to the rules, this lack of *zanshin* can result in no point being awarded. According to WKF rules: "Awareness (*ZANSHIN*) is that criterion most often missed when a score is assessed. It is the state of continued commitment in which the contestant maintains total concentration, observation, and awareness of the opponent's potentiality to counter-attack. He does not turn his face away during delivery of the technique, and remains facing the opponent afterwards."* Unfortunately, even in elite competition, this kind of behavior has become commonplace and is rarely penalized.

With even greater importance, students of *shodō* (Japanese calligraphy) also speak of and practice *zanshin*. At the completion of a brush stroke, there can be no hesitation, no distraction, no thought as the hand is lifted and brush leaves paper. The drops of ink that may fall from the brush after it releases from the paper are testimony to the remaining mind of the *shodōka*. If they continue the flow of the line, they are evidence of *zanshin*. H. E. Davey, a student of both Japanese martial arts and calligraphy explains:

> It is vital to maintain an unbroken flow of Ki and concentration throughout the artistic act. In *Budo* as well as *Shodo*, this is known as

* The official IKF Kendo Shiai and Shinpan Regulations describe the place of *zanshin* in its discipline: Section 2—Article 7. *Yūkō-datotsu* is defined as the accurate striking or thrusting made onto *datotsu-bui* of the opponent's *kendo-gu* with *shinai* at its *datotsu-bu* in high spirits and correct posture, being followed by *zanshin*."

> *zanshin* (literally 'remaining mind'), and it indicates a kind of 'mental follow-through' and unbroken condition of calm awareness. *Shodo* has been used in the past, as well as the present, as a way for Budōka to develop *zanshin* without the presence of an actual opponent.*

Takuan offered his samurai audience a description of the benefits of this mind, free from attachment and truly aware. "When facing a single tree, if you look at a single one of its red leaves, you will not see all the others. When the eye is not set on any one leaf, and you face the tree with nothing at all in mind, any number of leaves are visible to the eye without limit. But if a single leaf holds the eye, it will be as if the remaining leaves were not there."†

At the same time, Takuan explained that this is a very difficult level of mental activity. He was not prescribing a magic pill that will make mediocre martial artists unstoppable. First, the student must master his chosen discipline. Contrary to what certain celebrity martial artists conveyed in the twentieth century, one must start by learning the art. "If you do not train in technique, but only fill your breast with principle, your body and your hands will not function."‡ There is no shortcut. One absolutely must begin with technique with *kata*, with a style; those who are in a hurry to cast these aside will not progress very far.

If we are looking for action stars from martial arts movies to model *zanshin*, I believe the characters played by Jackie Chan exemplify this principle of "the mind not stopping" quite well. In any and every possible environment, his action sequences portray a mind that is free to respond fluidly to its environment without stopping... and with very little ego.

I have often heard people compare *zanshin* to being "in the zone." To be honest, I am not sure if this is a good comparison because I

---

* H. E. Davey, "Shodo: Budo and the Art of Japanese Calligraphy," *Furyu: The Budo Journal* (Spring-Summer 1995), cited in http://www.samurai.or.id/php/modules.php?name=News&file=article&sid=13.

† Takuan, 33.

‡ Ibid., 37.

am not sure what everyone means by "the zone." I suspect different people mean different things by this phrase, and so I avoid this comparison. I do, however, want to offer a couple of examples in order to help clarify what is, and what is not *zanshin*. Readers can then decide for themselves whether or not *zanshin* means being "in the zone."

A few years ago, I took a few of my students to a local martial arts tournament. One of my brownbelts , Anthony Losorelli, was performing the *kata shisochin*. Roughly halfway through his *kata,* an oblivious parent with a toddler strolled right through the ring where he was performing. It was obvious to everyone that it was too late to tell the parent to stop, and so we all watched to see what would happen. Knowing the *kata* as I do, I knew that if Anthony continued, he would not run into the two... but it would be close. Anthony never blinked; he continued his *kata* as well as ever, finished and bowed. The judges were impressed with his mental focus, as was I, and he was awarded first place. Afterwards, he was congratulated by a number of people, including his proud instructor, but he was confused by their comments. He had never seen the father and child in his ring. When he told me this, I laughed and told him I took back my compliment. That was not *zanshin*. To be so focused and self-absorbed as to no longer perceive one's environment is the opposite of what *zanshin* is about. Takuan taught, "You should not place your mind within yourself. Bracing the mind in the body is something done only at the inception of training, when one is a beginner."* If you are only aware of yourself, you are not aware at all.

Let us consider another example, this time of what *zanshin* actually looks like. This illustration, however, comes not from the world of martial arts, but from that of music. Several years ago I attended a concert here at Susquehanna University. The pianist, a student of mine, was performing his senior recital. My three year-old son was with me that day, so we only went into the hall after intermission and stayed for three pieces. During the second piece, my son sneezed,

---

* Ibid., 30.

although not very loudly. In fact, I suspected it was no more noticeable than the various coughing and rumbling that attend any such concert, and there was certainly no reaction from the pianist. However, the next day when I congratulated the young musician on his stellar performance, I jokingly apologized for my son's sneeze, not really thinking that he had heard it, much less remembered it. To my surprise, he remarked that he had indeed heard it and told me during which movement it had occurred.

It was not that the sneeze had interrupted his concentration; it was just part of his environment that he had perceived. He later explained to me that, while performing, he is aware of what people are doing in the audience. He does not mentally attend to what they are doing, but notices it, all while he plays some tremendously difficult compositions. His mind is not focused on what his fingers are doing, for he has already learned his art with great thoroughness. He is simply able to play his instrument with a mind free from attachment to any one thing while being calmly aware. That is *zanshin*!

Winston L. King, author of *Zen and the Way of the Sword,* used the same analogy. "Take the matter of playing the piano (or other solo musical instrument).... The master musician in concert (the 'moment of truth') becomes 'mindless,' that is, totally beyond the conscious thought of what notes to play, what fingers to use, or how vigorously or softly to deal with the successive notes."* This is the same goal as that sought by practitioners of *budō*.

If Sir Charles Eliot was correct in saying that "Zen is the Japanese character,"† and Inazo Nitobe, that bushido is the essence of the Japanese spirit, it is no wonder, then, that Japan continues to produce some of the best musical soloists in the world. It may also go a long way to explaining the Japanese fascination with figure skating, gymnastics, golf and baseball. In all cases, one can appreciate a single individual training intensely for years until that moment of truth

* King, 173.

† D. T. Suzuki, *Zen and Japanese Culture,* 85.

when an unattached mind must lead one flawlessly through motions of perfection.

How does one cultivate such awareness? There are simple physical exercises that discipline the mind in coordination with movement. There are countless such "games" that teachers use, and I do not pretend to know the best. I can, however, share one which I enjoy: Two people face one another in a horse stance, at a distance where they can reach out and touch their palms together. The exercise is then to try to disrupt the stance of the other with the only contact being palm to palm. Of course, I can pretend to push my opponent, and then move my hands out of the way when he tries to counter my strike, which may lead him to lose his balance, falling forward.

Such an exercise, familiar to many readers, can be a lot of fun to practice during class. It taps into students' competitive nature and forces them to concentrate on their balance and stance. However, students will also come to realize that there is a strong mental component involved. The more I anticipate my partner's movement, the worse I perform. The more I strategize, mentally attaching myself to a plan, the more often I am thrown off balance. The best mental approach involves little strategy and simply being observant, responding to the conditions as they present themselves rather than expecting a particular reaction. Taisen Deshimaru, the reader will recall, had this to say, "How does one choose the technique of attack? There is no choosing. It happens unconsciously, automatically, naturally. There can be no thought, because if there is a thought there is a time of thought and that means a flaw."* One must allow thoughts and distractions to pass from consciousness and simply be aware of one's environment. In such an exercise, one can get a taste of *zanshin*, or at least why it is important.

While such activities can allow students an introduction to the mindset and benefits of *zanshin*, practitioners of Zen-inspired martial arts have long recognized that a deeper grasp of this discipline

* Deshimaru, 32.

comes about through meditation. It is during *zazen* that we develop, practice, and experience a state wherein there is no mental fixation but only unfocused awareness of our environment.

Recall that Zen Buddhists, while practicing *zazen*, have their eyes half-open. They are not completely open, looking at particular things. They are not closed, shutting out the world. The eyes are partially open, aware of the world, but with an unfocused gaze, not becoming affixed to any one thing. This represents the spirit of *zanshin* as well.

Martial artists often speak of their *kata* as "moving meditation." The slow, meticulous performance of *sanchin kata* is often spoken of as "moving Zen." The same may be said of any *kata*. Indeed, if *kata* are performed with this mental state in mind, through them we may develop and participate in a state of *zanshin*. However, such a practice is quite demanding and not for the beginner. Initially, the *budōka* focuses his attention on the basic choreography. After this, he must spend countless hours learning and practicing the nuances of the *kata* until it may be said to be performed correctly. He may also practice *kata* while envisioning his opponent—a type of shadow-boxing—or in a performance for an audience. However, once the *kata* is learned and internalized, it may be performed without any mental attachment. There is no conscious thought of the next move, the grading panel, or one's peers. There is only a free mind as the individual performs *kata* with *zanshin*.

Sugawara Makoto explained it this way, "What mind can penetrate his opponent's mind? It is a mind that has been trained and cultivated to the point of detachment with perfect freedom. It is as clear as a mirror that can reflect the motions within his opponent's mind.... When one stands face to face with his opponents, his mind must not be revealed in the form of moves. Instead his mind should reflect his opponent's mind like water reflecting the moon."* Only the spirit remains.

---

* Makoto Sugawara, *Lives of Master Swordsmen* (Tokyo: East Publications, 1985), 95, cited in King, 108f.

One final example of this manner of awareness comes from the legendary swordsman Bokuden. The story is told that one day he wished to test the martial prowess of his three sons. He placed a pillow above a curtain that hung at the entrance to his room, so that anyone drawing the curtain back to enter would inadvertently knock the pillow down. He first called his oldest son, who, upon approaching the doorway, took down the pillow. After visiting his father he returned it to its position. The second son then came, but did not notice the pillow until it began to fall. He caught it in his hands, after which he carefully returned it. The youngest son came next. As he raised the curtain, the pillow fell, hitting him in the neck. However, before it hit the floor he drew his sword and sliced it in two.

Bokuden then addressed his sons. He praised the first, telling him, "[Y]ou are well qualified for swordsmanship." The second he cautioned, "Train yourself yet assiduously." The third was told that he was a disgrace to the family.*

We see, then, that there is no essential distinction between "no-mind" and the "remaining-mind." We are speaking of a mental state which cannot be captured by words or concepts, and so we use various images and metaphors to describe the indescribable. Each one offers us a particular perspective on the whole. So, *zanshin* can be spoken of in isolation, but is actually present as an expression of *mushin*. This is equally true of *isshin* and *fudoshin*.

Isshin

Isshin is translated as "one-heart" or "one-mind." The image of an individual hurling himself into an endeavor, completely committed to the cause, comes to mind. Whether it is an artist picking up her brush and attacking the canvas, a *judōka* fully committing to *tai-otoshi* in competition, or an Imperial Japanese soldier rushing in a banzai attack, there is a single-minded purpose and intensity in such an act. Of course, the action need not be aggressive, emotional, or

* D. T. Suzuki, *Zen and Japanese Culture*, 75f.

thoughtless. Rather, it is simply "to throw oneself wholly into the action,"* whether one is serving tea or striking down one's enemies. At the same time, it does not preclude awareness. Leggett points out that the classical schools of Japanese *budō* that speak of *zanshin*, see *isshin* as contained therein.† Single-minded attention does not exclude perception of one's environment. Just as I may have my full attention on my breathing or a *kōan* during *zazen*, this need not leave me oblivious to my surroundings.

As Deshimaru explained, "Training in concentration means gradually learning to concentrate all one's energies and faculties on one thing at a time and yet remain aware of everything else that is going on around one."‡

Fudōshin

This manner of relationship also exists with *fudōshin*. Often translated as "immovable heart" and presented as a mind that is immovable or imperturbable, *fudōshin* suggests to the martial artist an individual who has an indomitable spirit. Suzuki Shōsan wrote of such a person. "This mind is not hung up on things, it is unafraid, unshakable, undismayed, unfazed, undisturbed, and unchanged, master of all."§ We imagine the man who is fearless as bullets fly about him, staring down the enemy with a gaze that could bore holes in a rock. While this may be one manifestation of *fudōshin*, we would be in error if we limited it to such. A soldier manifesting such a mind on the battlefield may express himself in that way. A citizen with the same mental fortitude would appear quite different while testifying before a congressional panel, responding to a medical emergency, or meeting his mother-in-law for the first time.

Once again, we must appreciate that *fudōshin* is not a state essentially different from *mushin*, *zanshin*, or the mindfulness manifested

---

* Leggett, *Zen and the Ways*, 136

† Ibid.

‡ Deshimaru, 100.

§ As in Cleary, 46.

by an enlightened mind. When we return to our original mind, what is called our "Buddha-nature," we exist without fear, without mental attachment, without craving. *Fudōshin* is not different or distinct from *mushin*, but a singular expression of its mindfulness. The no-thought and no-mind of *zazen* must encompass *fudōshin*. Suzuki Shōsan once scolded his students for their "Empty Shell *Zazen*," warning them, "You even start to feel good sitting vacantly. But if you do that kind of *zazen* you'll lose your vigorous energy and become sick or go crazy. True 'no-thought, no-mind' *zazen* is just one thing—to have a dauntless mind."*

As an example of how the fearless, immovable mind is consonant with the serene, controlled psyche, I know of no better story than the legend of the teamaster and the *rōnin*. I hope the reader will pardon me as I quote D. T. Suzuki's telling of the tale at some length:

> Toward the end of the seventeenth century, Lord Yama-no-uchi, of the province of Tosa, wanted to take his teamaster along with him on his official trip to Yedo, the seat of the Tokugawa Shogunate. The teamaster was not inclined to accompany him, for in the first place he was not of the samurai rank and knew that Yedo was not a quiet and congenial place like Tosa, where he was well known and had many good friends....
>
> The lord, however, was insistent and would not listen to the remonstrance of the teamaster; for this man was really great in his profession, and it was probably that the lord harbored the secret desire to show him off among his friends and colleagues. Not able to resist further the lord's earnest request, which was in fact a command, the master put off his teaman's garment and dressed himself as one of the samurai, carrying two swords.
>
> While staying in Yedo, the teamaster was mostly confined in his lord's house. One day the lord gave him permission to go out and do some sight-seeing. Attired as a samurai, he visited Uyeno by the Shinobazu pond, where he espied an evil-looking samurai resting on a stone. He did not like the looks of this man. But finding no way to avoid him, the teaman went on. The man politely addressed

* As in Omori Sogen, *Zen Training*, 17f.

him: "As I observe, you are a samurai of Tosa, and I should consider it a great honor if you permit me to try my skill in swordplay with you."

The teaman of Tosa from the beginning of his trip had been apprehensive of such an encounter. Now, standing face to face with a rōnin of the worst kind, he did not know what to do. But he answered honestly: "I am not a regular samurai, though so dressed; I am a teamaster, and as to the art of swordplay I am not at all prepared to be your opponent." But as the real motive of the *rōnin* was to extort money from the victim, of whose weakness he was now fully convinced, he pressed the idea even more strongly on the teaman of Tosa.

Finding it impossible to escape the evil-designing *rōnin*, the teaman made up his mind to fall under the enemy's sword. But he did not wish to die an ignominious death that would surely reflect on the honor of his lord of Tosa. Suddenly he remembered that a few minutes before he had passed by a swordsman's training school near Uyeno park, and he thought he would go and ask the master about the proper use of the sword on such occasions and also as to how he should honorably meet an inevitable death. He said to the *rōnin*, "If you insist so much, we will try our skill in swordsmanship. But as I am now on my master's errand, I must make my report first. It will take some time before I come back to meet you here. You must give me that much time."

The *rōnin* agreed. So the teaman hastened to the training school referred to before and made a most urgent request to see the master....

The master quietly listened to the teaman, who told him the whole story and most earnestly expressed his wish to die as befitted a samurai. The swordsman said, "The pupils who come to me invariably want to know how to use the sword, and not how to die. You are really a unique example. But before I teach you the art of dying, kindly serve me a cup of tea, as you say you are a teaman." The teaman of Tosa was only too glad to make tea for him, because this was in all likelihood the last chance for him to practice his art of tea to his heart's content. The swordsman closely watched the teaman as the latter was engaged in the performance of the art. Forgetting all about his approaching tragedy, the teaman serenely proceeded to prepare tea. He went through all the stages of the art as if this were the only business that concerned him most seriously under the sun at that very moment. The swordsman was deeply impressed with the teaman's concentrated state of mind, from which all the superficial stirrings of ordinary consciousness were swept away. He struck his own knee, a sign of hearty approval, and exclaimed, "There you are! No need for you to learn the art of death! The state of mind in which you are now is enough for you to cope with any swordsman. When you see your *rōnin* outcast, go on this way: First, think you are going to serve tea for a guest. Courteously salute him, apologizing for the delay, and tell him that you are now ready for the contest. Take off your *haori,* fold it up carefully, and then put your fan on it just as you do when you are at work. Now bind your head with the *tenugui,* tie your sleeves up with the string, and gather up your *hakama.* You are now prepared for the business that is to start immediately. Draw your sword, lift it high up over your head, in full readiness to strike down the opponent, and, closing your eyes, collect your thoughts for combat. When you hear him give a yell, strike him with your sword. If will probably end in a mutual slaying." The teaman thanked the master for his instructions and went back to the place where he had promised to meet the combatant.

He scrupulously followed the advice given by the swordmaster with the same attitude of mind as when he was serving tea for his friends. When, boldly standing before the *rōnin,* he raised his sword, the *rōnin* saw an altogether different personality before him. He had no chance to give a yell, for he did not know where and how to attack the teaman, who now appeared to him as an embodiment of fearlessness, that is, of the Unconscious. Instead of advancing toward the opponent, the *rōnin* retreated step by step, finally crying, "I'm done, I'm done!" And, throwing up his sword, he prostrated himself on the ground and pitifully asked the teaman's pardon for his rude request, and then he hurriedly left the field.*

Mindfulness, alertness, awareness, openness, and an indomitable spirit—all of these exist within *mushin.*

* D. T. Suzuki, *Zen and Japanese Culture,* 189ff.

Chapter Seven

Zen, Budō and Ethics

"Through violence, you may 'solve' one problem, but you sow the seeds for another." –Tenzin Gyatsu, the 14th Dalai Lama

Buddhism and Violence

One of the most curious aspects of the relationship between Zen and *budō* is the ethical piece. In Buddhism, with its longstanding embrace of the principle of *ahimsa* (non-violence or non-harm), it seems rather bizarre that one's religious path may be so closely joined to the pursuit of martial discipline, developing the skill to slay one's enemies. Yet this is what we see in Japan, where pursuits such as *kyūdō, iaidō* and *karatedō* are the basis for the spiritual path of many men and women. How is it, then, that a religion which places such a high priority on the promulgation of peace is so readily associated with disciplines of violence?

To begin with, we should note that Buddhism in general is not focused on ethics in the same way that western religions are. For Jews and Christians, if God gives a moral decree, say in the Ten Commandments, then you do your best to follow that rule. Muslims find Allah's commands for righteous living in the Koran and live accordingly, no questions asked. Buddhism, on the other hand, has a different kind of relationship with ethical living. In general, one will not find lists of absolute moral laws. There is, rather, a greater emphasis on being in a right frame of mind, from which virtuous and compassionate behavior will flow.* When one eradicates crav-

* To be certain, one can find this kind of theology in western religion (cf. Martin Luther), but we are speaking here of emphases, not absolutes.

ing and realizes no-self, the lustful desires for money, power and glory give way to our true compassionate nature. The teachings of the Buddha in the *Abhidarma* (*Abhidhamma* in Pali) convey this emphasis on personal development over following rules. Rupert Gethin, a leading scholar of Buddhism at the University of Bristol, summarizes it this way, "*Abhidhamma*—and hence I think mainstream Buddhist ethics—is not ultimately concerned to lay down ethical rules, or even ethical principles. It seeks instead to articulate a spiritual psychology focusing on the root causes that motivate us to act: greed, hatred, and delusion, or nonattachment, friendliness, and wisdom."*

At the same time, Buddhism does not leave its adherents without ethical direction, trying to figure out what is virtuous, pulled along by nothing but good intentions. The heart of its moral teachings is found in the Five Precepts. Buddhists may pledge themselves to abstain from: (1) harming living beings, (2) stealing, (3) sexual misconduct, (4) dishonesty and (5) intoxication. In Peter Harvey's excellent introductory text on Buddhism, he explains, "The precepts are then regarded as quite weighty vows, so that a person may omit one if he feels he cannot live up to it (the first is never omitted, though)."† This first vow, which is our primary concern here, communicates a surprisingly rigorous moral requirement. As discussed briefly in the first chapter, following the first precept entails a life in keeping with the ideal of *ahimsa*. Those who take this vow are to avoid injuring or killing other human beings, as well as animals. Any action that intentionally leads to the injury of another is also forbidden, for example, hiring a hit-man or ordering a hamburger. Likewise, enabling or allowing others to violate the precept is itself a violation Thus, producing microchips that will be used in Air Force bombers is also seen as a violation of this precept.

---

* Rupert Gethin, "Can Killing a Living Being Ever Be an Act of Compassion? The analysis of the act of killing in the Abhidhamma and Pali Commentaries," *Journal of Buddhist Ethics* Vol. 11, 2004, 167-202.

† Peter Harvey, *An Introduction to Buddhism* (Cambridge: Cambridge University Press, 1990), 200.

What is interesting is that, according to the *Abhidharma,* it is an impossibility for one whose intentions are purified through Enlightenment to violate this precept. Gethin explains, "[T]he intention to kill is understood as exclusively unwholesome, and the possibility that it might ever be something wholesome prompted by thoughts of compassion is not countenanced."* It is a "psychological impossibility" that one who is entirely motivated by compassion could ever kill. The idea of a "just war," or "justifiable homicide" has no place in this traditional Theravadin interpretation of Buddhism. We can find this belief echoed in another famous teacher, who sought to live according to *ahimsa.* Mohandas Gandhi (1869–1948) declared, "Violence is simply not possible unless one is driven by anger, by ignorant love and by hatred."†

At the same time, the realities of this world make such an ideal difficult to implement. The millions of Buddhists in Laos, Vietnam and Korea, for example, are not all vegetarians. Clearly not all Buddhists feel obligated to abstain from meat. And while dietary restrictions can be difficult, the call for pacifism is an even tougher sell. Can nations of Buddhists, let alone individuals, not defend themselves against aggressors? We are certainly aware that countries whose citizens are primarily Buddhist do not lack a military. For example, the Royal Thai Army is held in high esteem by the Thai people for its role in serving and protecting the country.‡ The military in Sri Lanka goes even further, perceiving itself as protector of Buddhism on the sacred island.§ And of course, we have seen fighting monks on our televisions for years. Young men of my generation grew up watching Shaolin monks thrash the bad guys every Saturday afternoon on *Kung Fu Theatre.*¶ Indeed, there are numerous historical accounts of

* Gethin, 175.

† As in Raposa, 72.

‡ Harvey, 202.

§ Tessa Bartholomeusz, "In Defense of Dharma: Just-War Ideology in Buddhist Sri Lanka," *Journal of Buddhist Ethics* 6 (1999): 1-16.

¶ In separating fact from fiction regarding Shaolin, I know of no better book that Meir Shahar's *The Shaolin Monastery: History, Religion, and the Chinese Martial Arts.*

militias comprised of Buddhist monks in the history of China, Korea and Japan. It appears that Buddhists have often opted for pragmatism in their interpretation of the first precept.

In addition to this, we can even find some accounts of the Buddha himself appearing to put this principle on hold. The post-canonical *Upayakausalya Sutra* recounts how the Buddha in a prior life, a life during which he was called "Great Compassion," killed a man who was about to slay 500 righteous *bodhisattvas*. He did so in order to save the lives of these good men, but also to keep the potential murderer from going to hell. While the action is presented as morally wrong, and he would later suffer a thorn piercing his foot as punishment in a later life, we see that some wiggle room was being created in Buddhism as some followers preferred a more liberal approach to Buddhism's five traditional precepts.

Most people reading this book probably do not need much persuading to be convinced that violence can be used to accomplish greater goods. Pacifism may be a noble sentiment (or perhaps naïve), but it has not been all that popular among those who consider themselves realists. This applies whether one was raised in the United States, Germany, Sri Lanka, or Japan. When Buddhism became the dominant religion in certain nations, political and military rulers knew that a nation of pacifists could not exist for very long. As a result, Buddhists, especially in the Mahayana tradition, have found ways to bend the rules. Villagers in the valley of Kashmir, who were forced to deal with predatory wolves, would lure the animals into a high-walled trap, whereupon men threw large rocks over the wall, yet in such a way that no one knew for certain if he had killed the animal.* In Asanga's *Bodhisattva-bhumi*, it is claimed that a *bodhisattva* may kill a human being who is preparing to murder his or her parents or a monk.† Still, while there are exceptions and some flexibility in interpretation, the first precept is probably the closest thing Buddhism has to an absolute moral command.

---

* Harvey, 201.

† Ibid., 201f.

When we turn to Zen, we find a tradition that is even more flexible when it comes to ethical guidelines. To begin with, Japanese Buddhists in general have allowed more freedom in following, or interpreting, the precepts. In 1872, the Meiji government allowed Buddhist priests to marry, eat meat, grow their hair, and wear whatever clothing they desired. One year later this freedom was extended to nuns. While not all Buddhist clergy did so, such permissiveness must have shocked quite a few Buddhists on the Asian continent. Today, more than 90 percent of Buddhist priests in Japan are married.*

Zen itself is prone to considerable ethical liberty, even to the point of iconoclasm. The reader will recall that Zen values itself as being "a special transmission *outside the scriptures*, words, or letters." What matters most is perceiving the Buddha nature that is already present. This effectively means that Zen practitioners will focus their energies on discovering their True Self, spending less time on abstract theory and speculation. After all, the maturing self will necessarily become a more compassionate self. Moral rules and regulations can stand in the way of progress if your attention is drawn to various laws and your success or failure in following them. That approach can be dangerously dualistic, according to Zen thought. Becoming aware of one's True Nature, there is ultimately no need for external rules. Those who understand no-self respond freely with compassion and are not shackled by convention or others' expectations.

While Zen's lack of emphasis on written codes of conduct carries certain benefits, there are liabilities as well. Winston King explained, "For essentially Zen, with its slight regard for scripture and literary or ritual tradition, has no means of checking its 'Buddhist' quality from time to time or maintaining a consistent witness to a good or holy life-pattern. In a word, it has no intrinsic ethical quality or inner monitor, but … historically seems to be primarily a psychological technique for maximizing the visceral energies whatever their

---

* Ellwood, 220.

orientation."* King's point, while perhaps overstated, is important. Human beings need concrete ethical guidance. Let us grant Buddhism its claim that the enlightened individual will always act in keeping with compassion. The reality is that very few reach enlightenment. It may be true that external ethical codes can be dangerously dualistic and self-limiting, but they also help establish parameters for proper human conduct. The vast majority of us do not have the maturity that leads us to respond invariably with charity, justice and compassion; we remain ruled by our own greedy minds. Concrete rules may not be the ideal, but they are what most of us require. We will see below how this problem manifested itself during the period of Imperial Japan.

In addition to Zen's reluctance to embrace particular ethical mandates, it has long held a curious relationship with violence. There is, of course, its long association with *bujutsu* and *budō*, which has been treated in the previous chapters. In addition, Zen teachers are well known for their use of what some might consider "violence" in their teaching methods. We have already considered Zen masters who struck their students. The reader will also recall from the second chapter my first experience with *zazen* in Japan, and the posture-correcting slap I received.

Later, during that same session, the senior men came around with the *kyosaku*. A *kyosaku*, you will recall, is a wooden stick of varying lengths, sometimes referred to in English as an "encouragement stick." I was familiar with the concept of the *kyosaku* and its use to assist sleepy or distracted sitters. As the gentleman with the *kyosaku* slowly proceeded in front of me, I signaled that I would like to receive the four strikes across my back. At the time, I was driven in my decision both by curiosity and the desire to stretch my back, which is required when one moves into the correct position. I recall anticipating a sharp slap, along the lines of being hit with the flat side of a yardstick. The reality of the first strike was eye-popping! In a flash

* King, 190f.

I had three quick thoughts: 1. That really hurt! 2. I'm going to have a huge bruise down my back. 3. Oh no, there are three more coming! The gentlemen at Kozenji are not sadistic, but this is not a place for sweet affirmation and tender contemplation of oneself. One is to use this time wisely, rigorously and effectively. And nothing brings one into the present like a *kyosaku* wielded by an able *jikijitsu*. Many times, the continual use of the *kyosaku* during the intense training of a *sesshin* can prove too much, especially for westerners. As a result, signs may be placed above the heads of certain participants indicating that they wish to forego being struck.

As a brief postscript, I attended morning meditation at another well known *zendō* in Tokyo some time later where the *kyosaku* was administered far less severely. Not all *zendō* are identical in their practice, nor are *kyosaku* in size. If you want to know how hard practitioners are being struck at the facility you may be visiting—in order to determine your willingness to volunteer—you only need to listen to the sound of the blows falling on the trapezius and latissimus dorsi of your neighbors.

The use of violence in pedagogy is not limited to the *kyosaku*; tales abound of Zen masters slapping, kicking and striking their students with different objects. There is the story, also treated in the chapter 2, of Master Rinzai, who slapped the man who inquired as to the nature of Buddhism. Another story, of a Ch'an teacher in China, is told approvingly by D. T. Suzuki:

> Kuei-shan Ling-yu once made the following remark: 'Many masters have indeed an insight into Great Body, but they know nothing of Great Use.' Yang-shan, who was one of the chief disciplies of Kuei-shan, transmitting this remark to a monk living in a hut at the foot of the mountain, asked: 'What do you think of the master?' The monk said: 'Repeat that, please.' When Yang-shan was about to do so the monk kicked him down to the ground. Yang-shan reported the incident to the master, who gave a hearty laugh.*

* D. T. Suzuki, *The Zen Doctrine of No-Mind*, 85.

Such violence is, again, not mean-spirited, but is viewed as a truly effective approach to help people understand existential truths. This is not a religion of parroting beliefs or philosophical speculation. It is a religion of experience, and sometimes we need a serious jolt to pull us from academic musing into the present world in which we live.

We see, then, that Zen Buddhism developed in a culture in which violence was not something unequivocally bad, but could be used effectively as a tool for good. Early Buddhist prohibitions against harming other living beings needed to be interpreted more liberally. As we have seen, harming—or even killing!—another human being can be for that person's own good. Moreover, one needs to be realistic about the nature of this world we live in. The famous Rinzai Zen master and swordsman Omori Sogen Roshi (1904-1994) argued, "There can be no human life that does not participate in killing and death. The martial Ways must incorporate this somber fact."* From here, it is not a very big step to some manner of just-war theory. There will certainly be those who appreciate this kind of pragmatic realism, while others will perceive this move as a rejection of fundamental principles of the religion. Indeed, at times it appears that *ahimsa* vanished completely from the guiding values of some Zen teachers. In the early twentieth century, there were voices that should have been proclaiming, "Peace, peace!" but clamored for war instead.

The question remains, how have Zen adherents justified their association with and support of violence? In the preceding chapters we saw how the relationship between Zen and *budō* developed, from the period of the warring states through the peace of Tokugawa. We considered the contributions of some of the great men who realized the value of Zen training for the life and work of the samurai. With the passing of the samurai, we took a brief glimpse at how the warrior arts continued to be practiced for self-cultivation and national development after the Meiji Restoration. We must now consider the

---

* Hosokawa Dogen, 107.

closest and most controversial melding of Zen and violence: that which was intentionally carried out by soldiers of imperial Japan.

Violence in Context

While the Zen-*budō* relationship had existed for centuries, it intensified—in a curious way—during the period of Japan's imperialism. From the time of the first Sino-Japanese War (1894-1895) until the end of World War II, a great many Buddhist leaders supported the war efforts, while very few spoke up in favor of peace. What is more, Zen Buddhists were quite active in supporting the military through various publications, the training of officers and soldiers, and participation in combat themselves. (Admittedly, the price of dissent at this time was quite high.) The military drew upon themes in Zen practice to motivate soldiers and civilians, and Zen leaders encouraged the war effort to the very end.* In fact, Omori Sogen Roshi admitted that he attempted to sabotage the emperor's radio broadcast of surrender, as he "wanted to resist till the end."†

So how is it that Zen became so closely associated with violence? How does forging one's body in steely strength and deeply studying the arts of injuring and killing others becomes a spiritual path? In order to understand what some regard as a contradiction, we need to take a step back. Recall that there are a great many activities that westerners regard as secular, that function as religious disciplines in Japan. *Shodō*, calligraphy, or the way of the writing, is one. *Chadō*, the way of tea, known around the world as the Japanese tea ceremony, is another. *Kadō*, or *ikebana*, that is, flower arranging, is yet another. While these are the most familiar, we could add the practice

---

* The two books by Brian Daizen Victoria remain the standards for the history of Buddhist complicity with the military at this time: *Zen at War* (New York: Weatherhill, 1997) and *Zen War Stories* (New York: RoutledgeCurzon, 2003).

† Hosokawa Dogen, 51. He later stated, "When one forgets his biological origins and characteristics, he separates himself from the multi-faceted nature of human existence. Such are the peace activists who call for 'Peace!' in their hollow and feeble way. The current reality for all humans is truly severe: eat or be eaten. In the face of these conditions, it is time to unfold the great lessons of these teachings from *Budo*." (114)

of music, sculpture, or dance. These may all hold a certain relationship to Zen.

It is in these disciplines that one develops self-discipline and self-understanding and undertakes the pursuit of truly living. In the second chapter of this book we saw that Zen is not about getting in touch with some external power or entering into a relationship with a divine being. Buddhists seek to live an authentic human existence. How better to learn to live such a life than to undertake worldly tasks with precision and the pursuit of perfection? In the Introduction of Eugen Herrigel's celebrated book, D. T. Suzuki clarified, "One of the most significant features we notice in the practice of archery, and in fact of all the arts as they are studied in Japan and probably also in other Far Eastern countries, is that they are not intended for utilitarian purposes only or for purely aesthetic enjoyments, but are meant to train the mind; indeed, to bring it into contact with the ultimate reality."*

Omori Sogen Roshi also explained, "There is ... the Zen of sewing, the Zen of cutting vegetables, the Zen of keeping accounts, the Zen of typing. It is all right to have all kinds of Zen."† (In fact, Sogen reached his moment of realization in the bathroom, hearing his urine splash in the toilet.) He went on to say, however, that it is important for those serving tea or arranging flowers not to limit their discipline to the time of their particular practice. What is practiced and learned while doing calligraphy or picking tea leaves should be joined with the rest of one's life. If one comes to grasp the nature of oneself in one area, the same wisdom can be brought to bear on one's every action. In the words of Miyamoto Musashi, "From one thing, know ten thousand things."‡

If such mundane activities hold the potential to shed light on the true nature of human existence, how much more so those activities in which one is forced to stare mortality square in the face? Seventeenth century samurai-turned-monk, Suzuki Shōsan, explained,

---

* Eugen Herrigel, *Zen in the Art of Archery* (New York: Pantheon Books Inc., 1953), 9.

† Dogen, 116.

‡ Miyamoto Musashi, 21.

"Now the life of the samurai is especially one in which birth-death (*samsara*) cannot but be comprehended. And when one does understand birth-death, inevitably the Way [of Buddha] is there."* For the samurai, their study offered not only physical disciplines that require great mindfulness, as do the other disciplines discussed above, but also the necessity that one come to grips with the existential issue of one's death, which for the samurai could be at any time, and possibly by one's own hand. It is no wonder, then, that Japanese warriors have long believed that spiritual discipline strengthens the corporeal, while corporeal discipline strengthens the spiritual.

These Zen warriors also believed that the physical and religious progress that one makes also translate into virtue. Those who overcome their attachment to the world and self will necessarily be compassionate and less likely to pursue unjust gain. There were other samurai, in addition to Suzuki Shōsan, who gave up their swords for the tonsure in their later years. Likewise, many modern martial artists have taught the same. Gichin Funakoshi, founder of shotokan karate, taught, "Karate-do is not only the acquisition of certain defensive skills but also the mastering of the art of being a good and honest member of society."† Becoming proficient in the use of violence does not necessarily lead to greater violence. If governed wisely, the converse is true.

Takuan provided the standard Japanese Buddhist differentiation between the sword that kills and the sword that gives life. "[T]he accomplished man uses the sword but does not kill others. He uses the sword and gives others life. When it is necessary to kill, he kills. When it is necessary to give life, he gives life."‡ What began as a Buddhist embrace of *ahimsa* ended up in Japan as a just-war theory. This line of thinking led Rinzai Zen master Nantembō (1839–1925) so

---

* Quoted in King, 185.

† Gichin Funakoshi, *Karate-Do: My Way of Life* (New York: Kodansha, International, 1975), 101.

‡ Takuan, 115. This theme finds considerable articulation in D. T. Suzuki's, *Zen and Japanese Culture*, 1959.

far as to say, "There is no *bodhisattva* practice superior to the compassionate taking of life."*

In addition to the development of such justification for violence, Zen Buddhism's iconoclastic spirit makes it possible to overlook moral rules, when needed. While the precepts may appear to be deontological ethics (that is, absolute moral principles), they are not. Mahayana ethics consider moral commands to be useful tools to control our lustful predispositions and to direct compassionate efforts. However, when a situation presents itself in which compassion and love are best served by stepping outside of the rules, then so be it. Moral commands may be set aside in the interest of the greater good. Moreover, enlightenment is not found in virtuous behavior; overemphasis on ethics is counterproductive. Those who hold the true faith will act with compassion motivated by gratitude, doing the good spontaneously.

There is also another difference between the traditional western notion of religious ethics and those of eastern traditions. Religions like Judaism, Christianity and Islam typically teach certain moral rules and then expect everyone to follow them. For example, the Ten Commandments apply to everyone, not just rabbis or priests. Eastern religions tend to describe ethical living along a continuum. So, vegetarianism may be the ideal, but not everyone is expected to refrain from meat. If your family is poor and undernourished, and someone offers you a chicken to eat, eat the chicken! So, while it is morally superior to refrain, it is understood that many will consume meat in this lifetime. Perhaps they will have the luxury of pursuing the more devoutly religious path in their next lifetime. The same may

---

* Victoria, *Zen War Stories*, 36. Likewise, Sōtō Zen Master Yasutani, in *Dōgen Zenji to Shūshōgi*: "That is to say, of course one should kill, killing as many as possible. One should, fighting hard, kill everyone in the enemy army. The reason for this is that in order to carry [Buddhist] compassion and filial obedience through to perfection it is necessary to assist good and punish evil. However, in killing [the enemy] one should swallow one's tears, bearing in mind the truth of killing yet not killing.

Failing to kill an evil man who ought to be killed, or destroying an enemy army that ought to be destroyed, would be to betray compassion and filial obedience, to break the precept forbidding the taking of life. This is a special characteristic of the Mahāyāna precepts." (72)

be said of those born into warrior castes. The religious ideal forbids violence, but many will not be able to enjoy such a life this time around. For them, they should fulfill their calling honorably in this lifetime; perhaps the next will allow them to live in peace.

Even within the realm of violence, there exists a range of better and worse behaviors. It is a greater moral wrong to kill a larger animal with greater mental acuity than a smaller one with less. Thus, choosing chicken over steak may be better for both body and soul. Also, we find something similar playing out within *budō*. Less violence is always better. Avoiding bloodshed is the ideal, and for this reason we find celebrated stories of *bushi* like Bokuden Tsukahara, the renowned Japanese swordsman of the sixteenth century: While crossing Lake Biwa in a rowboat, a young arrogant samurai was trying to stir up trouble. Bokuden remarked to him, "My art is different from yours; it consists not in defeating others, but in not being defeated." As more words were exchanged, the young man challenged Bokuden to fight. The latter accepted, but suggested that they first stop at a certain solitary island, so as not to injure the others on the boat. The young samurai agreed. However, once they reached the island, Bokuden quickly jumped back in the boat, leaving the man stranded. As the boat pulled away, Bokuden smiled and called to the man, "This is my 'no-sword' school"* While Bokuden could have easily struck the man down, it was the young samurai's arrogance and lust for victory that ultimately doomed him.

One can find the same value communicated in the history of Okinawan karate. Funakoshi's *Karate-Dō: My Way of Life*, contains a number of stories of great masters who responded to violence without resorting to violence in return. One of my personal favorites tells of his teacher Ankō Itosu (1831–1915):

> Indeed, Itosu was so well trained that his entire body seemed to be invulnerable. Once, as he was about to enter a restaurant in Naha's amusement center, a sturdy young man attacked him from the rear,

---

* Suzuki, *Zen and Japanese Culture*, 74f.

aiming a hearty blow at his side. But the latter, without even turning, hardened the muscles of his stomach so that the blow glanced off his body, and at the very same instant his right hand grasped the right wrist of his assailant. Still without turning his head, he calmly dragged the man inside the restaurant.

There, he ordered the frightened waitress to bring food and wine. Still holding the man's wrist with his right hand, he took a sip of the wine from the cup that he held in his left hand, then pulled his assailant around in front of him and for the first time had a look at him. After a moment, he smiled and said, "I don't know what your grudge against me could be, but let's have a drink together!" The young man's astonishment at his behavior can easily be imagined.*

In this same book, Funakoshi recounted an event where he himself responded to a threat of violence without resorting to his physical training. When he related the event to his teachers, Itosu and Ankō Azato (1827–1906), he received unprecedented praise. Funakoshi recalled, "I tried to smother my pride. Although the two masters had never praised a single kata that I executed during our practice sessions, they were praising me now, and mingled with the pride was an abiding sense of joy."†

At times, however, violence may be the only option in order to avoid a greater evil. Funakoshi, when he was around eighty years old, was assaulted by a young thief. He responded by ducking under the attack and grabbing hold of the young man's testicles. He released the man shortly thereafter into the custody of a policeman. Even here, Funakoshi regretted his use of violence against a man who was most likely a returning veteran with no means to support himself financially. Again, there can be greater and less use of force. While the ideal is non-violence, when compelled to use force one should be deliberate in the attempt to use as little as possible.

Back in 2008, I was invited to a *jōdō* training seminar at the Budōkan in Tokyo one afternoon. Before attending, I tried to learn

* Funakoshi, 16f.

† Ibid., 54.

as much as possible about this short-staff fighting style as I could with Youtube and a mop that was in our kitchen. Nonetheless, I knew essentially nothing upon my arrival. While I was instructed in the art's physical performance, I was also given an introductory lecture on the history and use of the *jō*. Two points stand out in my mind. First, I was taught that the *jō*, being made of wood, provided an opportunity for an individual to respond to an attacker wielding a sharp metal *katana* with less violence. Rather than counter with a blade, one could answer with the "peaceful" rejoinder of the *jō*. The same gentleman, at another point in the class, explained to me how hitting properly with the end of the *jō* could split open a man's skull. Apparently, "peaceful" is a relative term. His teaching was not self-contradictory, however. While we in the West may prefer to draw a distinct line between war and peace, my instructor perceived more shades of gray. While he could certainly have killed me with his *jō*, his weapon of choice also gave him the ability to respond with far less force. In that respect, when compared to the alternatives of wielding a steel blade or allowing oneself to be cut down, the *jō* looks like a rather peaceful proposition.

Returning to Buddhism's flexible understanding of the use of violence, a brief word about karma is necessary. Karma will ensure that violent behavior will be punished at some point, in this life or the next. This is certainly true in Buddhism. However, an individual who is born into a calling where violence is necessary, e.g., *bushi*, can respond to his occupation's demands in different ways. One who actively seeks to use as little violence as necessary may be reborn with an opportunity to live a life devoid of bloodshed, practicing a higher calling of the spiritual life. Those who shed blood indiscriminately can count on a rebirth into a life of suffering.

Finally, Buddhism's understanding of karma suggests that the enlightened no longer accrue positive or negative karmic effects because of their behavior. The actions of such a person are beyond moral critique. When one acts freely from one's true nature, there is no fruit of karma. According to D. T. Suzuki, "[Such a mind] cannot be held responsible for its deeds. They are above moral judgments, for there is no deliberation, no discrimination. The valuation of good and bad presupposes discrimination, and where this is absent, no such valuation is applicable."*

What Went Wrong?

In theory, the Zen-inspired warrior should be a model of virtue and restraint in situations of potential violence. Through the eradication of craving he curtails the pursuit of wealth, prestige and honor, which are so often the source of bloodshed. In understanding no-self, he overcomes the impetus to accumulate things of this world at the expense of others. As Morihei Ueshiba wrote, "If you have not linked yourself to true emptiness, you will never understand the Art of Peace."† Moreover, those who achieve excellence in martial skill have no need to prove their valor to themselves or others. Like an adult being pestered by a child, one can respond to provocation without resorting to violence. Shoshin Nagamine expressed it this way:

> Cultivating indomitable fortitude is a necessary prerequisite for any and all *budoka* who aspire to transcend the immediate results of physical training and overcome the source of human weakness and suffering. Needless to say, it is through such inner achievement that one can become impervious to abusive provocation, and hence never be reduced to physical violence.‡

So what went wrong? The imperial Japanese military was instructed, inspired and disciplined by Zen teachers who sought to

---

* Suzuki, *The Zen Doctrine of No Mind*, 116. In addition, "According to this, when your mind functions with Nature, being no more harassed by the dualistic thoughts of good and bad, just and unjust, merit and demerit, Heaven and Hell, but inevitably as fire burns and water soaks, you are not responsible for whatever deeds you commit, and consequently no course of karma is attached to them. You behave like the wind, and who blames the wind when it leaves havoc in its wake?" (118)

† As in Raposa, 31.

‡ Shoshin Nagamine, *Tales of Okinawa's Great Masters*, trans. Patrick McCarthy (Boston: Tuttle Publishing, 2000), 125.

strengthen their fighting men with noble principles. All Japanese soldiers, regardless of class, were now the new samurai: warriors of courage, principle and bravery. They were fighting in brutal wars, yes, but wars understood through the lens of religious duty and calling. Killing an enemy can be an act of compassion. Fighting to the death for a just cause can be virtuous. Nitobe discussed "the tenderness of a warrior" and explained, "Benevolence to the weak, the downtrodden or the vanquished, was ever extolled as peculiarly becoming to a samurai."* And yet, the legacy of Japanese soldiers is not only how mentally tough and determined they were, but how merciless as well.

The rape of Nanjing, the Bataan Death March and Cabanatuan, the use of Korean comfort women, all of these and more make it crystal clear that Japanese officers and men did not live up to the legendary samurai code of bushido. Why not? There are, of course, a great many reasons, but I would like to address a few that relate to the practice and principles of Zen.

We begin with the Japanese disdain for weakness. This found its most obvious expression in the practice of military surrender. For the Japanese soldier, there was no greater dishonor. Death in the service of one's sovereign should be expected, not avoided. It said as much in the Japanese *Field Service Code*, a text that, according to Brian Victoria, had its foundation in Zen thinking.† It is no wonder, then, that there were such high casualty rates among the Japanese in the battles of the Pacific: 97% at Saipan, 98.8% at Attu, 99.7% at Tarawa.

Americans and their allies who preferred surrender to death were regarded as despicable, and they were treated as such. While Buddhism teaches that spiritual maturity necessarily increases compassion, a different psychological factor was at work here. When one's righteousness is determined through one's own efforts, as it is in Buddhism,‡ the result is often arrogance. For the Japanese soldier, his

---

* Nitobe, 43.

† Victoria, *Zen War Stories*, 108.

‡ The exception being Pure Land Buddhism.

own hard-earned mental toughness, in perceived contrast to the Allies, created such arrogance. It expressed itself in disdain for captives, who he believed were not worthy to live.

Moreover, the concept of *mushin*, or no-mind, that Zen seeks to cultivate, was corrupted by some for the perceived benefit of the nation. Instead of helping young men to recognize an absence of self and thereby cultivate selflessness, wisdom and compassion, *mushin* was taught in order to create unquestioning obedience. Even D. T. Suzuki argued, "[S]oldiers must, without the slightest hesitation or regret, offer up their lives to the state in carrying out such religion-sanctioned punishment;"* There is no room for a soldier to morally evaluate the orders he receives. In Zen, what is important is to act, not to spend time ruminating. Suzuki also informed his readers, "Philosophy may be safely left behind with the intellectual mind; Zen wants to act, and the most effective act, once the mind is made up, is to go on without looking backward. In this respect, Zen is indeed the religion of the samurai warrior."† For the Japanese soldier, however, others made up his mind for him.

In relation to this, the related principle of one's mind "not stopping," that one finds in Takuan, was similarly abused. Ishihara Shummyō, a Sōtō Zen priest, associated this concept with immediate and unquestioning obedience. "If ordered to face right, one simply faces right as quickly as a flash of lightening. This is proof that one's mind has not stopped."‡ Presumably, this would also apply when ordered to engage in pointless banzai charges or war crimes.

The eagerness to cultivate this cheap *mushin*, in order to ensure obedience and willingness to sacrifice one's life, may have been militarily expedient, but it was not the best expression of the teachings of Buddhism. Missing from the rhetoric of the time were the words of Nitobe, "Death for a cause unworthy of dying for, [is] a 'dog's death.'"§

* Victoria, *Zen War Stories*, 25.

† As in King, 189.

‡ Victoria, *Zen at War*, 102f.

§ Nitobe, 29f.

Admittedly, Rinzai Zen places more emphasis on no-self than the precepts, but, one might wonder, where in all of this was the teaching that one should eradicate craving? Where was the censure of lusting after the human construct of honor? Where was the careful attention to ensure that violence was justified? Victoria may exaggerate things, but his point is important:

> [I]t is clear that Japan's wartime Zen leaders did everything in their power to turn not only Japanese soldiers, but nearly the entire civilian population, into a mass collection of 'walking dead.' They did so by interpreting the Buddhist doctrine of the non-existence of the self, coupled with the oneness of life and death, in such a way as to produce an unquestioning willingness to die on behalf of the emperor and the state.*

Perhaps it is human nature to co-opt what is virtuous to serve what is vicious. While the code of bushido has been needlessly glamorized, it does present a model of noble martial ethics with the potential to inspire. These elements were simply overlooked. As Takuan wrote, "A half-baked martial art is the foundation of great injury."† Still, there is reason for optimism. Ueshiba's teachings have a place of honor among *budōka* today. He wrote, "In the old days, martial arts were used for destructive purposes—to attack others in order to seize more land and possessions. Japan lost the war because it followed an evil, destructive path. From now on, martial arts must be used for constructive purposes."‡

Today, fanatic loyalty to the Japanese emperor has been consigned to the annals of history. Fidelity to one's sovereign has often shifted to the modern Japanese company, which rarely asks its employees to fight to the death. (Work themselves to death, maybe.) As a result, in the world of martial arts, uncritical allegiance to the will of another has largely passed. Those practicing traditional archery,

---

* Victoria, *Zen War Stories*, 143.

† Takuan, 106.

‡ As in John Stevens, *The Philosophy of Aikido* (New York: Kodansha International, 2001), 69.

swordplay, or judo do so for self-cultivation. Those seeking spiritual maturity through such disciplines, likewise, do so for their own benefit, not in order to become a more efficient killing machine at the disposal of another. *Mushin* is no longer abused to create unthinking warriors, but is once again understood as the overcoming of a false sense of self. Without those who would hijack these principles of Zen for the sake of violent conquest, we find martial artists returning to the practice of Zen as a way to foster humility, respect, self-discipline and compassion in themselves and their students. While such practitioners remain in the minority, in Japan and abroad, the positive influence of Zen is ubiquitous in the world of *budō*. This is fortunate, for today there is a new threat to the spirit of martial arts as *dō*. In the final chapter we will consider the contemporary world of Japanese martial arts, the role of sport, and the place of *dō* in today's interconnected world.

Zen and Confucian Ethics

It would be a mistake to leave the reader with the impression that Zen and *budō* are devoid of ethics. Proper ethical conduct is obviously of paramount concern among *budōka,* and Zen does not simply promote libertinism, leaving to each his own. As we have seen, however, the disciplines of *bujutsu* did not necessarily require a moral code of conduct, and Zen trusts in the cultivation of the individual to bring out the good that is inherent in human nature. So where does a moral code of conduct derive from among Zen-inspired *budōka*? The answer must take us back to China, to a man named Kong Fuzi, better known in the West as Confucius. It is from Confucius, and the subsequent schools of thought that bear his name, that we find the foundation for ethical principles in *budō*. His teachings extended far beyond the borders of China to much of East and Southeast Asia. Confucius' teachings have directed emperors and peasants, the elderly and children, generals and laundry women in how to conduct themselves with one another in society. To do so, Confucius did not write volumes of canon law, detailing good and bad behavior.

His approach was often to describe what kind of person each of us should be. He taught something called "virtue ethics."

Virtue ethics is an approach to moral deliberation where one looks to "character" for guidance more than to the consequences of an action or fixed rules of conduct. Here, personal qualities (e.g., prudence, justice, restraint, courage and piety) are the touchstones for determining proper behavior. Rather than ask about rules or consequences, here one chooses one's actions based on their adherence to these virtues. For example, drunkenness is not consistent with restraint, cheating is not compatible with justice, disrespect for parents is not an act of piety. Louis P. Pojman, former ethicist at the United States Military Academy, sums up virtue ethics nicely. This approach "emphasizes being, being a certain type of person who no doubt will manifest his or her being in actions or nonaction. For traditional duty-based ethics, the question is 'What should I do?' For virtue ethics, the question is 'What sort of person should I become?'"*

In the *Analects,* Confucius repeatedly described the conduct of a "gentleman" or "good man," who was often contrasted with the "small man." He did not give his students a list of virtuous behaviors, but described what sort of people they should become:

> "A gentleman can see a question from all sides without bias. The small man is biased and can see a question only from one side." (II, 14)
>
> "A gentleman takes as much trouble to discover what is right as lesser men take to discover what will pay." (IV, 16)
>
> "The good man does not grieve that other people do not recognize his merits. His only anxiety is lest he should fail to recognize theirs." (I, 16)

In addition to descriptions of how a virtuous person behaves, Confucius spent considerable time addressing the relationships that exist in society. The five most important are: Ruler-subject, father-

* Louis P. Pojman, *Ethics: Discovering Right and Wrong* (Belmont, CA: Wadsworth, 2002), 160.

son, husband-wife, elder-younger brother, and friend-friend. He firmly believed that members of a society must know how to interact with one another; they must know their place, responsibilities and obligations within society. When this is the case, a community can thrive.

Again, making this happen is not as easy as providing an inventory of expected behaviors, listing all the acceptable and unacceptable actions that an individual should know. To do so is impossible, as the interconnectedness of people forms an infinitely complex web of human relations. Rather, it is enough for one to learn the desired qualities of each category of people and then behave in accordance with those virtues when interacting with others. For this reason, when asked about good governance by Duke Ching, he replied, "Let the ruler be a ruler, the subject a subject, the father a father, the son a son." It is virtue, then, rather than law, that should be the basis for government. In the classic *Great Learning*, Confucius explained, "... when the will is sincere, then the heart is set right; when the heart is set right, then the personal life is cultivated, then the family life is regulated; when the family life is regulated, then the national life is orderly, and when the national life is orderly, then there is peace in this world."*

Confucianism made its way into Japan in the third century AD. However, it was later neo-Confucianism—a philosophy which combined elements of Daoism and Buddhism to the thought of Confucius and his disciples—that played an enormous role in the development and ideal of *bushido*. The principles of duty, obligation, service and self-sacrifice that have come to be associated with the samurai class find their foundation in neo-Confucian thought.†

In neo-Confucianism, the social rituals (*li*) taught by Confucius came to be understood as an expression of the Dao, the divine reality

* Quoted in John M. Koller, *Asian Philosophies* (Upper Saddle River, NJ: Prentice Hall, 2002), 276f.

† For further reading on the influence of Confucianism and neo-Confucianism on Japanese military history, I recommend *Training the Samurai Mind: A Bushido Sourcebook*, Ed. and Trans. Thomas Cleary.

which animates existence. That is to say, observing your place in your community means acting in accord with the Divine. And when we live and act in accord with the Divine, we find the meaning, maturity and fulfillment that we all desire in life. Observing one's place in society is, therefore, necessary in progressing on the way toward spiritual development. Ellwood explains:

> Neo-Confucianism had definite political and social implications, for it envisioned a coherent cosmos in which the nature of ultimate reality, the universal *li,* is expressed reflexively in society and the human individual. These two are not at odds, but ultimately harmonize; an individual's *li* is that of his or her place in the social order. The human family functions well when everyone moves harmoniously in accordance with his or her true inner nature, as though in a great dance. One's true inner nature, and that of the universe, can become known through self-discipline and clear-eyed introspection, and the wise person will undertake self-examination.*

In this respect, the Japanese who is born a samurai had an obligation to live the life of a warrior. More than that, in the pursuit of this livelihood, the samurai undertook the spiritual path appropriate for this lifetime. By embracing his call to be a warrior, driven by a sense of duty and governed by virtue, he was living in accordance with *dō*; no more can be asked or sought. Ellwood continues, "One can no more change society than one could change the laws of nature. Acceptance of one's role—parents over children, husband over wife, older brother over younger brother; one's social rank and one's duties as a subject of the state, with mutual obligations all around—is simply like accepting gravity. To reject them is to go against nature, which can only bring dire consequences."†

This is reminiscent of the famous Hindu story told in the *Bhagavad Gita,* in which Prince Arjun is reticent to go to war against the Kauravas, recognizing that great suffering comes from warfare. His

* Ellwood, 159.

† Ibid.

charioteer and advisor at the time is Krishna, who tells him that he has a duty, as a prince, to protect his people. He must fight. Krishna explains, "Now you shall hear how a man may become perfect, if he devotes himself to the work which is natural to him. A man shall reach perfection if he does his duty as an act of worship to the Lord."

Within the Japanese framework, the duties of the *bushi* are not governed by lists of moral commands, but ideals of virtue. This meshes quite well with Zen, and explains the compatibility between Zen's self-cultivation and Confucian moral teaching. Both believe that proper human conduct stems from an effort to live in accord with *dō*, not obedience to sets of ethical precepts.

Religion for the samurai did often involve prayers at Shinto shrines, appeals to Amida Buddha, and seated meditation in the Zen tradition. However, it was Confucian ethics that bound them together. It was this influence that governed their daily conduct, formed their identity, and directed their lives. While Shinto and Buddhist rites were important, neither formed the principal philosophy for most *bushi*. The way of the warrior, celebrated by Zen, was one of action, not rumination. Such a life favored a focus on ethics rather than questions of theology, metaphysics, or soteriology (the study of salvation). Along these lines, we find Inazo Nitobe, in his influential Bushido, explaining, "As to strictly ethical doctrines, the teachings of Confucius were the most prolific source of Bushido."* Likewise, according to religion scholar Robert Ellwood, "[T]he real 'religion' of the Tokugawa government, though the house formally embraced Pure Land [Buddhism], was Confucianism."†

Virtue Ethics in Contemporary Dojo

While Japanese life today is not governed by the fanatic sense of duty, obligation and self-sacrifice observed in earlier times, and the

* Nitobe, 15.

† Ellwood, 159.

previous social caste system has long been discarded, these virtues are still revered in contemporary society. For many Japanese, the study of *budō* is a way to reconnect with the traditions and values of a prior age. It is a way to forge oneself physically and mentally, to pursue a spiritual path, and to revivify something of the Japanese spirit and tradition. The person who facilitates this, then, is the teacher. It is this person who should model correct behavior—physical, emotional, moral and spiritual. One's *sensei* leads by example in all of the above. Students are not directed to read books, peruse the internet, or watch Youtube videos. They watch their teacher and copy what they see. They attempt to emulate the traits of their teacher in their path toward self-perfection. This applies to the physical performance of the art as well as personal conduct.

The dojo *kun,* which obviously communicates a concern for the moral behavior of those studying, is a set of rules for students to follow. My friend Hideyuki compared them once to the Ten Commandments, and there are indeed similarities. However, a look at these "rules" points to an important difference as well. At Hideyuki's dojo, the *kun* includes these five directives:

> Work to perfect your character.
> Always act with good manners.
> Refrain from violent and uncontrolled behavior.
> Cultivate a spirit of endeavor and perseverance.
> Have fidelity in seeking a true way.

What we do not find here are specific rules or regulations. The Ten Commandments tell you: Do not lie; Do not commit adultery; Do not covet; Do not murder, etc. This stands in contrast to the *kun* above which describes virtuous character, not particular acts.* The *kun* tells you what kind of person to be, the Ten Commandments what behaviors to practice or avoid.

---

* The commandment to honor father and mother may be closer to virtue ethics, but the general trajectory of the Decalogue is clearly toward absolute and specific moral commands.

In Japan, the teacher also understands that he or she is doing something more than providing a service in exchange for compensation. As a result, training fees are generally handled quite differently in Japan than the United States. To begin with, it is considered in bad taste to discuss payment with one's *sensei*. Part of this may date back to a general distrust of merchants, who provide something of value in exchange for money. This stands in stark contrast to the *bushi* who offered his service, his very life, out of duty. For a teacher of *budō* to be seen fussing over how much he or she is paid is unseemly; what is being provided by the teacher is of greater value than currency. Moreover, accepting money for something akin to mentoring is also unbecoming. And while currency must enter into the equation, it is only one part of payment to one's *sensei*, and perhaps a necessary evil at that.

During my time in Japan I was shocked at how small my training fees were compared to what I have seen and experienced in the US. Moreover, very often I found that questions regarding payment, and the actual transaction itself, take place through a senior student, not the instructor. Small gifts, however, are always appreciated … and often expected. A token of one's appreciation for what has been taught, the gift is more of a "thank you" than payment. For this reason, I was told that it is not always proper to bring a gift to the first training session with a teacher.

Merits and Liabilities

Virtue ethics, as with any approach to ethics, carry certain advantages and disadvantages. To be sure, any person who undertakes training and reflection in the realm of ethics is likely to benefit. Even when differences of opinion on what is most virtuous arise between individuals, the effort to think critically, determine the Good, and seek to live in accord with one's principles is always time well spent.

There are considerable merits to the approach we call virtue ethics. To begin with, it is clear that modeling behavior is important.

Virtue ethics often direct one to emulate a person of virtue, a flesh and blood individual who is worthy of, and can inspire, imitation. The student is not left to consider what rules from the Koran, Talmud, or Vatican apply to a given situation, but can observe how another human being behaves and extrapolate from that how he should behave.

Additionally, this modeling of behavior creates responsibility for the teacher as well. In a community governed by virtue ethics, those in positions of authority cannot say, "Do as I say, not as I do." It is understood that they, like it or not, are role models. Teachers must then keep an eye on their own behavior, knowing that others will be watching and imitating what they see.

Another attractive feature of virtue ethics is their flexibility. Concrete rules, while often easy to understand and implement, can provide difficulties in unusual situations. We are told, "Do not lie." Yet we wonder if that is good advice when an angry female holding a meat cleaver comes to the door and asks, "Is your cheating, no-good roommate home?" Virtue ethics direct us to be people whose lives are characterized by values such as humility, compassion, or integrity. With guiding principles of that kind, we have freedom to respond to life's difficult moral dilemmas with creativity and resourcefulness, rather than slavish devotion to rules. In our day, when the authority of absolute moral rules is often questioned, and utilitarianism can appear cold and calculating, there is a real attractiveness to virtue ethics. Moreover, the ethical considerations that surround violence are extremely complex. When am I justified in defending myself or others? Is "teaching someone a lesson" good for society if it discourages future menacing behavior? Do I have a moral obligation to train in a martial art that develops the ability to control aggression without injuring one's assailant? A book of rules is unlikely to be helpful in this regard, but asking oneself, "What would sensei do?" may be helpful.

Lastly, virtue ethics inculcates a respect for our elders, for those who have gone before. It helps us appreciate the virtue and character that have been developed and nurtured by others over the decades of their lives. The passions of youth and misplaced priorities of young adulthood often give way to greater perspective among our seniors. While some never outgrow their craving for prestige and honor, time teaches many what is truly important in life. Here, the elderly may be truly appreciated. When virtues are valued more than rules or logical consequentialism, people are valued. Unfortunately, in cultures obsessed with youth, beauty and style, those with more experience and perspective are often overlooked.

I recall watching a demonstration of international martial artists perform at the Budōkan in Okinawa. There were a variety of very impressive performances that day. However, what brought the crowd to their feet were the *kata* performed by the most senior men in attendance. In their seventies, they did not have the spring, speed and athleticism of the young adults. Outsiders would likely have appreciated their being "in shape" in their later years, but what was esteemed by the audience that day was that these men demonstrated that they had dedicated their lives to an art, a way of living. They continued their pursuit of excellence into their later years. They had taught countless students, passing on this mental and physical discipline to multiple generations. If any of them had taken the microphone to offer some advice to the audience, all would have listened and responded with the greatest respect, far greater than what would be afforded to the young dynamos who amazed us with their physical prowess.

At the same time that we find much to appreciate in virtue ethics, there are liabilities to be aware of as well. When a community establishes its moral framework around emulating virtues personified in certain individuals, what happens when those individuals fail to meet our expectations? Whether through human foibles or monumental disgrace, the toppling of an icon may have a profound effect on those who pattern their lives after their hero. Fallible human beings can point to absolute principles as the standard, thereby assuring the ideal if they should fail. But what happens when that human being exists as the model and then proceeds to display immoral behavior? Communities operating within a virtue ethics framework must be careful not to associate their prescribed virtues too closely to the example of any one person.

Furthermore, when a person in a position of authority recognizes that she is not only respected for her knowledge and physical abilities, but has become the model for her students' moral and spiritual journey, there is danger as well. Power corrupts. Being a teacher carries with it a certain authority and influence, but becoming a spiritual mentor carries this to a whole new level. The incumbent power that accompanies such a position can easily go to one's head. Very often in the West we see teachers trying to imitate the Asian model of teacher and student. These teachers then proceed to relish the clout they now have—often displayed with ridiculous belts, ranks and titles—as they lord it over their juniors. The corrupting influence associated with a morally dubious teacher extends beyond the effects on the students, but to the teacher as well.

A system wherein students are encouraged to look to their teacher as the example *par excellence* of physical, mental, spiritual and moral maturity also runs other risks. There is the danger of students uncritically accepting their teacher's instruction, a problem ubiquitous in Japan. Whether in the physical performance of the art or in conduct outside of the dojo, critiquing the "one who has gone before" is strongly discouraged. While this social rule does encourage young know-it-alls to keep their mouths shut, fostering humility, it may also perpetuate mediocrity. No one wants to tell their *sensei* that the *bunkai* he just demonstrated is completely unrealistic. Likewise, if the conduct of one's *sensei* is morally bankrupt, behavior which senior students never question or critique, junior students are more likely to duplicate his example.

This esteem and deference to the respected instructor certainly serves the purpose of maintaining tradition, keeping young half-baked martial artists from thinking they know better than their teacher and running off to start a new dojo, organization, or style. However, it can also stifle creativity. When the imitation of one's sensei is the highest ideal, originality and imagination suffer. This need not be the case. A good *budō* instructor will encourage his or her students eventually to explore possibilities and transcend the strict form of the art. Here we may appreciate the words of the eighteenth century Japanese scholar Izawa Nagahide, "You should detach from arts when you have mastered them. If you do not detach from arts, you are not an artist."*

Budō as Religion?

Some may ask, at this point, whether *budō* is a religion. We have seen that there are a significant number of common traits between the two: Japanese *budōka* are often part of a close-knit community of—shall we say—believers, who trust in the efficacy of a chosen practice to shape them into virtuous, whole and principled human beings. There is likely no consideration of an afterlife, but as with many eastern religions, there does exist a desire for an enlightened understanding of the self and the world. Moreover, the role of ethics, particularly virtue ethics, is quite strong. Students look to their *sensei* for guidance, not simply as one who conveys knowledge, but one who draws out of the student what existed from the beginning. In all these ways, we see that *budō* may indeed function as a religion, if we use the term broadly.

This is not to say that the student who throws himself completely into *budō* culture, within the traditional framework described above, has made a choice to have *budō* as his religion. He can certainly have his ultimate concern grounded elsewhere. He may find purpose and meaning in life in another religious tradition and still be inspired by—and perhaps even revere—his *sensei*. Dedication to *budō* and any particular religion are not mutually exclusive.

For some, however, *budō* does function in the place of conventional religion. One may find under the guidance of an exceptional teacher an authority figure who offers direction and inspiration on the Way toward human fulfillment and purpose. As with any belief

* Cleary, 118.

system, there are dangers to navigate and virtues to be cultivated in the pursuit of what may make us whole. Whether or not a *kyūdōka* will find the Absolute through the austere discipline she has chosen is difficult to say. Perhaps the answer we give simply betrays our own beliefs. What she certainly has, however, is the opportunity to develop herself as a person of virtue.

Chapter Eight

The Contemporary World of Budō

"Void of its spiritual foundation, karate is reduced to common brutality. It is of the utmost importance that physical training be balanced by philosophical assimilation and methodological introspection as a single practice." –Shoshin Nagamine

Overcoming Self, Overcoming Others

In the early twenty-first century, *budō* has become an international phenomenon. Martial art programs, many with roots in Japanese disciplines, are ubiquitous worldwide. In my small town in Pennsylvania, I would wager that children spend more time practicing tae kwon do than playing Little League baseball. Judo and Tae kwon do are now Olympic sports, and there is increasing momentum for kendo and karate to join their ranks. At the same time, traditionalists are also found in every corner of the world, from *iaidōka* in Botswana to those training in Okinawan goju-ryu in the Czech Republic.

Many practitioners regard Japan as the Mecca of their tradition, longing to visit the place of its birth and experience firsthand the legendary training that still goes on there. Perceiving—correctly in many cases—that their own studies are limited due to incomplete understanding of the art or deleterious external influences, a great many people believe that returning to Japan will enable them to reconnect with the "true" practice of their discipline. However, many come to realize that Japan is not immune to the corrupting influences that have watered down *budō* around the world. In many cases, the distortions and damage began within Japan itself.

We have discussed *budō* as comprising two essential elements: the physical techniques of the particular art and the spiritual/mental discipline we associate with *dō*. The physical aspects of a discipline may be kept constant—for historical or cultural reasons—or they may evolve. (Of course, not every change is an improvement. A conscious change in an art's performance is considered progress by the one doing the change, despite the fact that great harm has been perpetrated by brash "masters" who seem to know better than all their predecessors.) Without passing judgment on these changes, it need only be noted here that the physical techniques of an art can and do change. Some of these changes reflect a conscious decision, while others creep in inadvertently. In Japanese philosophy, the *dō* remains constant; what changes is the seriousness with which it is considered.

Over the centuries, we've seen a kind of boomerang effect within the world of *budō*. What began as physical disciplines of martial science, practiced for the sake of defeating one's enemies, became *shugyō*, austere mental and physical disciplines by which one seeks to overcome oneself. In many cases today, these arts have shifted back to become, once again, nothing more than exercises for overcoming others. Today, of course, we typically practice these arts to overcome others in the sports arena rather than on the battlefield.

If we consider judo and karate, this boomerang effect seems to have been espeically strong over the last hundred years. In the case of the former, the tension between Jigorō Kanō's vision of judo as a vehicle for personal transformation and its current manifestation as an Olympic sport is a topic of considerable discussion. In regard to Okinawa's most well known export to the world, Shoshin Nagamine taught: "Karate is a discipline which surfaced from man's instinctive efforts to defend himself. As the discipline continued to grow it came to address the issues surrounding life and death. As karate ultimately unfolded as an art form it provided a spiritual path on which its followers could discover and conquer the sources of human weakness."* Of course, a quick look inside many contemporary dojos—littered with trophies, focused on scoring points, aesthetically

* Nagamine, 108f.

pleasing *kata*—betrays the only goal of many practitioners: beat the other guy.

We must be careful, however, to remember that we are speaking here in generalizations. We should be mindful of stereotypes, in which we imagine earlier *budōka* as enlightened sages while focusing only on today's most absurd cases of sports-frenzy. It is true, in Donn Draeger's words, that "budo are considered to be not instruments for killing but vehicles through which individuals can aspire to moral perfection."* However, it is naïve to imagine that young men wielding their *bokken* or drawing the string on their *yumi* during the Meiji era did not do so with determination to better their peers. While *karateka* in Okinawa did not practice competitive sparring one hundred years ago, as we do today, I cannot imagine that they were not trying to outdo one another hitting the *makiwara*. In the 1950's, a young Morio Higaonna regularly practiced free sparring with Sutayachi Matayoshi, which he recalls would "start out amicably enough, but as soon as one of us landed a punch or kick, the other would get angry. Soon the exercise would escalate into a full fledged brawl."† This kind of competition appears hardwired into our brains, and young men especially will obsess with it. On the other hand, today's emphasis on sporting contests has not completely overshadowed interest in *budō* as *shugyō*, as you, the reader of this book, attest.

Nevertheless, while *budō* has always existed with the tension between overcoming others and overcoming oneself, emphases shift. The young will generally favor the former, while the more mature will recognize the greater value of the latter. What changes is the concern and intent of those in positions of authority. It is they who lead by example and set precedents and curricula for those who follow. In modern sport-oriented *budō*, winning in competition has been permitted to become the *telos*—the aim or goal—which dictates the practice of the entire discipline. Those in charge have often conceded

* Draeger, *Classical Budo*, 36.

† Morio Higaonna, *The History of Karate: Okinawan Goju-Ryu* (Dragon Books, 1995), 152.

to this inferior purpose. The result when this happens, as we shall see, is the tail wagging the dog.

The role of competition in training

If we consider those martial arts that have come to play a significant role in the modern sports world—judo, kendo and derivatives of Okinawan karate—we find that competition has always been an element within their training. Various types of "free-sparring" often had some place in the curriculum, whether *randori, irikumi*, or *jigeiko*. Testing and developing one's own skill outside the confines of pre-arranged exercises has had a place. However, the popular practice of competitive free-sparring that we see in today's dojos was not always the norm. *Karateka* bouncing around, looking to rack up more "points" during their two minutes on the mat, is a more recent phenomenon. Without dissecting the different approaches to competitive practice in various arts throughout history, I believe we can see an essential difference between competition then and now. The earlier model utilized competitive free-sparring as a tool to a greater end. Today, winning in competition has often become the end in itself.

An example of this kind of thinking was expressed in a conversation I had at the Ozawa Tournament a few years ago. This traditional karate tournament brings in talented athletes from around the globe. As the tournament was underway, I had the chance to chat with one of the vendors. I remarked that while I was indeed competing that day, I belong to an organization that is not really oriented toward sport. "We really don't focus on competition," I explained to him. The look on his face betrayed a complete lack of comprehension, as if I had just told him that I like to play tennis, but not against other people. In his mind, karate exists for the sake of competition. Why else would one do it?

When these art forms had a closer connection to their more brutal and lethal applications, a primary focus on competition would have seemed odd. It is no wonder that competitive fighting was so rare. Chojun Miyagi is reported to have said, "Karate is dangerous. As far as kumite training is concerned, *yakusoku kumite* (pre-arranged sparring) and *kakie* (push hands) are all that one needs."* Goju-ryu's *kakie* allows for wonderful competitive exchanges with a partner, while providing a much safer format than *irikumi*. At the same time, it is not particularly conducive to "keeping score," thereby offering a healthier framework for competition without as many of the distractions that come from counting points, winners and losers.

In my early years practicing karate, I found myself falling prey to a misconception that is rampant among *karateka*. Somewhere I got the idea that all of our training was ultimately put to the test in sparring. That was where the rubber hit the road; here I would find out how good of a martial artist I had become. And so, I would bounce around, looking at my opponent over my shoulder, throwing out sidekicks and backfists while trying to avoid getting tagged by the other guy. (I'm still not sure what I thought would happen if I actually struck somebody in the skull with an *uraken*—either to my fist or his head.) I had confused this kind of competitive game with actual fighting, and subsequently the purpose of my discipline. I had managed to minimize the curriculum of my art, develop all manner of bad habits, and delude myself about what would keep me safe in a real life conflict. I am thankful that I eventually stumbled into Roberto Schipp's dojo in Nashville and had the opportunity to understand the serious limitations of that approach and have the opportunity to train in something far more meaningful and effective.

Of course, my superficial karate was particularly bad. And my point is not to suggest that all competitive fighting is shallow and ineffective. The vast majority of today's competitive MMA fighters practice disciplines with great depth. Moreover, I am sure that they are quite capable of defending themselves and their loved ones when push comes to shove. At the same time, Kanō's warning about sport rings true:

* Ibid., 70.

> But that object of competitive sport is a simple and narrow one, whereas the objective of Judo is complex and wide. Competitive sport pursues only one part of the objective of Judo. Of course, Judo can be treated simply as competitive, and it may be all right to do so. But the ultimate objective of Judo cannot be attained in that way. So while we recognize that there is a demand these days to treat Judo on the lines of a competitive sport, on the other hand we must not forget what the real essence of Judo is and where it lies.*

Aside from the effect on the "spirit" of *budō*, sport changes the practice of the art as well. We all understand why precautions are taken to make sport-training safe. Fists are wrapped, certain strikes are forbidden, referees are present. While this is all necessary and good, it must be acknowledged that important elements of the original arts are thereby passed over as well. If everything serves the purpose of sport-fighting with gloves, why practice with the *makiwara*? If leg kicks are forbidden, why practice them? In kendo, if strikes with the *shinai* are limited to targets covered with armor, why practice hitting the seams? In all these examples, the focus on competition has led to the loss of fundamental elements in the art. We see this in the rise of "strong kendo," focused on sport, at the expense of "correct kendo" which expresses its traditional practice.† The same is taking place in other arts, from karate to *kyūdō*. As a result, the historical discipline itself is sacrificed for the sake of sport.

Fortunately, there do remain teachers who perceive a different *telos* to their training. In discussing the role of traditional Okinawan karate in the twenty-first century, Isamu Arakaki (1941–) remarks, "We are not preoccupied with the thought that a training partner may one day face us in the competition arena, only that we improve as karateka, as human beings and, therefore, as citizens of the world."

---

* As in Leggett, *The Spirit of Budo*, 100.

† Alexander Bennett, "Kendo or Kumdo: The Internationalization of Kendo and the Olympic Problem," *Budo Perspectives*, Ed. Alexander Bennett (Auckland, New Zealand: Kendo World Publications, 2005), 327f.

Perhaps it is my own personal bias, but I am inclined to see more of this emphasis among Okinawan *karateka* than their counterparts in mainland Japan. There is some irony in this, as it was the Japanese philosophy of *dō* that was responsible for shaping the fighting system of Okinawan *te* into the *budō* art of *karatedō*. Now, it appears that karate in mainland Japan has undergone a reversion to the primary goal of overcoming others. This should not be surprising, however, given the role of martial arts in both Japanese militarism and the place of sport in today's society. Okinawa has certainly not been immune from these influences, but there appears to be a genuine difference in martial cultures. Arakaki Sensei continues, "For us the karate dojo is a sacred place where its members rejoice in the strength and skill they have acquired, while admitting their weaknesses, and resolving to overcome them. This is true of everyone from the most junior to the most senior. Thus the dojo is not a place of conflict, (exemplified by draconian discipline and senseless brutality), but of a perfect harmony created by the mutual effort of people with identical goals and aspirations."*

At the same time, lest obvious generalizations deteriorate into stereotypes, it is worth quoting Fukuoka-born Shotokan legend, Teruyuki Okazaki (1931–). "I'm training now for over 55 years. But [I'm] still not good enough. That's why I have to challenge myself to be a good human being. Then I have to show my students a good example—how to practice continuously, to develop yourself.... That is how to aim everyday's training to be a good human being."†

To this we might add the advice of Gichin Funakoshi, the patron saint of Japanese karate, whose advice to his students nearly a century ago remains invaluable. "One thing I often say to my young pupils they find confusing. 'You must,' I tell them, 'become not strong but weak.'"‡ There are teachers who understand and communicate

---

* Isamu Arakaki, "The Future of Traditional Karate," *Classical Fighting Arts* Vol. 2, No. 17, (2009), 9-12.

† Teruyuki Okazaki, http://www.youtube.com/watch?v=iKDdXBOJDBo, June 10, 2010.

‡ Funakoshi, 114.

these values still today, but they seem to be in shorter supply, in Japan and throughout the world.

Olympic Budō?

To those outside of *budō* traditions, the decision of whether or not to become an Olympic sport must appear to be a no-brainer. Why wouldn't you want your discipline to be featured in the most celebrated athletic venue in history? Therein lie opportunities for tremendous recognition, resources and respect. International coverage, promotion and relationship building appear to be unequivocal goods. However, we know that such universal support is far from reality among *budō* practitioners; the opinions are split.

What Alexander Bennett calls "the Olympic problem" is an epic struggle in the world of kendo. The International Kendo Federation (FIK; previously IKF), headquartered in Tokyo, has expressed little interest in joining the Olympic movement. The Korean World Kumdo Association (WKA), on the other hand, is pursuing inclusion in the Olympics with a vengeance. Many in the kendo community look at Olympic judo, however, and do not like what they see. Bennett explains, "We see incidents of doping, money for winning, cheating (suspicious *dōgi*), point system instead of clean *ippon* which is seen to advantage brute strength over technique, unbridled emotional outbursts in victory or defeat when the essence of *budō* is said to be to control emotion and show respect, death threats (by Japanese) to international referees who are perceived to have made flawed judgments, raucous crowds of the kind seen at football matches, and so on." Many among the Japanese see this as sufficient reason to stay out. Among the Koreans, the good is perceived to outweigh the bad. It is possible, strangely enough, that because of this tension we may see *kumdo* rather than kendo as an Olympic sport.*

The karate community is split as well. There are those who as-

---

* *Kumdo* is the Korean version of *kendo*, which some in Korea actually claim originated in their homeland before it was exported to Japan. Cf. Alexander Bennett, "Kendo or Kumdo."

pire to see World Karate Federation (WKF) athletes featured in the Olympic Games, and others who see such inclusion as the death knell for the art. Differences of opinion, however, do not lie simply between sport karate enthusiasts and the traditionalists. I had the chance to speak with one of the USA national coaches at the WKF world championships in Tokyo, 2008. She expressed to me her hope that karate would not be accepted as an Olympic sport. The corrupting effects of money were what concerned her most. Along with the problems in contemporary judo, discussed above, she was concerned that financial incentives would attract too many unsavory characters who would not appreciate that they were learning an art which is "dangerous." Karate holds, after all, the potential to hurt others. When economic opportunity brings in people with little respect for the ethics ingrained in the discipline, a real danger presents itself. It was interesting to me that her reservations had to do with ethical conduct among participants, as opposed to preservation of authentic *karatedō*. Nevertheless, if such concerns are present among the elite in sport karate, it is not surprising that the traditionalists are adamant in their opposition.

While Olympic *budō* could invite the corrupting influences of money, fame and recognition, there is another important consequence as well. As we have seen, adapting *budō* arts to sport affects the very nature of the discipline. In one conversation with Sogen Sakiyama Roshi, he asked me what I thought of karate in the Olympics. I paused, recognizing that our language barrier precluded the possibility of some long, drawn-out discourse on the difficult relationships between sport, tradition, culture and *dō*. I looked at the table in front of us, which held various plates, bowls, cups and implements. I gestured at the table, indicating that all of these various items could represent the different aspects of karate. I then picked up one cup and said, "If karate enters the Olympics, it will become only one thing." Sogen Roshi smiled. I was quite gratified to know that he both understood my answer and approved.

If karate becomes an Olympic sport, those pursuing the discipline will have no need of *makiwara* training; they wear gloves. There will be no need to practice with stone levers, gripping jars, or iron *geta*, as those are not particularly conducive to the expertise needed in sport karate. Fighters will have no need of *kata*. Those doing *kata* need not train with a partner. And no one needs to understand what is actually taught in *kata*. Practices like *kakie* may disappear as participants become expert in either scoring points or matching a certain aesthetic in their performance of forms. The art could be reduced to two courses of study: choreographed dance or hitting another karateka in a highly controlled environment before being hit. All of this is rather different from the multifaceted arts that were designed to keep people safe from those who would do them harm. Olympic karate has the potential to make itself into a remarkably narrow discipline.

On the one hand this is regrettable, for reasons of respecting, maintaining, and passing on this remarkably sophisticated art form. It would be shameful if traditional karate were to be lost for the sake of sport. On the other hand, a narrow curriculum is not at odds with an art form being a vehicle for self-cultivation. Disciplines like *iaidō* and *kyūdō* do not have the breadth of their predecessors, yet are highly respected *budō* arts which many people practice as transformative *shugyō*. A contracted curriculum does not interfere with a martial art holding a relationship to personal development. It might not be all that useful in a bar-fight, but it can certainly remain connected to the spirit of *budō*. In fact, as discussed in earlier chapters, and as Donn Draeger lamented, the transition from "*jutsu*" to "*dō*" has often involved a narrowing of the discipline.

At the same time that I insist that a contracted curriculum does not preclude a relationship between *budō* and Zen, there is another factor to be considered when the narrowing that takes place is dictated by sport. What we see with the increase of sport-karate, for example, is not simply an emphasis on *kata* and point-sparring, but a focus on winning contests. Doing so requires speed, athleticism and strength—in other words, youth. When the *telos* of the discipline is winning competitions, one reaches the apex of "ability" at a relatively young age. As in all Olympic sports (with the exception of curling), few athletes continue competing into their mid-30's, let alone 40's. When the peak has been reached at that point, little is left to do but coach. Lost is the lifelong endeavor to progress, both in the discipline and in life. We are less likely to be inspired by masters in their 60s, 70s and 80s who continue to exert themselves in the effort to improve. This is also lost when an art is defined chiefly by victory over others.

Is it all bad?

It is a reasonable question to ask whether *budō's* increasing embrace of sport and competition is entirely bad. While winning a contest may not represent the pinnacle of achievement, are there not valuable lessons to learn in healthy competition? Moreover, the corruption of a practice does not mean the practice itself is flawed. Sport may be distorted by some, but that does not imply that it is worthless for the rest. Personally, I love participating in sports and competition. As a young person, it provided me with countless good habits, memories and discipline. Still today, it drives me to improve and has provided me with wonderful opportunities to meet and learn from a variety of people.

There are certainly practitioners of traditional *budō* who look with great skepticism at their arts becoming linked with sport. Draeger was one. He argued, "It is patent that no sport can ever be a true classical dō form; no classical dō form can ever house a sport entity."* For the sake of the individual's pursuit of self-cultivation, one must not be distracted by the call to overcome others. He goes on to say, "To become a classical dō a sports entity must drop all notions of competition and record-breaking, or immediate results for championships, of garnering group prestige, and concentrate upon the individual's self-perfection as the end point of training."† Draeger saw these two activities as mutually exclusive.

---

* Draeger, *Classical Budo*, 125.

† Ibid.

Sōtō Zen master Taisen Deshimaru, whose *The Zen Way to the Martial Arts* is required reading on this subject, influenced a large number of martial artists around the world with respect to how they understand the relationship between their disciplines and Zen. Perhaps as a result of the carnage he witnessed, wrought by the Japanese military in Banka, Indonesia during World War II, he held serious reservations about those with strong desires to overcome others. He wrote, "I have nothing against sports, they train the body and develop stamina and endurance. But the spirit of competition and power that presides over them is not good, it reflects a distorted vision of life. The root of martial arts is not there .... In the spirit of Zen and Budo everyday life becomes the contest. There must be awareness at every moment—getting up in the morning, working, eating, going to bed. That is the place for the mastery of self."*

Alongside this advice we may place the approach that I have found among many Okinawan karate teachers. When I was at the Ozawa Tournament in 2006, Higaonna Sensei was conducting a teaching seminar one day before the competition. The room was filled with *karateka* who came to compete—teenagers and adults from various countries around the world. Sensei looked at us and offered the following assessment of sport karate: "Competition is good ... for children." I could not help but laugh. While I was laughing at the others—adults from around the world who had traveled all the way there to beat each other—I was also laughing at myself. I had wanted to come and compete—to prove something to myself, to feel accomplished, to overcome the demons of the elementary school playground. I could not help but think he was right. Competition does have something to offer, but it is not nearly as important as we think it is. And it is an expression of our immaturity when we grant it great importance.

Competition and sport have their place in the world of *budō*. They provide additional motivation, especially for the young, and

* Deshimaru, 2f.

are a wonderful advertising mechanism. They hold the power to draw people in, hopefully long enough that they can discover the lifelong path offered by these various arts. Of course, when they obscure one's view of that path, there is a problem.

Yasuhiro Yamashita (1957–), a 1984 Olympic Gold medalist in judo, recalls his *sensei's* advice when he was a boy: "You are all training for the moment to become champions. But, the most important thing is to become human beings who can go out into the big wide world and make your way, not only for your own sake, but for the benefit of others in society. Of course, it is important for you to strive to become a judo champion. But it is just as important for you to utilize what you learn in judo to [become] a champion of society as well."* Here we find an example of the school of thought which places great value on competition while teaching that "it is just as important" to cultivate oneself for the sake of society. Indeed, Yamashita's *sensei* appears to have communicated some exemplary moral values to his promising young student, including this counsel: "I often see it at competitions, be they high school students, university students, or even the police; pompous idiots who think they are special because they win tournaments. They walk across the floor like they own the world. Whatever you do, don't turn out like that."†

This early guidance appears to have had a lasting effect on Yamashita. His work with the All Japan Judo Federation and the Kōdōkan to bring about the "Judo Renaissance" in 2001 points to the values he still maintains, after an illustrious competitive career. The "Judo Renaissance" sought to promote, through the visual arts, the role of judo in "helping youth follow their dreams, make friends, learn respect, and challenge themselves. We are also trying to encourage judo practitioners to reconsider Kanō Jigorō's ideas and motives for creating judo. I am referring to his ideals of utilizing judo as a means

---

* Yamashita Yasuhiro, "The Role of Judo in an Age of Internationalization," *Budo Perspectives*, Ed. Alexander Bennett (Auckland, New Zealand: Kendo World Publications, 2005), 404.

† Ibid., 405.

for self-improvement."* Thus, the goal of personal development for the sake of others is not to be lost in the fury of sport training. It remains an essential part of the discipline.

We must also consider the role that sport plays in the popularization of the art. Older generations of men and women endlessly practicing the fundamentals of their art for the sake of pursuing perfection, whether in karate, calligraphy, or the tea-ceremony, are unlikely to attract young people to their discipline. Given the choice between overcoming oneself through endless *kihon* or a spirited game of baseball, it is not difficult to guess which will win out. The same holds true for executives at the local television station; sport competitions will draw far more viewers than documentaries about antiquated art forms. If the latter will survive, for the benefit of culture and the individuals who practice them, they need new blood. Sport and competition are wonderful ways to attract interest and support. It may be true, as Trevor Leggett points out about judo, that its "practice can be no more than an introduction to the much deeper Budo spirit."† However, if you never get people to the door of the dojo, that first step cannot be taken. Without Olympic judo, far fewer people would ever walk through that door.

This approach to generating interest is currently being extended to disciplines often considered to be immune to the competition-bug. Thanks to Eugen Herrigel's famous book on *kyūdō*, there has been a mystique surrounding Japanese archery, especially throughout the West. While this form of *budō* maintains its sober practice and traditional Japanese atmosphere, it functions as a sport among young Japanese today as much as basketball or badminton. A few years ago, I had the chance to spend some time with the *kyūdō* team at Senshu university. As with the judo and kendo dojos, there was a *kamidana* at the front of the dojo and an aura of austere tradition. However, just as in those other university clubs, spirituality was not much of a concern for the young people there, who were busy train-

---

* Ibid., 406.

† Leggett, *The Spirit of Budo*, xi.

ing for their next competition. While there seemed to be recognition among the *kyūdōka* that there is something a bit different, or potentially different, in studying a *budō* art—in contrast with the university's western archery club—it was only expressed in terms of "tradition." I asked one student if he would continue practicing *kyūdō* if there were no more competitions for him to join. Responding to what he perceived to be a rather strange question, he let me know that he would not. And so, while his instructor may hope that he will one day come to practice archery without thoughts of beating others, in the meantime it keeps him engaged.

We can even see the same embrace of competition among young people who practice calligraphy. The Japanese newspaper *The Asahi Shimbun* ran an article entitled, "Rewriting Calligraphy as a Performance Art."* It detailed the growing popularity of high school *shodō* clubs throughout Japan with their intense embrace of competition. With recruiting beginning as early as fifth grade, teams often practice four hours daily. At Mishima High School, the thirteen female members of the team begin practice with a 2-kilometer run, push-ups, sit-ups, and other exercises before preparing their ink. Young people are throwing themselves into the discipline in hopes of winning national titles. The art itself has changed as well with the popularization of "performance shodo," calligraphy of lyrics brushed to music. According to the article, "This shodo isn't like the shodo that their grandparents were taught: a solitary pursuit of perfection. Rather, it is as exciting as playing on a sports team." And while one wonders how much *dō* is left in this *shodō*, it may offer what is necessary to bring in students who discover its value for a lifetime. The Matsuyama Joshi High School team's motto is *Ippitsu nyukon* ("The whole soul in every line"). The teenagers on that team may not yet understand fully what that entails, but they are getting the introduction that may one day lead them to a more complete understanding.

Competition, then, is not necessarily a bad thing. It is a lesser

---

* *The Asahi Shimbun*, Sep. 29, 2008, 30.

good that should not be permitted to overshadow higher goods. Instructors may use it wisely to motivate students and gain popularity for the discipline, while waiting until the time is right to introduce students to the more profound aspects of *budō*. Anton Geesink, the heavyweight gold medalist at the 1964 Tokyo Olympics and a judo legend, explains, "[I]f judo can be experienced and practiced according to the specific needs of exponent [sic] according to their stage of judo maturity… we can do full justice to the totality that judo offers, not at once, but as a natural progression."*

While there is certainly truth in what Geesink articulates, and a principle that many traditionalists can embrace, there is a fundamental problem that Geesink ignores. In many cases, the focus on competition has completely overshadowed everything else. The time to move on to more reflective study of the art never comes. The seniors who are supposed to exemplify the spirit of *budō* are caught up in the destructive spirit of sport that Deshimaru Roshi warned us about.

Geesink, in his same address, goes on to say, "Young people aim to become the best, to become a champion through training long and hard, and for the most part have little interest in the traditional or historical aspects of judo. Most regard these aspects as tedious and an inconvenience. This lack of appreciation for history or culture is not unique to young judo people, but youth in general, and we should acknowledge it honestly as we consider judo education."† In this comment, Geesink offers a rather depressing view of the contemporary world of judo. First, he has no confidence that young people have the maturity to perceive and value what lies in judo beyond technique. This is not so much a sad commentary on today's youth but on the teachers who completely underestimate their students… and their own ability to inspire them. Second, he betrays that his own understanding of what judo offers, outside of physical disci-

* Anton J. Geesink, "The Paradox of 'Judo as an Olympic Sport' and 'Judo as Tradition,'" *Budo Perspectives*, Ed. Alexander Bennett (Auckland, New Zealand: Kendo World Publications, 2005), 382.

† Ibid.

pline, is only tradition, history and culture. It confuses me why a man awarded the rank of *judan* in judo would express Jigorō Kanō's ideals and philosophy in such a superficial way. Fortunately, for us and for Geesink, the book in which his lecture appears includes a wonderful article on the subject by Naoki Murata entitled "From '*Jutsu*' to '*Dō*': the Birth of Kōdōkan Judo."

Geesink goes further and encourages judo to continue as nothing more than sport. He continues, "For the judo-*ka* that desires to compete, only those techniques and skills required for winning matches are necessary. Anything else at this stage of their career is superfluous."* When the most senior practitioners and representatives of a *budō* art decide to buy wholesale into the world of sport, what hope is there for the next generation?

Yamashita, our other Olympic gold medalist *judōka*, expresses a greater appreciation for his art as *dō*. In regard to tradition, he offers, "One of my favorite maxims is, 'tradition is not just a matter of preserving form. It is to preserve the soul, the spirit.'"† In language that would have made his own *sensei* proud, he argues, "Putting *dōjō* experience into actual practice in society is what lies at the heart of judo."‡ However, one has to wonder if Yamashita—and many like him—has still allowed himself to get caught up by the spirit of sport competition. After a conversation with his *sempai* Geesink, both men agreed that the practice of judo needs to change if judo is to survive and prosper. Yamashita explains, "Thus, it was obvious to me that we really have to make efforts to make judo simple to follow.... My responsibilities as the Education & Coaching Direction of the IJF are to ensure that every effort is made to promote judo internationally, and make it interesting for spectators who may not have ever even stepped in a dōjō before."§

---

* Ibid., 383.
† Yamashita, 405.
‡ Ibid., 409.
§ Ibid., 413.

The question is, how much is enough? How much promotion, support, money, attention and showcasing are necessary? Is its Olympic standing really not enough? Are we in danger of seeing judo disappear from Japanese culture because of insufficient exposure? Or is the tail wagging the dog? Kanō's dreams of self-realization, cultivation, and contributions to society through judo are hardly discernible today, and a primary reason for this is the paramount focus on sport. To suggest that more of the same will improve the situation is absurd.

EPILOGUE

Is it really Zen?

"Though realization be not attained, a sitting of zazen *is a sitting of Buddha"* –Daikaku

Where's the Zen?

There are many who understand the practice and culture of *budō*, and appreciate the concepts that have been discussed in this book, but will ask the very important question, "Yes, but is it really Zen?" There are elements in *budō* that derive from Zen, are consistent with Zen, or bear similarities to Zen, but does that mean that we can truly speak of Zen in the arts of *budō*? This is an important question, as there have been quite a number of mischaracterizations and distortions, along with romanticizing, of the place of Zen in the world of *budō*. Is it really Zen, or even Buddhism, for that matter? This question deserves our attention.

It appears that authentic Zen is not typically expressed in *budō*. With very few exceptions, we do not find practitioners of Japanese martial arts undertaking the lifelong discipline of Zen under a qualified teacher, let alone teaching about their interconnectedness. Our romantic notions of Zen in *budō* culture may be shattered when we realize that people like Eugen Herrigel were expert in neither, while others, like D. T. Suzuki, could only speak with authority on one side of the equation. Those who have been well trained in both Zen and *budō* are quite uncommon; their rarity speaks to the fact that we have overstated the relationship between the two.

When looking at the history of *budō* as a spiritual discipline, we find little if any discussion of *satori,* overcoming duality, perceiving reality in its "as-it-isness," *nirvana, inka* or dharma transmission, dependent co-arising, let alone the four noble truths, precepts, or sutras. Even meditation itself often appears perfunctory and superficial. We do come across discussions of principles like *mushin* and its progeny, present-ness and concentration. What we often find in these cases, however, are only select attributes that are particularly conducive to becoming a better fighter. Is it really fair to call that Zen?

Moreover, many of these aspects of *budō* discipline are found in Daoism, the Wang Yang-ming school of Confucianism, or Shugendo. As we have seen, many of the ethical dimensions we associate with bushido derived from traditions quite distinct from Buddhism. Automatically to associate Zen with the spirit of *budō* is problematic, especially when we consider *budō* in the twenty-first century. Tetsushi Abe explains, "To many Japanese, regardless of whether or not they are *budō* practitioners, kendo or judo invoke notions of education and character development.... The image that '*budo* = education' is prevalent in the minds of many Japanese."* To attribute such characteristics of *budō* solely to Zen is not academically credible.

It appears that Zen is not an essential component of the spirit and tradition of *budō*. However, to the contrary, I believe it is indeed an indispensable element in both its history and current practice. Fundamental concepts of *budō* find their origin, expression, and continuing relevance when understood through their Zen roots. Moreover, while it is true that one rarely finds dedicated *budōka* who are also committed practitioners of Zen, the undertaking of their discipline has placed them on the same road. The *budō* "way" directs the traveler in the same direction as those beginning the "way" of Zen. Even when starting off, we are on a particular path, even if we do not realize it or where it leads. It is true that *budō* is not Zen; but Zen is still there, woven into the fabric of the discipline. For all of his faults, Herrigel was right when he wrote, "So understood, the art of archery is rather like a preparatory school

---

* Abe Tetsushi, "Cultural Friction in Budō," *Budo Perspectives*, Ed. Alexander Bennett (Auckland, New Zealand: Kendo World Publications, 2005), 135.

for Zen."* Some will recognize it, others will continue in it, and still others will cast it aside. This is as it should be. In the remainder of this epilogue, I will lay out my argument as to why Zen is a constituent part of *budō,* while acknowledging the exaggerated place it has held, especially in western culture.

The embellishment of the place of Zen

Over the past two centuries, misconceptions, hyperbole and fiction have worked their way into the story of *budō* and Zen. While much of this is the result of overactive imaginations and romanticism, some of the responsibility must be laid at the feet of scholars. There is a need to respond to the charge that the role of Zen, historically and today, has been exaggerated. John P. Keenan, who has a solid grasp of the subject matter, goes so far as to argue, "[T]he spiritual ethos surrounding martial arts practice is in fact a warmed-over Taoism, quite different from Mahāyāna Buddhism."† (The spirited exchange between Keenan and Stewart McFarlane on this issue, in *Japanese Journal of Religious Studies* from 1989-1991, is excellent reading on the subject.) Keenan has overplayed his hand, but there is value in drawing our attention to the exaggerated emphasis on Zen in Japanese martial arts. Some of the most influential authors who wrote about Zen and *budō* have overblown their interrelatedness.

Herrigel went to Japan looking for Zen, thought he found it in Awa Sensei's *kyūdō,* and announced it to the world. In reality, Herrigel probably had some communication problems with his teacher, a man who was not a practitioner of Zen but whose philosophy had a "close connection" with Wang Yang-ming Confucianism.‡ As Shōji Yamada has argued, but perhaps overstated, the German philosopher is a poor resource for anyone desiring to learn about either *kyūdō* or

---

* Herrigel, 27.

† John P. Keenan, "Spontaneity in Western Martial Arts: A Yogācāra Critique of *Mushin* (No-Mind), *Japanese Journal of Religious Studies,* 16, no. 4 (1989), 286.

‡ Suzuki Sadami, "Twentieth Century *Budō* and Mystic Experience," 27.

Zen.* Herrigel saw the teaching he received from Awa through Zen-colored glasses, a distorted vision he passed on to us.

D. T. Suzuki opened the eyes of many in the West, including this author, to the study and practice of Zen. We are certainly indebted to him for his substantial work, but his books paint a picture of Japanese culture in which Zen influences every stroke of the brush. British diplomat Sir Charles Eliot (1862–1931) shared this misperception, and Suzuki enthusiastically reported his recollection of Eliot's remark that "Zen is the Japanese character."† Winston King, in his academic work as an historian, cited this in turn and shared in this amplification of the role of Zen.‡ Even the great Kakuzo Okakura, author of *The Book of Tea*, was probably guilty of exaggeration when he wrote, "All of our great tea-masters were students of Zen and attempted to introduce the spirit of Zennism into the actualities of life."§ The truth of the matter has been overstated. During my time in Japan, it was often pointed out to me that few Japanese *budōka* undertake the study of Zen. Shōji Yamada points out the same in regard to *kyūdō*, "[A]mong modern practitioners of Japanese archery those people who approach it as one part of Zen training are extremely unusual in Japan."¶ The fact that this holds true for *kyūdō* suggests that it applies to other *budō* arts—judo, karate, kendo—all the more.

To be certain, amplification and embellishment of Zen's role in Japanese culture, the life of the samurai, and *budō* arts has indeed occurred. Influences from Shinto, Confucianism, neo-Confucianism, Shugendo, among others have played significant roles in these various cultural phenomena. However, there has been an overreaction to the exaggerations as well. This is also unfortunate.

---

* Shōji Yamada, "The Myth of Zen in the Art of Archery," *Japanese Journal of Religious Studies*, 28, no. 1-2, 1-30.

† Suzuki, *Zen and Japanese Culture*, 85.

‡ King, 180.

§ Kakuzo Okakura, *The Book of Tea* (Berkley: Stone Bridge Press, 2006), 59.

¶ Yamada, 2.

There have been those who insist that Herrigel knew nothing of *kyūdō* or Zen, and that his teacher was only a marginal and eccentric individual. Suzuki's great scholarly contributions are dismissed by some because of his exclusive focus on Zen. I have come across senior *budōka* who roll their eyes whenever they hear mention of Zen. On the one hand, I can sympathize with this. The term has often become meaningless through overuse and abuse, and a lot of young people get too big for their britches after reading through a book or two on the subject. However, overreaction does not get us closer to the truth.

We need to remember that scholars often focus intensely on their particular areas of interest, creating a skewed picture of the whole. Jewish scholars speak almost exclusively of the 6 million dead Jews, while giving short shrift to Gypsies, Jehovah's Witnesses, Christian clergy, Russian civilians, homosexuals and countless others who died during the Holocaust. Black American historians can narrowly focus on slavery when discussing the Civil War. Books about World War II by Russian scholars certainly have a different emphasis than those written by Italian or British authors. Scholars dwell on their own interests and can thereby misrepresent the reality they seek to describe. It is unfortunate, but it is forgivable. Throwing the baby out with the bathwater is not the answer.

Zen in the Arts of Budō

What we see in budō disciplines are practices that derive from, or are expressions of Zen. Throughout this book we have seen teachers in various traditions develop these themes: *mushin, zanshin, fudōshin,* overcoming attachment, fluidity of thought, concentration, existing in the instant, freedom of action, decisiveness, simplicity, austere mental and physical discipline, and a preference for action over rumination. While claiming that they all find their foundation in Zen alone is obviously erroneous; denying a significant influence from Zen is equally absurd.

It is true that many Japanese study *budō,* undertaking the discipline as a serious personal *shugyō,* without perceiving Zen as a factor in what they do. Explicit study and practice of Zen is indeed quite unusual among *budōka*. However, there need not be conscious awareness and intent for a person to be acting in accord with a particular set of beliefs or principles. We in the West are greatly influenced by Plato, for example. Our typical assumption of a body-and-soul dualism is one place where our beliefs and actions are quite Platonic, despite the fact that one rarely comes across a person who recognizes this. Likewise, a typical Korean teenager does not think of himself as Confucian. He does not view his life as being in accord with the teachings of a man who lived 2500 years ago in China. However, we would be grossly mistaken if we thereby concluded that his daily social interactions are not profoundly influenced by Confucius. So, when *kendōka* tell us that they have no understanding of Zen, they may be truthful but overestimating their ignorance. Many elements of *budō* are indeed expressions of Zen.

Bearing this in mind, we can understand why Miyamoto Musashi's *A Book of Five Rings* is considered a Zen-inspired classic, despite the fact that there is no explicit reference to Zen in the book. Tanchū Terayama, professor at Nishōgakusha University, argues, "*Gorin no sho*, often translated into English as *A Book of Five Rings*, is heavily influenced by the Zen teaching of *Go-I* or the 'five degrees of enlightenment.'"* He points to Musashi's use of terms like *jikishin* (true-mind) and *ginmi* (to know through practice and experience) as evidence of the direct influence of Zen.† Thus, while Musashi does not present himself as a scholar of Zen, and one could read the entire book without noticing any association with Zen, the absence of direct references do not mean there was no influence. Musashi's formal study of Zen with Obuchi Ōsho, if Terayama is right, certainly had a profound influence on the swordsman and subsequently his countless readers over the last 500 years.

---

* Terayama Tanchū, "Ken-Zen-Sho: An Analysis of Swordsmanship, Zen, and Calligraphy and their Relevance Today," *Budo Perspectives*, Ed. Alexander Bennett (Auckland, New Zealand: Kendo World Publications, 2005), 108.

† Ibid.

Philip Kapleau's Zen master, Haku'un Yasutani, commended those who undertake *zazen* without any consideration of its philosophy or religion. While he obviously did not believe such people availed themselves of all he had to offer, he still considered them to be engaged in the practice of Zen. Even when practiced for reasons of mental and physical health alone, it is still Zen; it is *Bompu* Zen. In fact, Yasutani describes "five varieties of Zen,"* which embrace varying levels of Zen teaching and practice. They are all still Zen. Even without belief in or concern with the ultimate *telos* taught by the Buddha, it is still Zen.

Lastly, when trying to determine whether or not it is truly Zen in the history and practice of *budō*, it is important to acknowledge differences between western and eastern approaches to religion. In the West, we generally practice exclusive religions. Adherents either belong to one religion or another, and they are expected to believe and practice according to the teachings of that religion. Thus, a Christian cannot simultaneously be a Muslim. She is expected to believe certain central doctrines of the Church (e.g., what is found in the Apostle's Creed) and try to live according to the moral imperatives in the Bible. Failure to do so might lead others to conclude that she is not really a Christian.

In the East, religions are generally not exclusive. In Japan, for example, many people practice elements of both Buddhism and Shinto simultaneously without any perceived conflict. Moreover, there is no expectation that one will strive to live by all principles of the religion. As we saw, there were samurai who recognized that violence is not in keeping with the teachings of the Buddha, but believed they had an obligation to fulfill their duty as members of the warrior caste. The ideal of *ahimsa* would have to wait for another time or another life. Still, they were not excluded from Buddhist practice and community. The same principle is at work throughout Buddhist countries

---

* Kapleau, 44ff. The remaining four are: *gedo*—"Zen related to religion and philosophy but yet not a Buddhist Zen;" *shojo*—"the vehicle or teaching that is to take you from one state of mind [delusion] to another [enlightenment] [but]only one's self;" *daijo*—"a truly Buddhist Zen;" *saijojo*—"the highest vehicle, that culmination and crown of Buddhist Zen."

today. A woman in Thailand may be completely unfamiliar with the eightfold path, meditation, or the sutras. The subject of enlightenment might not concern her in the least, and her visits to the temple might be quite infrequent, but her community still considers her a Buddhist. Having no interest in the final goal of Buddhist practice does not disqualify someone from belonging to the community. People may live a partial expression of the Buddhist ideal, but still be considered practicing Buddhists.*

As we have seen throughout this book, people embraced certain elements within Zen. They did not need to embrace the entire discipline, join the *sangha,* and seek enlightenment in order to be bona fide Buddhists. One can be an adherent of Zen without undertaking the whole of what Zen has to offer. Even fragments of Zen are still Zen. As Daikaku explains in his *Zazenron,* "Though realization be not attained, a sitting of *zazen* is a sitting of Buddha, a day of *zazen* is a day of Buddha, a life of *zazen* is a life of Buddha."†

Certainly there are those who prefer to define terms more strictly. Some will argue that the woman in Thailand or the California businessman who meditates for purposes of health are not actually practicing Buddhism. In the same way that Orthodox Jews may not view their liberal counterparts among the Reform Jews as truly practicing Judaism, or regular church-goers may argue that Easter/Christmas Christians are not really Christians, so there are those who will dispute whether *Bompu* Zen or "Folk Buddhism" are truly Buddhism. However, I prefer a more inclusive understanding of what we may call Zen and Buddhism. For these reasons, I must answer the question in the affirmative. Yes, it is indeed Zen in *budō.* It may not be explicit. It may not be complete. It may not even be recognized. But it is Zen nevertheless.

---

* In the West, the traditional Roman Catholic differentiation of the lay and religious life bears a strong similarity to what we perceive here in the East. Monks and nuns follow a higher calling, while the laity follow a less rigorous path. The latter may not concern themselves with the *telos* of heaven, content with the prospect of purgatory before reaching the beatific vision. Still, both groups are considered "Christian."

† As in Leggett, *Zen and the Ways,* 44.

Bibliography

Abe Tetsushi. "Cultural Friction in *Budō*." *Budo Perspectives.* Alexander Bennett, ed. Auckland, New Zealand: Kendo World Publications, 2005: 125-140.

Arakaki Isamu. "The Future of Traditional Karate." *Classical Fighting Arts* 2, No. 17, (2009): 9-12.

Austin, James H. *Zen and the Brain.* Cambridge: The MIT Press, 1998.

Bartholomeusz, Tessa. "In Defense of Dharma: Just-War Ideology in Buddhist Sri Lanka." *Journal of Buddhist Ethics* 6 (1999): 1-16.

Bennett Alexander. "Kendo or Kumdo: The Internationalization of Kendo and the Olympic Problem." Alexander Bennett, ed. Auckland, New Zealand: Kendo World Publications, 2005: 327-349.

Broughton Jeffrey L. *The Bodhidharma Anthology: The Earliest Records of Zen.* Berkeley: University of California Press, 1990.

Cleary, Thomas, ed. and trans. *Training the Samurai Mind: A Bushido Sourcebook.* Boston: Shambhala, 2008.

Davey, H. E. "Shodo: Budo and the Art of Japanese Calligraphy." *Furyu: The Budo Journal* Spring-Summer, 1995

Deshimaru, Taisen. *The Zen Way to the Martial Arts.* New York: Compass, 1982.

Draeger, Donn F. *Classical Budo: The Martial Arts and Ways of Japan.* Boston: Weatherhill, 1973.

Draeger, Donn F. *Classical Bujutsu: The Martial Arts and Ways of Japan.* Boston: Weatherhill, 1973.

Ellwood, Robert. *Introducing Japanese Religion.* New York: Routledge, 2008.

Friday, Karl. "Off the Warpath: Military Science and *Budō* in the Evolutions of Ryūha Bugei." *Budo Perspectives*. Alexander Bennett, ed. Auckland, New Zealand: Kendo World Publications, 2005: 249-265.

Funakoshi, Gichin. *Karate-Do: My Way of Life*. New York: Kodansha, International, 1975.

Geesink, Anton J. "The Paradox of 'Judo as an Olympic Sport' and 'Judo as Tradition.'" *Budo Perspectives*. Alexander Bennett, ed. Auckland, New Zealand: Kendo World Publications, 2005: 379-401.

Gethin, Rupert. "Can Killing a Living Being Ever Be an Act of Compassion? The analysis of the act of killing in the Abhidhamma and Pali Commentaries." Journal of Buddhist Ethics 11, 2004: 167-202.

Goldberg, Michael. *A Zen Life: D. T. Suzuki*. Japan Inter-Culture Foundation, 2006. Video documentary.

Harvey, Peter. *An Introduction to Buddhism*. Cambridge: Cambridge University Press, 1990.

Henning, Stanley E. "The Imaginary World of Buddhism and East Asian Martial Arts." *Classical Fighting Arts* 2, no. 12, 37-40.

Herrigel, Eugen. *Zen in the Art of Archery*. New York: Pantheon Books Inc., 1953.

Higaonna, Morio. *The History of Karate: Okinawan Goju-Ryu*. Thousand Oaks, CA: Dragon Books, 1995.

Hosokawa, Dogen. *Omori Sogen: The Art of a Zen Master*. New York: Kegan Paul International, 1999.

Hyams, Joe. *Zen in the Martial Arts*. New York: Jeremy P. Tarcher/Putnam, 1979.

Irie Kōhei. "Budō as a Concept: An Analysis of Budō's Characteristics." *Budo Perspectives*. Alexander Bennett, ed. Auckland, New Zealand: Kendo World Publications, 2005: 155-169.

Kapleau, Philip. *The Three Pillars of Zen: Teaching, Practice, and Enlightenment.* New York: Doubleday, 1980.

Keenan, John P. "Spontaneity in Western Martial Arts: A Yogācāra Critique of Mushin (No-Mind)." *Japanese Journal of Religious Studies* 16, no. 4 (1989): 285-298.

King, Winston L. *Death Was His Kōan: The Samurai-Zen of Suzuki Shōsan.* Fremont, CA: Asian Humanities Press, 1986.

King, Winston L. *Zen and the Way of the Sword: Arming the Samurai Psyche.* New York: Oxford University Press, 1993.

Koller, John M. *Asian Philosophies.* Upper Saddle River, NJ: Prentice Hall, 2002.

Kushner, Kenneth. *One Arrow, One Life: Zen, Archery, Enlightenment.* Rutland, VT: Tuttle Publishing, 2000.

Leggett, Trevor. *Zen and the Ways.* Boston: Routledge & Kegan Paul, 1978.

Miyamoto Musashi. *The Book of Five Rings*. New York: Bantam Books, 1982.

Molloy, Michael. *Experiencing the World's Religions.* Mountain View, CA: Mayfield Publishing Company, 1999.

Nagamine, Shoshin. *Tales of Okinawa's Great Masters.* Patrick McCarthy, trans. Boston: Tuttle Publishing, 2000.

Nitobe, Inazo. Bushido: *The Soul of Japan.* Rutland, VT: Tuttle Publishing, 1969.

Okakura, Kakuzo. *The Book of Tea.* Berkley: Stone Bridge Press, 2006.

Pilgrim, Richard B. *Buddhism and the Arts of Japan*. Chambersburg, PA: Anima Books, 1981.

Pojman, Louis P. Ethics: *Discovering Right and Wrong.* Belmont, CA: Wadsworth, 2002.

Rahula, Walpola. *What the Buddha Taught.* New York: Grove Press, 1974.

Raposa, Michael L. *Meditation and the Martial Arts.* Charlottesville: University of Virginia Press, 2003.

Ray, Reginald A. *Indestructible Truth: The Living Spirituality of Tibetan Buddhism.* Boston: Shambhala, 2002.

Ray, Reginald A. *Secret of the Vajra World: The Tantric Buddhism of Tibet.* Boston: Shambhala, 2002.

Shahar, Meir. *The Shaolin Monastery: History, Religion, and the Chinese Martial Arts.* Honolulu: University of Hawai'i Press, 2008.

Silk, Jonathan A. "The Fruits of Paradox: On the Religious Architecture of the Buddha's Life Story." *Journal of the American Academy of Religion* 71:4, (2003): 863-881.

Sogen, Omori. *An Introduction to Zen Training.* Dogen Hosokawa and Roy Yoshimoto, trans. Rutland, VT: Tuttle Publishing, 2001.

Stevens, John. *The Philosophy of Aikido.* New York: Kodansha International, 2001.

Stevens, John. *Zen Bow, Zen Arrow: The Life and Teachings of Awa Kenzo.* Boston: Shambhala, 2007.

Strong, John S. *The Experience of Buddhism: Sources and Interpretations.* Belmont, CA: Wadsworth, 2008.

Sugawara, Makoto. *Lives of Master Swordsmen.* Tokyo: East Publications, 1985.

Suzuki, D. T. *The Zen Doctrine of No-Mind: The Significance of the Sūtra of Hui-neng.* Boston: Weisner Books, 1969.

Suzuki, Daisetz T. *Zen and Japanese Culture.* Princeton: Princeton University Press, 1959.

Sadami, Suzuki. "Twentieth Century *Budō* and Mystic Experience." *Budo Perspectives.* Alexander Bennett, ed. Auckland, New Zealand: Kendo World Publications, 2005: 15-44.

Suzuki, Shunryu. *Zen Mind, Beginner's Mind.* New York: Weatherhill, 1973.

Takuan Sōhō. *The Unfettered Mind: Writings from a Zen Master to a Master Swordsman.* William Scott Wilson, trans. New York: Kodansha, 2002.

Terayama Tanchū. "Ken-Zen-Sho: An Analysis of Swordsmanship, Zen, and Calligraphy and their Relevance Today." *Budo Perspectives.* Alexander Bennett, ed. Auckland, New Zealand: Kendo World Publications, 2005: 105-122.

Uozumi Takashi. "Research of Miyamoto Musashi's Gorin no sho—From the Perspective of Japanese Intellectual History." *Budo Perspectives.* Alexander Bennett, ed. Auckland, New Zealand: Kendo World Publications, 2005: 45-67.

Victoria, Brian A. *Zen at War.* New York: Weatherhill, 1997.

Victoria, Brian A. *Zen War Stories.* New York: Routledge, 2003.

Yagyu Munenori. *The Life-Giving Sword.* William Scott Wilson, trans. New York: Kodansha, 2003.

Yamada, Shōji. "The Myth of Zen in the Art of Archery." *Japanese Journal of Religious Studies* 28, no. 1-2, (2001): 1-30.

Yamamoto Tsunetomo. *Hagakure: The Book of the Samurai.* William Scott Wilson, trans. New York: Kodansha, 2002.

Yamashita Yasuhiro, "The Role of Judo in an Age of Internationalization," *Budo Perspectives.* Alexander Bennett, ed. Auckland, New Zealand: Kendo World Publications, 2005: 403-415.

Yokoi, Yūhō. *Zen Master Dōgen: An Introduction with Selected Writings.* New York: Weatherhill, 1976.

Glossary

Agura (Jpn): A seated cross-legged position where neither foot is elevated on the other thigh.

Ahimsa (Skt, Pali): The religious or philosophical principle of non-harm, non-injury, and non-violence established in Hinduism and also embraced in Buddhism.

Atman (Skt): The Hindu notion of the self or soul that animates a body.

Banzai (Jpn): From "Tennōheika banzai!" A battle cry among Japanese soldiers during World War II meaning "May the emperor live 10,000 years."

Bodhi (Skt, Pali): A general term, often used as a prefix, that refers to enlightenment, awakening, or wisdom.

Bodhidharma (Skt): c. 5-6th century C.E. Also, Dharma, Daruma, Tamo. The legendary 28th patriarch of Ch'an Buddhism who is said to have brought his sect of Buddhism from India to China and created the prototypes for quan fa.

Bompu Zen (Jpn): Meaning "ordinary" Zen, it is discussed by Philip Kapleau as one of the five varieties of Zen. This is a discipline of Zen for the sake of physical and mental health, separate from any religious or philosophical principles.

Budō (Jpn): The category of martial arts or "ways" developed in Japan and often practiced for the sake of personal cultivation. E.g., kendo, judo, aikido.

Bujutsu (Jpn): The category of fighting disciplines developed in Japan for the sake of combat. E.g., kenjutsu, jujutsu, aikijutsu.

Daimyo (Jpn): A Japanese feudal lord and member of the samurai class.

Daoyin (Ch): An early Daoist exercise regime, utilizing meditation, breathing techniques, and physical movement to facilitate health. It is believed to be a precursor or prototype for later qigong.

Dhyana (Skt): Meditation—the seventh undertaking of the eightfold path. It is the root word for Ch'an (China), Son (Korea), and Zen (Japan).

Dō (Jpn): From the Chinese Dao, meaning "Way," suggesting the path one should follow in order to live in harmony with certain religious or philosophical principles.

Dōjō (Jpn): Literally, the place for training in the "Way." Typically refers to the training halls used in Japanese budō.

Dukkha (Pali): Meaning suffering, anguish, or frustration, it is used to describe the essential nature of life in the Four Noble Truths.

Fudōshin (Jpn): An indomitable, imperturbable, unmovable mind.

Gaijin (Jpn): A foreigner, non-Japanese. In common usage it is limited to foreigners whose ethnicity is Caucasian.

Gasshuku (Jpn): A training seminar.

Geta (Jpn): Traditional Japanese footwear, typically wooden and resembling sandles or clogs.

Go and **Ju** (Jpn): Literally "hard" and "soft," these two complementary principles are developed in balance with one another in various martial arts, most notably, Goju-ryu.

Gun fa (Ch): Chinese staff fighting.

Hara (Jpn): The abdomen or belly, symbolically and literally the center of one's being. Sometimes used interchangeably with the word tanden.

Harai-goshi (Jpn): A sweeping hip throw in Judo.

Hizaguruma (Jpn): The knee wheel throw in Judo.

Ichigyo-zammai (Jpn): One act concentration, where one's attention is singularly focused on one particular activity or phenomenon.

Ikken hissatsu (Jpn): The principle or ideal in martial arts of "one strike, one kill."

Ikkyo (Jpn): The first technique in Aikido, involving a controlled manipulation of the opponent's outstretched arm.

Ino (Jpn): See Jikijitsu.

Jikijitsu (Jpn): The individual who wields the kyosaku during zazen.

Jō (Jpn): A Japanese short staff, slightly more than four feet in length, used in the martial arts of jōjutsu, jōdō, and aiki- jō.

Joriki (Jpn): The power of concentration that is developed and nurtured in meditation.

Judō (Jpn): Literally "the gentle way," a grappling martial art developed by Dr. Jigoro Kano in the early twentieth century. Based on various older arts of jujutsu, judo is a martial art that was intended to be oriented toward self-cultivation of the practitioner.

Judōka (Jpn): One who practices judo.

Kake (Jpn): The final step in a judo throw, the actual execution of the throw.

Kakie (Jpn): A pushing hands drill practiced with a partner in Okinwan Goju-ryu karate.

Kamae (Jpn): A generic term for any of a large number of fighting postures in Japanese martial arts.

Kami (Jpn): The gods, goddesses, spirits, or forces of nature in Shinto, the indigenous religion of Japan.

Kamidana (Jpn): A small family-altar or shrine used in the religion of Shinto, often found in homes and in the front of a martial arts dojo.

Karate-dō (Jpn): Literally "the way of the empty hand," a martial art that developed in Okinawa, was popularized throughout mainland Japan, and which finds it roots in China.

Karateka (Jpn): One who practices karate.

Keisaku (Jpn): See Kyōsaku.

Kendō (Jpn): Literally "the way of the sword," a modern martial art in which practitioners typically duel with split-bamboo swords called shinai.

Kendōka (Jpn): One who practices kendo.

Kata (Jpn): A pre-arranged form of movements, often found in martial arts, which one practices extensively in order to learn and internalize the physical performance of the art form.

Kiai (Jpn): Often translated "spirit yell," a shout from one's diaphragm that correlates with certain movements in martial arts, often at a point of particular focus.

Kihon (Jpn): The basic techniques of an art form, e.g. punches, kicks, blocks, and stances in karate.

Kinhin (Jpn): A formalized walking meditation practiced in the Zen tradition.

Kōan (Jpn): An apparently illogical question, riddle, or statement used primarily in Rinzai Zen with the intention of helping the practitioner achieve insight through non-discursive thought.

Kun (Jpn): A statement of values that are taught and expected of students, often found in martial arts dojos.

Kuzushi (Jpn): The first step in a successful throw in judo, which involves unbalancing the opponent. Once unbalanced, the judoka can "fit in" and then execute the technique.

Kyōsaku (Jpn): The "awakening stick" used in Zen meditation, for the purpose of rousing those who may have become sleepy or distracted, serving the purpose of abruptly bringing them back to the moment.

Kyūdō (Jpn): The formal art of Japanese archery.

Mahayana (Skt): Literally "large vehicle," and one of the three major divisions of Buddhism to which Zen belongs.

Mai-ai (Jpn): The distance or spacing between opponents in budō.

Mandala (Skt): Literally "circle," Tibetan Buddhists are famous for constructing these elaborate depictions of the cosmos and the beings therein, often with colored sand. Found in various sects of Buddhism and Hinduism, they hold great religious and ceremonial value and are used as a teaching mechanism.

Mantra (Skt): A sound, word, or phrase that may be repeated during meditation in order to focus the mind.

Meijin (Jpn): Literally a "brilliant man," it may be translated into English as one who is a "master" in a particular art.

Mu (Jpn): The focal point of the famous kōan often referred to as Joshu's Mu, the word means literally "nothing, non-existence, negation."

Mudra (Skt): A symbolic gesture, typically performed with the hands and fingers, that is often used in esoteric Buddhist meditation.

Mushin (Jpn): Literally "no-mind," it is a mental state cultivated in Zen meditation and practice. It is characterized not by an absence of thought, but by cutting off the discursive mind.

Nirvana (Skt): Impossible to define, it is the state of one who has overcome attachment and reached enlightenment.

Parinirvana (Skt): The state that an enlightened being attains after death in one's final lifetime.

Qigong (Ch): A Chinese mental and physical discipline wherein one fosters health, clarity of mind, and spiritual insight.

Quan fa (Ch): A broad term for Chinese martial arts, better known as kung-fu or wushu.

Ram muay (Thai): A pre-fight ritual in Muay Thai kickboxing used to demonstrate the fighter's skill.

Rōnin (Jpn): A samurai who is not in the service of a particular lord. He was hired, at times, as a kind of mercenary.

Rōshi (Jpn): Literally, "old teacher," it is an honorary title for a Zen teacher who has practiced for many years and may be considered a "master."

Ryūha (Jpn): A particular school, or style, within a larger disciplinary tradition. E.g. Goju-ryu is one particular ryūha within the broader category of karate-do.

Sabi (Jpn): The Japanese aesthetic value associated with age and wear, which illustrates the impermanence of things.

Sadhu (Skt): An ascetic, wandering monk in the Hindu tradition who has dedicated his entire life to spiritual discipline.

Samadhi (Skt): A state of calm single-minded awareness cultivated in meditation.

Samsara (Skt): The endless cycle of birth and rebirth in which humans find themselves.

Sangha (Skt): The Buddhist community of believers, and one of the three jewels of Buddhism.

Satori (Jpn): Enlightenment or awakening, often conceived to happen in an instant in the Zen tradition.

Seiza (Jpn): The formal Japanese seated position—lower legs on the floor with one's heels under the buttocks.

Sempai (Jpn): The senior person in a junior-senior relationship.

Sesshin (Jpn): An extended period of intense meditation in the Zen tradition, often lasting several days.

Shiai (Jpn): Competition.

Shikan-taza (Jpn): A practice of meditation most associated with Sōtō Zen in which the mind is aware yet free from thought.

Shinai (Jpn): A sword made of split bamboo, used in kendo competition and practice.

Shugyō (Jpn): An austere mental and physical discipline for the sake of self-cultivation.

Suki (Jpn): Literally a break or gap. The word is used in martial arts to refer to a mental disconnect which leaves one momentarily susceptible to an attack.

Sutras (Skt): Buddhist scriptures containing the teachings of the Buddha.

Tanden (Jpn): The physiological center of a person, located roughly three finger widths below the navel. Sometimes used interchangeably with the less specific hara (belly).

Tanha (Pali): Desire, craving, thirst.

Tantras (Skt): A set of scriptures with their roots in the Hindu tradition that provide means for an accelerated path toward enlightenment through esoteric religious practices.

Tsukuri (Jpn): Positioning one's body, or "fitting in," for a throw in judo.

Ukemi (Jpn): The skill required in being an uke (one who receives an attack) in the martial arts; knowing how to roll or fall when thrown as to avoid injury to oneself.

Wabi (Jpn): The Japanese aesthetic value associated with simplicity in form and appearance, often represented by imperfections (e.g. asymmetry) in the work of art.

Wai khru (Thai): A pre-fight ritual in Muay Thai kickboxing in which appreciation for teachers is expressed.

Yamabushi (Jpn): Japanese religious ascetics who live in the mountains.

Yin and **Yang** (Ch): The two opposite yet complementary forces that function in harmony with each other throughout the natural world.

Yoga (Skt): A spiritual and physical discipline, for strengthening mind and body, that developed within Hinduism in India.

Zafu (Jpn): A cushion for sitting during Zen meditation.

Zanshin (Jpn): Literally "remaining mind," it refers to the mental state wherein a practitioner does not mentally "check out," but remains aware, after completing a particular activity.

Zazen (Jpn): Seated meditation, the primary practice of Zen.

Zendō (Jpn): A room, or hall, set aside for the practice of zazen.

Index